THE CRESCENT
DICTIONARY OF
AMERICAN
POLITICS

THE
CRESCENT
DICTIONARY OF
AMERICAN
POLITICS

by Eugene J. McCarthy

Oscar Tarcov, General Editor

THE MACMILLAN COMPANY • NEW YORK
MACMILLAN NEW YORK • LONDON
A Division of The Crowell-Collier Publishing Company
1962

Library of Congress catalog card number: 62-10644

First Printing

The Macmillan Company, New York
Brett-Macmillan Ltd., Galt, Ontario

Printed in the United States of America

To Sam Rayburn

Speaker of the United States House of Representatives
1940-1947, 1949-1953, 1955-1961, who contributed much to
the meaning of democracy and to the significance of
its institutions and to the definition of its terms.

INTRODUCTION

It is my hope that this *Dictionary of American Politics* will contribute in some measure to a better understanding of American government and American politics. It is intended to supplement textbooks on civics and on government and also on current history by providing definitions of terms current in political thought and action.

In selecting terms for definition I have excluded those which, in my judgment, are purely legal and those which have lost importance in relation to contemporary governmental and political problems. I have tried to limit the number of terms to those most frequently used and those which have the greatest significance.

This dictionary of politics includes not only terms relating to the structure and form of government at all levels, that is, to the institutional aspects, but also includes those subject to change and which reflect the changing processes of government and politics. Our government is one of men as well as law, and politics is the practical art by which men arrive at political decisions and by which they determine policies.

In determining the style and content of the dictionary, I have attempted to meet high school and college students' needs for a convenient reference in the field of government and politics. Some of the definitions reflect the classical or traditional meaning of the terms. Others are contemporary and contain what, in my judgment, is the meaning given them by men in government and politics today. They reflect, I hope, something of the knowledge and experience I have gained in thirteen years of serving in the Congress of the United States, in both the House of Representatives and the Senate, and my experience in the practical fields of political party activities and political campaigns.

For advice and counsel and assistance in the selection of material in the dictionary and in preparation for publication I am indebted to the members of my senatorial staff, especially to Mr. Emerson Hynes, formerly on the faculty at St. John's University in Collegeville, Minnesota, and to Mr. William Gerberding, now on the faculty of the Political Science Department, University of California, Los Angeles, and to Miss Jean Stack for typing and reading the manuscript.

Eugene J. McCarthy

CONTENTS

Introduction vii
A Guide to the Use of the Dictionary x
The Crescent Dictionary of American Politics 1
Supplements
    States, Territories, and Possessions 173
    Campaign Memorabilia 183
    Seals of Departments of the Government 184
    Charts
        A County Government 186
        A Council-Manager Government 187
        A Strong-Mayor Government 188
        A Weak-Mayor Government 189
        Government Under a State Constitution 190
        The Government of the United States 191
        Executive Branch of the Government 192
        Department of Agriculture 193
        Department of State 194
        The United Nations and Related Agencies 195

A GUIDE TO THE
USE OF THE DICTIONARY

All entries have been entered in strict alphabetical order.

Boldface type has been used throughout for all words and terms for which definitions are included. The cross references are planned to facilitate fuller exploration of a subject beyond an initial specific question. Therefore, in addition to main entry words and explicit cross references, all words and terms used within the body of a definition for which separate entries exist are printed in boldface type.

Italics have been used to emphasize certain words and phrases within the body of the definition.

AAA See **Agricultural Adjustment Act.**

Agriculture, Department of See **Department of Agriculture.**

Agriculture, Secretary of See **Department of Agriculture.**

ABA See **American Bar Association.**

ABC Warfare An expression used to describe the destructive types of weapons developed by modern science..The letters ABC stand respectively for atomic, bacteriological, and chemical forces available for use in modern wars. See **War.**

Mauldin, St. Louis Post-Dispatch, 1961.

"GOOD NEWS, MEN—WE'RE GOING BACK TO CIVILIZED WARFARE."

Absentee Vote A vote cast by someone unable to appear at his polling place on election day; such votes may be mailed in on ballots supplied in advance or deposited with the city clerk or some other recognized official.

Absolute Majority See **Majority.**

Academies (Navy, Army, Air Force) The three educational institutions established by the federal government to train the professional officer corps of the Army, Navy, and Air Force. The Military Academy is at West Point, New York; the Naval Academy, at Annapolis, Maryland; the Air Force Academy, at Colorado Springs, Colorado. The President of the United States, United States Senators and Representatives, and others may select candidates who must meet rigid physical and intellectual requirements before they are admitted to these schools. Graduates are awarded commissions as ensigns in the Navy or second lieutenants in the Army and Air Force.

Academy, United States Coast Guard An educational institution (New London, Connecticut) operated by the federal government to train men to become officers in the United States Coast Guard. Candidates must meet high physical and intellectual standards, and they are selected on the basis of competitive examinations. Upon graduation they are commissioned as ensigns. They receive the same pay and allowances as officers of comparable rank in the other armed services. See **Coast Guard.**

Academy, United States Merchant Marine An educational institution (King's Point, New York) operated by the federal government to train men to become officers in the United States Merchant Marine and the United States Naval Reserve. Candidates must meet high physical and intellectual standards. They are nominated by United States Representatives and Senators, with a quota assigned to each state based on its population. Graduates are awarded a bachelor of science degree and a com-

1

mission as ensign in the United States Naval Reserve. See **Merchant Marine.**

Accord   An agreement reached between two contending parties, for example, labor and management, competing companies, or nations.

Acquittal   The formal judicial determination by a court or a jury that the accused is not guilty of the offense with which he is charged.

ADC   See **Aid to Dependent Children.**

Adjournment   The ending of a **legislative day.** Regular adjournments set the date for the next meeting. A *recess* also concludes legislative business on a given day and sets time for the next meeting, but it does not mark the end of the legislative day. *Adjournment sine die* literally means "adjournment without a day." This marks the end of the legislative session, since it does not set a time for reconvening.

Adjournment sine Die   See **Adjournment.**

Adjudication   The process of giving a legal judgment in a dispute after notice to the parties and after a court hearing.

Admiralty Law   That body of law having to do with controversies arising out of actions performed upon the high seas or relating to the sea. Modern admiralty, or maritime, law has evolved primarily from usage and customs in the ancient Mediterranean seacoast states and cities. In England maritime law is administered by the admiralty courts, but in the United States by federal courts, generally called admiralty courts when dealing with maritime problems.

Administration   **(a)** The organization and procedures by which the executive branch of government carries out its functions. Within limits administrative decisions have the force of law. Administration is the level at which government and citizens most frequently meet. Within the broad policy framework set by statute, administrators can operate rather freely and their day-by-day interpretations and decisions are very important. The problems of dividing responsibility within the executive branch and of coordinating policy as well as of securing able administrators has become a major challenge and test of good government.

(b) A popular term used to identify the executive branch, especially that of the federal government. The Administration represents the authority of the President and his policy-making appointees. Generally the Administration position is taken to be the official policy of the political party in power, but it is not unknown for the Administration position to be opposed by the party leaders in Congress. See **Administrative Procedure Act of 1946.**

Administrative Procedure Act of 1946   A federal law enacted to clarify and restrain executive authority in making administrative regulations and decisions. The size and scope of national problems has required the Congress to delegate partial legislative and judicial functions to executive agencies and commissions. Protests about arbitrary and excessive exercise of administrative authority led Congress to impose more specific and uniform procedures for making and changing administrative regulations, for publicizing changes and for safeguarding the rights of interested persons affected by the regulations. The law of 1946 also enlarged the area of judicial review of certain administrative decisions by an appropriate federal court.

Ad Valorem A base used for computing a tax, especially a duty on imported goods. An *ad valorem* tax on property or imported goods is determined by taking a certain percentage of the value of the property or goods. This method of levying the tax is in contrast to a specific duty, that is, a fixed amount imposed on each article of a class of property without consideration of its value.

AEC See **Atomic Energy Commission.**

Affidavit A written, sworn statement made voluntarily under oath. The oath is taken before a person authorized to administer oaths, such as a notary public, and it attests to the facts contained in the document. An affidavit can sometimes be used as evidence in court.

AFL-CIO See **American Federation of Labor and Congress of Industrial Organizations.**

Agricultural Adjustment Act (AAA) (1933) A complicated law designed to reduce agricultural production so that prices for farm products would rise. Farmers who reduced production were to receive cash payments, the money to be provided by a tax on food processors. The Supreme Court declared the act unconstitutional, and new laws were passed designed to bolster the farm economy. See **New Deal.**

Agency for International Development (AID) The agency established in 1961 to replace the **International Cooperation Administration** and to conduct the general nonmilitary foreign

aid program of the United States. The **Development Loan Fund** is administered within the agency. See also **Mutual Security Program.**

Agricultural Trade Development and Assistance Act A program for the disposal of surplus agricultural commodities established in 1954 and generally referred to as Public Law 480. While the immediate purpose of the program is reduction of government-held surplus commodities, it is also conceived of as a "food for peace" project to alleviate poverty and malnutrition throughout the world. The principal title of the act provides for the sale of surplus commodities to friendly nations for their own currency—"soft currency"—instead of dollars, which the United States deposits in banks of the nation involved. These funds may be used only for limited purposes such as grants and loans for economic development and to meet common defense costs.

Under the act the United States also may give surplus commodities to foreign governments to relieve famine and to combat malnutrition. Grants of surplus agricultural commodities are likewise made to voluntary nonprofit groups in the United States which distribute the products, free, to needy persons abroad. Several billion dollars' worth of surplus commodities have been disposed of through operations under Public Law 480.·

Aid See **Agency for International Development.**

Aid to Dependent Children (ADC) A program for granting aid to children of needy mothers established under federal-state assistance provisions of the Social Security Act of 1935. The purpose of the plan is to   **3**

provide better care for dependent children, to keep them out of orphanages, foster homes, and other public institutions, and to try to provide a home environment insofar as possible.

Air Force, Department of See **Department of Defense.**

Alderman The title used in some cities for a member of the city council. An alderman usually represents a political and geographic subdivision of the city, sometimes called a ward. The aldermen acting together function as the legislative body of a city.

Alien A resident who is not a citizen of the United States. Aliens within the territory of the United States are entitled to its protection, but they do not have all the rights and privileges of a **citizen.**

WONDER HOW LONG THE HONEYMOON WILL LAST?

Berryman, 1939. Library of Congress.

Alliance An agreement, usually by treaty, between two or more nations for diplomatic and military support of a common policy against another state or bloc of states. Secret alliances were denounced after World War I as fac-

tors contributing to war, but the open alliance between Germany and Italy in 1936 provided evidence that open covenants do not necessarily insure the peace. Alliances are sometimes formed in the course of a war for the joint conduct of military activities.

Alliance for Progress A ten-year, $20-billion program for economic and social development of Latin American countries proposed by President Kennedy. The United States and 19 Latin American countries reached agreement on the general nature of the program in 1961. The economic aid in the program is to be related to internal economic, political, and social reform within the participating countries.

Alternate A person at a political convention who is authorized to act on behalf or in place of an official **delegate** if the delegate is not present.

Ambassador The highest ranking diplomatic official appointed by the head of state to be his personal representative at the capital of another nation. Under ordinary circumstances, he is the official channel for political negotiations between the two states. He also represents his government at important state and social affairs in the host country. In traditional usage, the ranking diplomat to a major country is called *ambassador extraordinary* or *plenipotentiary* and to a less important state *minister plenipotentiary*. A *minister resident* is sent to minor nations. For more than a century the United States was represented by ministers plenipotentiary, but in 1893 several ministers were made ambassadors. At present the United States sends ambassadors to about 100 nations. Frequently the appointment as an ambassador is a reward for political party support. See also **Embassy, Diplomat.**

Amendment A formal change made or proposed to be made in a bill, motion or constitution. An amendment may propose a minor change in the wording of the bill or rather insignificant modification. On the other hand an amendment may propose very basic changes, sometimes bringing about a reversal in the meaning and intent of the legislation. A constitutional amendment is a much more complicated process than amending legislative bills and generally requires some form of ratification in addition to approval by the legislature, for example, by vote of the people. The federal Constitution provides two methods of initiating and of ratifying amendments (Article V).

American Bar Association A voluntary professional association of lawyers in the United States. It is generally concerned with establishing standards for the practice of law and in some measure policing its members. Bar associations often conduct plebiscites, polling their memberships, when candidates for appointment to judgeship are being considered at the local, state, or national level. The American Bar Association generally speaks for the legal profession on questions of licensing members of the legal profession, standards for law schools, and legislation relating to courts as well as appointments to the court.

American Farm Bureau Federation An organization of farmers and others interested in the agricultural economy. It has approximately 1.5 million members. The Farm Bureau, as it is usually called, has local organizations in all sections of the United States but is concentrated among the more prosperous farm units in the corn-and-cotton-producing regions of the Midwest and South. It is closely tied to the agricultural extension programs of the land-grant colleges. It tends to support conservative farm policies such as a reduction in government price supports for farm products and a general restriction on governmental interference with the farm economy, as well as with the general economy. Compare with the **National Grange** and the **National Farmers Union.**

American Federation of Labor and Congress of Industrial Organizations (AFL-CIO) A federation of most of the labor unions in the United States, with a membership of approximately 13.5 million men and women. It is the product of the merger in 1955 of the AFL and the CIO. The old AFL was made up primarily of craft unions, whose membership was skilled in a particular craft such as carpentry or plumbing. The CIO, which came into existence in the thirties, was organized along industrial, rather than craft lines; that is, all workers in a given plant or industry, representing many different skills or crafts, were organized into one union. The AFL-CIO is one of the most influential organizations in public life, especially on matters directly affecting organized labor. It generally supports liberal policies aimed at providing greater welfare and security.

American Foreign Policy The characteristic actions and attitudes of the United States government toward other nations and groups of nations. The original policy as stated by President Washington in his *Farewell Address* was to avoid foreign entanglements and to confine our activities to   **5**

domestic stability and growth. This position was modified somewhat by the **Monroe Doctrine** (1823) by which we asserted our intention of excluding political interference by European powers in the affairs of independent North and South American nations.

World War I, a break with the past, committed us to support the cause of democratic governments in Europe and cooperate to secure world peace. The internationalist position of President Wilson, however, did not prevail, and after the war the United States remained outside the **League of Nations** and the **World Court** and on the whole returned to an isolationist position.

Despite efforts at neutrality we were drawn into World War II, and since 1945 our foreign policy has been to assume international leadership. Membership in the **United Nations** and affiliated organizations has involved us in support of programs for world health, agricultural development, montary stability, loans to underdeveloped countries, and cultural and scientific exchange. Through the **Marshall Plan,** the **Mutual Security** program, and various treaties and alliances, such as **NATO,** we have extended military and economic aid to countries around the world. Besides assistance to needy nations and peoples, American foreign policy since 1947 has also been directed at containment of the Soviet Union and at stopping communist imperialism.

American Legion The largest war veterans' organization in the country with a membership of approximately 2.8 million men and women. The Legion attempts to influence public policy on veterans' benefits, strong national defense, and measures affecting the nation's internal security.

American Medical Association (AMA) An organization of approximately 175,000 physicians. Because of its resources, the prestige of the medical profession, and the size of its membership, the AMA and its state organizations are extremely influential in all public policy—national, state, and local—which bears on the practice of medicine. The AMA generally supports conservative policies, resisting such things as government health insurance plans and the inclusion of doctors in the Social Security program.

Amnesty See **Pardon.**

Anarchism A theory that governmental authority is unnecessary and bad. Philosophical anarchism is an old idea but it came into greater prominence in the nineteenth century. It was associated by some with the idea of the natural goodness of man, but it also was supported by those who advocated and used violence and terror to destroy government.

Anarchy A condition in which there is no effective government. A society is said to be in a state of anarchy when the government has collapsed and no instrument for interpreting and applying law has been developed.

Antitrust A term applied to actions taken under the Clayton Act of 1914 and the Sherman Act of 1890 and under other state and federal statutes designed to curb monopolies, trusts, or other restraints on trade. The Antitrust Division of the United States Department of Justice enforces these acts.

Appeasement The name given to the policy which attempts to satisfy another nation by conceding or granting most or all of its demands. Traditionally, appeasement was accepted as a defensible and even honorable method of avoiding armed conflict. But within recent decades it has acquired a negative connotation and is generally applied with reference to such policies as that followed by Great Britain and France when they permitted Germany to take over part of Czechoslovakia just prior to World War II. Whereas the word *appeasement* now applies specifically to unsuccessful or dishonorable policy, it is somewhat uncritically applied to any proposal which is in the nature of compromise or concession.

Page, Louisville-Courier Journal, 1939.
THE MILLENNIUM

Appellate Courts (State) Intermediate courts between the general trial courts and the state supreme court. These courts usually consist of three judges who sit together as *the* court for the purpose of hearing appeals from the trial courts. They help relieve or prevent congestion in the supreme court. The appellate courts decide only questions of law without

a jury and have limited original jurisdiction.

Appellate Jurisdiction See **Jurisdiction.**

Apportionment Allocation by law of legislative seats according to some established formula. See also **Reapportion, Gerrymander.**

Appropriation The act of providing money by a legislature in order to meet expenditures of the government. Ordinarily a legislature passes a bill which authorizes that a certain amount of money be appropriated—this is an *authorization bill*—and later passes an appropriation bill which provides the money. The appropriation may be somewhat less than that which is originally authorized. An appropriation bill is sometimes referred to as a "money bill."

Appropriation Bill See **Appropriation.**

Arbitration The process whereby two parties to a dispute agree in advance to accept a compromise solution to be worked out by a third party called an "arbiter." Arbitration is used in both international and domestic controversies. What distinguishes arbitration from **mediation** and **conciliation** is the advance agreement to accept the compromise.

Aristocracy A system of government in which a very few people in the population exercise political control. In current usage this small percentage would most likely be composed of "old established families" or the very wealthy. The term is also used today to describe a small ruling class or the "best families" of a community.

Arms Control A form of **disarmament** which, in the face of failure to **7**

bring about general disarmament, seeks to limit and reduce armaments and subject the development and experimentation to some kind of control and inspection. See **Disarmament.**

Goldberg, 1947. Wide World Photos.

Arraignment A procedure in criminal law by which the accused is brought before the court and asked to plead guilty or not guilty after the charge contained in the indictment has been read to him.

Articles of Confederation The constitutional basis for the loose affiliation of the American revolutionary colonies. The Articles were adopted in 1781, but proved to be inadequate. They were abandoned in favor of the Constitution proposed in 1787. Under the Articles of Confederation, each of the newly independent colonies, large or small, had one vote in the Congress. Each was jealous of its sovereignty. The central government provided by the Articles of Confederation was feeble and ineffective. It lacked

an executive branch to enforce the laws and had no power to regulate commerce, to tax, or to compel state compliance with acts of Congress.

Assessor A public official, elected or appointed, whose duty is to fix or assess the value of property upon which property taxes are to be based.

Assistant to the President See **White House Office.**

Atlantic Charter The program agreed upon by President Franklin D. Roosevelt and Prime Minister Winston Churchill at their meeting aboard ship in the North Atlantic, August 14, 1941. Although the United States had not yet entered World War II, the declaration was of psychological value, encouraging, as it did, hope of victory over the Axis. The Atlantic Charter contained an eight-point declaration of principles for postwar reconstruction. For example, peace with freedom from fear was assured; territorial gains were renounced; the right of all peoples to choose their own form of government was asserted; and disarmament and world-wide economic cooperation were pledged. On January 1, 1942, the 26 nations united in the war effort against the Axis powers signed the declaration of purposes and principles embodied in the Atlantic Charter.

At Large The election of a member of the House of Representatives by the entire state instead of by a **congressional district** made up of part of a state. Those states that have only one member in the House of Representatives obviously elect that member at large. If the number of representatives from a state is increased after a decennial census and the state legislature cannot agree on a plan to redistrict that state, then the addi-

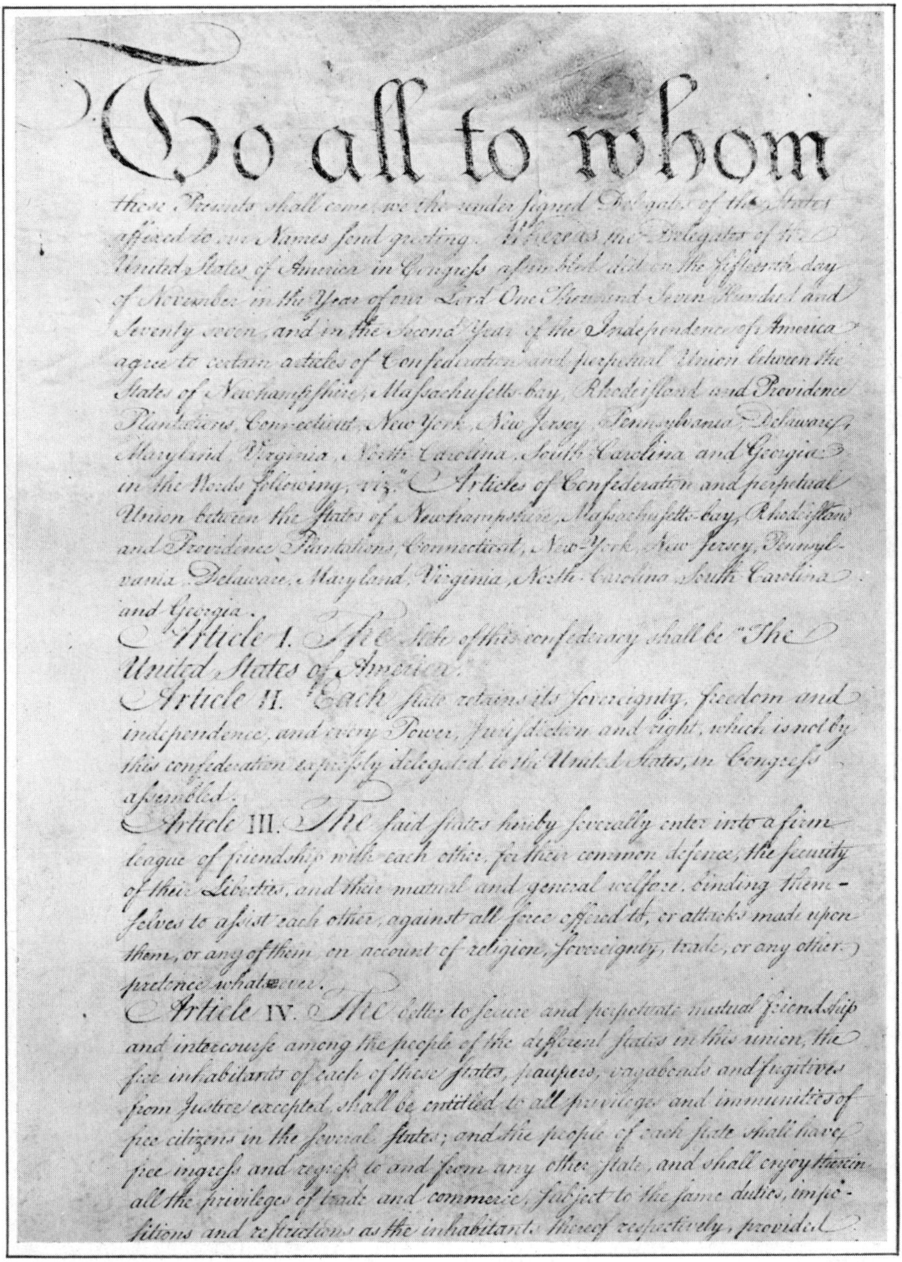

To all to whom these Presents shall come, we the under signed Delegates of the States affixed to our Names send greeting. Whereas the Delegates of the United States of America in Congress assembled did on the fifteenth day of November in the Year of our Lord One Thousand Seven Hundred and Seventy seven, and in the Second Year of the Independence of America agree to certain articles of Confederation and perpetual Union between the States of Newhampshire, Massachusetts-bay, Rhodeisland and Providence Plantations, Connecticut, New York, New Jersey, Pennsylvania, Delaware, Maryland, Virginia, North Carolina, South Carolina and Georgia in the Words following, viz. "Articles of Confederation and perpetual Union between the states of Newhampshire, Massachusetts-bay, Rhodeisland and Providence Plantations, Connecticut, New-York, New Jersey, Pennsylvania, Delaware, Maryland, Virginia, North-Carolina, South Carolina and Georgia.

Article I. The Stile of this confederacy shall be "The United States of America".

Article II. Each state retains its sovereignty, freedom and independence, and every Power, Jurisdiction and right, which is not by this confederation expressly delegated to the United States, in Congress assembled.

Article III. The said states hereby severally enter into a firm league of friendship with each other, for their common defence, the security of their Liberties, and their mutual and general welfare, binding themselves to assist each other, against all force offered to, or attacks made upon them, or any of them, on account of religion, sovereignty, trade, or any other pretence whatever.

Article IV. The better to secure and perpetuate mutual friendship and intercourse among the people of the different states in this union, the free inhabitants of each of these states, paupers, vagabonds and fugitives from Justice excepted, shall be entitled to all privileges and immunities of free citizens in the several states; and the people of each state shall have free ingress and regress to and from any other state, and shall enjoy therein all the privileges of trade and commerce, subject to the same duties, impositions and restrictions as the inhabitants thereof respectively, provided

Library of Congress.

ARTICLES OF CONFEDERATION

Berryman, 1943. Library of Congress.

tional representatives are ordinarily elected at large. If the state's representation in Congress has been decreased and the state legislature has not redistricted, then all of the representatives must be elected at large. Occasionally a state will continue to elect a representative or representatives at large for an indefinite period, although normally this is a temporary arrangement. In some cities a proportion of members of the *city council* may also be elected at large. See also **Redistrict** and **Reapportion.**

Atomic Energy Commission (AEC) An independent agency consisting of five commissioners appointed by the President with the consent of the Senate, serving five-year, staggered terms. Because of its great potential, Congress determined to maintain governmental control over atomic energy after its development by the government as a part of the military effort during World War II. Congress therefore created the AEC. To date its

most important function has been building and stockpiling nuclear weapons for the armed forces. The AEC is also charged with the development of the peacetime uses of atomic energy. One of the government's most powerful and important agencies, it spends huge sums of money and influences decisions ranging all the way from such things as who should develop the nation's power resources to the intricate problem of disarmament as it relates to atomic weapons. The Congress maintains a continuous review of AEC operations through its *Joint Committee on Atomic Energy.*

Attaché An officer assigned to a diplomatic office. An attaché usually accompanies the ambassador on a mission of state and acts as his secretary. An attaché may represent one of his government's special interests, such as the army, navy, air force, commerce, cultural affairs, and so on.

Attorney at Law A person licensed by the supreme court of the state to practice law in the courts of the state. Attorneys may be appointed or elected to be legal officers at various levels of government. The Attorney General of the United States is the chief legal officer of the federal government, head of the Department of Justice, and a member of the cabinet. He appears in person or through an assistant in all cases before the Supreme Court in which the United States is a party or has an interest. He also furnishes legal advice to the President and the various executive departments. The Attorney General of the individual states performs similar functions at the state level. The United States District Attorney is the lawyer for the United States in a particular district of the nation, and each state has one or more district attorneys. Some states have judicial districts with a state district attorney as the chief legal officer of that area. The County Attorney is the chief legal officer of a county. He is generally known for his prosecution of criminals in the county courts, although he does handle civil cases as well. A City Attorney is the chief legal officer of a city and represents the city in court in civil and criminal cases.

Attorney General See **Attorney at law, Department of Justice.**

Auditor The official charged with the supervision of the accounts of all other government offices which collect or disburse funds. The auditor is elected in thirty-nine states, and generally his office is more powerful and more important than that of state treasurer. At the municipal level the auditor is generally called "comptroller." The position of auditor is common at both the state and county levels.

Australian Ballot A method of voting used since 1888 wherein the ballot is provided by the government and the marking of the ballot is done in secret. Before the adoption of the Australian ballot, most paper ballots were printed with distinctive markings for each political party, and it was easy for party workers to see what kind of a ballot any voter put into the ballot box. The Australian ballot insures that all ballots look alike on the outside and that they are marked in secret before being placed in the ballot box.

Authorization Bill See **Appropriation.**

Backdoor Spending A term used by opponents of the policy of financing a federal program without going through the normal procedure of making an appropriation. In such cases the Congress establishes an agency to make loans for specific purposes and permits the agency to borrow its capital directly from the Treasury rather than receive an appropriation from current revenues. The practice began in 1932 when the Congress created the Reconstruction Finance Corporation and in effect directed the Treasury to lend the RFC money from funds raised by sale of United States bonds. This procedure in one form or another has since been used to provide funds for a number of agencies including the **Export-Import Bank,** the Home Owners Loan Corporation, the **Commodity Credit Corporation,** and the Public Housing Administration. In authorizing these programs the Congress, of course, specifies the conditions of operation and sets the maximum that can be borrowed from the Treasury. The policy is defended on the basis that establishment of a government lending agency is not strictly an appropriation since the money will be repaid. The term *backdoor spending* is quite inappropriate as a description of this procedure.

Background Conference An informal, unofficial, and private meeting between a high government official and representatives of the press. It is designed to give officials an opportunity to provide reporters with an explanation of the reasons for certain government policies. Reporters present are permitted to print all or most of what they are told, but usually cannot divulge the source of their information.

Baghdad Pact See **Central Treaty Organization.**

Bail The amount of money a person accused of a crime must offer as assurance or security that he will present himself before a court at the assigned time. If one fails to offer bail when it is required, or if he is unable to raise bail, he is ordinarily detained in jail or in prison. The person accused of a capital crime is not given the privilege of being released on bail.

Balance of Payments In the United States the difference, stated in terms of dollars, between the economic value of our exports and imports. An unfavorable balance of trade results when the value of (a) goods and services brought into the country, (b) goods and services purchased and consumed by Americans overseas, (c) American overseas investments, and (d) grants and loans to foreign governments is greater than money received for (a_1) goods and services exported, (b_1) goods and services purchased and consumed in the United States by foreigners, (c_1) foreign investments in our country, and (d_1) foreign debtors' payments on loans. A continuing unfavorable balance can affect the value of a nation's currency on the world market and force a revision in trade and investment policies or in domestic economic and fiscal policies.

Balance of Powers A political and military policy based upon the assumption that alliances of nations will prevent any single nation from threatening the integrity of other nations or dominating international policy. This principle was the basis for the agreement reached in the treaty of Vienna in 1815, and throughout the nineteenth century was advanced particularly by England. It was recognized in some measure in the Treaty of Versailles following World War I and was referred to, also, in the **North Atlantic Treaty Organization.**

Ballot The actual piece of paper, or the recording device in a voting machine, on which a vote is recorded. The word is sometimes used with reference to the right to vote. In this sense it is said that most aliens in this country "do not have the ballot."

Sometimes used simply as a verb —to vote.

Ballot, Australian See **Australian ballot.**

Ballot, Long An election form by which candidates for a great many offices, important and unimportant, are placed before the voters. A long ballot is characteristic of states and communities in which there are very few appointive positions and most offices are filled by a vote.

Ballot, Short An election form by which candidates for only the most important offices or major issues are placed before the voters. A short bal-

12

lot may be achieved by holding federal, state, county, or local elections at different times. The purpose of the short ballot is to focus attention on each election or on each issue and on each candidate. The short ballot can be achieved only if many minor posts are filled by appointment and if only major issues are brought before the citizens for decision by voting.

Bandwagon A political campaign which seems likely to be successful. To "jump on the bandwagon" is to associate oneself with what appears to be a winning campaign. In campaigns the "bandwagon technique" is the attempt to make one's own candidate look like a certain winner so that the undecided voter will "jump on the bandwagon" lest he back a loser.

Bankruptcy The financial condition under which an individual's (person or business firm) liabilities so far exceed his assets that the courts take over control of his property on behalf of the creditors. The federal government and the states have concurrent jurisdiction in establishing procedures whereby a business or an individual either voluntarily or involuntarily may be absolved from all liabilities incurred prior to the filing of the original petition of bankruptcy, with a provision for *pro rata* disposition of assets to the creditors. A procedure of this sort is justified as a means of giving overburdened debtors an opportunity for a fresh start.

Bar In the United States, the term is applied to the whole body of attorneys and members of the legal profession. The word is derived from the bar or barricade in a courtroom which served to keep the general public out of the well of the court.

Bench The term applied to all judges. It originated with the bench which judges occupy in the courtroom. Today it retains this specific meaning as well as the more general one.

Bicameral Having two chambers, as most legislatures in the United States. See also **Unicameral.**

Big Stick An expression taken from the statement of President Theodore Roosevelt that American policy should be to "speak softly and carry a big stick." "Big stick" had reference to a strong military establishment which would back up policy decisions.

Bill A proposal which is formally introduced into a legislature and if approved becomes law. In a recent session of Congress, for example, over 12,000 bills were introduced and slightly over 600, or about 5 per cent, of these were enacted into law. Of course, among the 12,000 there were many duplications. See also **Resolution.**

Bill of Attainder A law designed to punish an individual without due process of law. As late as the seventeenth century, it was common practice for the English Parliament to pass laws which condemned persons to the scaffold without any judicial review of their cases. Many of these bills were hastily drawn and were extremely unjust. In the French Revolution, too, many people were condemned without any kind of fair trial or judicial review of their cases. The Constitution prohibits both the national and the state governments from enacting bills of attainder. The term has been broadened in scope to apply to legislation designed so as to punish or cause hardship to a single person.

Bill of Rights The first ten amend-   13

ments to the federal Constitution. They were adopted in 1791. When the Constitution was first proposed in 1787, there was widespread dissatisfaction because it did not contain guarantees of certain basic freedoms and individual rights. To counter these objections and encourage the states to ratify the Constitution, supporters of the Constitution guaranteed that the first Congress would submit a Bill of Rights in the form of amendments for ratification by the states.

Some of these ten amendments are now relatively unimportant, such as the Second which relates to the right to bear arms, and the Third which prohibits the quartering of soldiers in private houses in peacetime without the consent of the owners. But others, especially the First, the Fourth, the Fifth, the Seventh, and the Eighth, continue to be of great importance and significance. See also **Palko v. Connecticut.**

Bipartisan An action or movement which includes members of both major political parties. See also **Nonpartisan.**

Marcus, 1954. New York Public Library.

TEA FOR TWO

Birth Registration The act of recording every birth in the Bureau of Vital Statistics or Department of Health in the town, city, or county where the birth occurred as well as in the state health office. Usually a registrar is in charge of the bureau, and physicians are required by law to file a birth certificate giving the names of parents, address, date, time, place of birth, and sex of the child.

Black Belt **(a)** Any area where there is a heavy concentration of Negroes in the population. In cities it generally reflects a pattern of segregation. **(b)** Those parts of the South where there is a heavy concentration of Negroes.

Black Market A marketing operation in which products are bought and sold in violation of the law. There are black markets in such things as narcotics and drugs in most areas of the world. In wartime, black market operations were extended to include almost any commodity in short supply or rationed or controlled in some way by the government.

Bloc A group of legislators who have certain interests in common and who vote together on most matters affecting that interest. In the United States Congress there is common reference to the farm bloc, although it is difficult to isolate this bloc, and also to the Southern bloc, which on the issue of civil rights is quite solid and firm.

Blue Law A law relating generally to behavior and conduct. Often the term refers to laws on the books for many years but out of step with current community tastes and values. Examples of blue laws are those re-

BILL OF RIGHTS

quiring that Sunday athletic contests end at 6:00 P.M., and those which prohibit the sale of liquor at certain times or in certain areas.

Board of Education An elective or appointive body which directs a municipality's education system. The board's functions include selecting a superintendent, purchasing land and buildings, letting contracts for school construction, and operating the schools. City schools generally include primary schools, secondary schools, vocational schools, junior colleges, and sometimes senior colleges and universities.

Bolshevism That particular brand of **communism** whose advocates won control of the Russian communist movement and ultimately seized control of the government during the Russian Revolution of 1917. The term is now sometimes used as a synonym for communism, especially Russian communism. Bolshevism emphasizes such communist principles as the necessity in a given country of overthrowing the capitalist regime rather than cooperating with it, the inevitable struggle between economic classes, and the effectiveness of a small, highly disciplined party instead of a large, unwieldy, and unreliable group.

Bond **(a)** A certificate of indebtedness issued by a government or a business in return for money which it has borrowed. Most governments or their subdivisions, such as school districts, obtain some of the money they require by selling bonds bearing fixed rates of interest and extending over a long period of time.

(b) A financial guarantee posted with a court by one charged with a crime to insure his appearance in court.

(c) A financial guarantee posted by a contractor (performance bond) to insure that he will perform his contract. If he does not perform, the bond is subject to forfeiture.

Boom A favorable trend in a political candidate's prospects, usually accompanied by extensive promotion on the part of his followers. The term is also used to describe a time of great business activity and economic growth.

Boomer One who takes long chances in politics.

Boondoggle Any job or project, especially a government job or project, which involves very little work or is nearly useless or is wasteful. The term arose in the days of the Great Depression when the government embarked upon a vast public works program to help relieve unemployment.

Bootleg The act of assisting in the sale or distribution of goods, primarily liquor, after such sale or distribution has been declared illegal. Bootlegging in liquor was widespread during **Prohibition** and continues on a limited scale even today.

Border State A state which borders on both the North and the South and has some of the characteristics of each region. States ordinarily called border states are Delaware, Maryland, West Virginia, Kentucky, Missouri, and Oklahoma. Tennessee is also sometimes included in this group; its eastern mountainous region refused to support the Confederacy during the Civil War and today remains a strongly Republican area in a Democratic state.

Boss A political leader who controls a strong organization or **machine** or has the reputation of controlling it. The term *boss* is often used with reference to opposition leaders, especially in convention contests or primary contests or within one or the other political party.

Boycott An organized refusal to deal with a person, organization, or nation. Examples in recent years have been labor union boycotts of products made in nonunion shops, boycotts by Negroes of stores practicing segregation, and the American boycott on goods made in Communist China. Boycotts are designed to bring economic or social pressure to bear in order to change the policies of the person, organization, or nation against which the boycott is directed. The term originated from the ostracizing of a land agent, Captain Boycott, by his Irish neighbors during the Land League troubles in 1880.

Brain Trust A group of advisers to a high public official. The term originated during the election campaign of 1932 as a description of the many Franklin Roosevelt advisers who were college professors. It is used today to describe any group of advisers composed largely of professors or other experts and specialists. It is sometimes used in a derogatory sense.

Breach of Contract The failure to perform, without sufficient legal cause, a promise which constitutes a part or the whole of a contract. The remedy of the injured party lies at law, where he may sue the nonperforming party for damages or for specific performance of the contract. In the latter instance, the court will direct the party to fulfil the broken promise. See also **Tort.**

Brown _v._ Board of Education (1954) A case in which the Supreme Court ruled that racial segregation in public schools is unconstitutional and thus reversed the "separate but equal" application of **Plessy _v._ Ferguson** (1896). It was one of the most important and far-reaching decisions in the history of the Court. At issue was the segregation by race of children in public schools of many southern states. The Fourteenth Amendment requires that no state shall "deny to any person within its jurisdiction the equal protection of the laws." Like "due process of law," and other vague phrases, the term _equal protection of the laws_ means different things to different people. Because of this uncertainty and because of the difficulty of drafting legislation which covers every conflict, the Supreme Court has been called upon in many cases to decide the meaning of this clause. In the case of Brown _v._ Board of Education, a unanimous Court held that segregated schools deprived children in a minority group of equal educational opportunities. "Separate educational facilities are inherently unequal," the decision declared.

Budget Message An annual message from the President to Congress submitted near the beginning of each new session. It contains a detailed explanation of the President's proposed budget. The message itself is usually a very comprehensive document, about the size of a large city's telephone book. It is usually approved by the President's own party and greatly criticized by members of the opposition party, who usually charge that the budget message underestimates expenditures and overestimates anticipated revenue. See also **Budget system.**

Budget System In the federal government, the complex series of actions and decisions to determine how much money will be spent and for what. **17**

The process begins about May in the various departments and agencies as they decide how much money they will need for the coming fiscal year and why. Their proposals all go to the **Bureau of the Budget,** a part of the **Executive Office of the President.** The Bureau accepts some requests, rejects others, and demands explanations for most. After months of pulling and hauling between the Bureau of the Budget and the departments, the Bureau consults with the President. The final decisions make up the President's budget.

After the President sends his **Budget Message** to Congress, it is referred to the congressional committees having jurisdiction over the various matters, and the legislative process begins. By the time Congress acts, more than a year has usually elapsed since the agencies first started working on their budget requests.

Marcus, 1952. New York Public Library

Building Code   The set of laws, rules, and regulations of a municipality or of another unit of government which prescribe the specifications to which houses and buildings must be built. Generally the building code contains fire and safety regulations about such things as fire escapes, stairs, elevators, sprinklers, electric wiring, plumbing, and heating equipment which may be used, and also the manner in which these may be installed.

Bull Moose Party   See **Progressive Party.**

Bunting *v.* Oregon (1917)   A case in which the Supreme Court held by a five to three vote that an Oregon law which established a maximum ten-hour day for all industrial employees was a legitimate health safeguard and not a violation of individual rights. This decision marked a turning point in the Court's interpretation of the Constitution. In such fields as hours, wages, and working conditions, a state's right to act under the **police power** clause of the Constitution is now almost universally accepted.   See also **Lochner *v.* New York.**

Bureau   A subordinate administrative division within a government agency. Among the most important and best known is the **Federal Bureau of Investigation** in the Department of Justice. Among the more obscure is the Bureau of the Chief of Postal Inspectors in the Post Office Department.

Bureaucracy   A highly centralized system of administration. Historically the term is applied to the administrative system developed in France after the first Napoleon. Today, however, bureaucracy implies a unit of government with more or less permanent authority, unresponsive to political changes, to public opinion and to the attitudes of the people.

Bureaucrat One who technically is employed in a bureau. The word is often used, however, in a derogatory sense to imply that such an employee exercises authority arbitrarily.

Bureau of the Budget One of the fiscal control agencies of the federal government. When it was created in 1921, it was placed nominally in the Department of the Treasury, but since 1939 it has been a part of the **Executive Office of the President.** The Bureau of the Budget, acting through the Director of the Budget, prepares the President's budget. It passes judgment on all legislation introduced in the Congress, determining whether it is in conformity with the President's program and making estimates as to the possible cost of the program. The Bureau of the Budget has grown in importance through the years to a point where in many cases clearance by the Budget is almost essential to passage of the legislation, and disapproval by the Bureau of the Budget is considered a good indication, at least in major legislation, of a possible presidential veto.

In addition to performing fiscal functions, the Bureau of the Budget is the overseer of the administrative organization for the entire executive branch of the government and makes recommendations for improvement when necessary. Critics of the increased power of the Bureau of the Budget have charged that oftentimes the bookkeeper is running the country.

Bureau of the Census See **Department of Commerce.**

Bureau of Employment Security See **Department of Labor.**

Bureau of Indian Affairs See **Department of the Interior.**

Bureau of Labor Statistics See **Department of Labor.**

Bureau of Mines See **Department of the Interior.**

Bureau of Public Roads See **Department of Commerce.**

Bureau of Standards See **Department of Commerce.**

By-Election An election held in order to fill a vacancy created by the death or resignation of an officeholder.

Bylaw A rule or regulation of a corporation, private or public, designed to regulate its internal and external affairs. Less formal groups, such as political parties and private clubs, may also adopt bylaws to regulate their activities.

CAB See **Civil Aeronautics Board.**

Cabinet An advisory group to the President which has developed by custom rather than constitutional provision. It is made up of the heads of the ten major executive departments and in recent years it has included also the United States representative to the United Nations. The Vice President likewise participates in cabinet meetings. The cabinet members in order of their rank are the Secretary of State, the Secretary of the Treasury, the Secretary of Defense, the Attorney General, the Postmaster General, the Secretary of the Interior, the Secretary of Agriculture, the Secretary of Commerce, the Secretary of Labor, and the Secretary of Health, Education, and Welfare. This is the order in which they would succeed to the presidency after the Vice President, the Speaker of the House of Representatives, and the President Pro Tempore of the Senate.

Cabinet members are appointed by the President with the consent of the Senate. They can be removed at any time by the President. The President usually meets with the cabinet once a week, and traditionally the cabinet has been regarded as important not only as an administrative body, but also as an advisory body.

The influence of the cabinet itself and of individual cabinet members varies from one administration to another. Much depends upon the manner in which the President of the United States decides to use his cabinet. In those cases in which the cabinet is considered to be ineffective, other groups of individuals who are close to the President and considered to be his advisers are often identified by such labels as the **kitchen cabinet** or the shadow cabinet.

Calendar   **(a)** A list of cases pending before a court.

(b) In legislatures, a list of the bills pending before a committee or a legislative chamber. There are different kinds of calendars, varying from one legislative chamber to another, but their basic purpose is the listing of measures to be considered.

Campaign   All of those activities conducted in behalf of a candidate for public office. A campaign usually begins with seeking party nomination. It may carry on to a primary within one's own party and then through a general election. The duration, cost, and technique of a campaign may vary from one office to another. A campaign for the office of county coroner may be rather brief and inexpensive, since the issues are generally quite restricted, while campaigns for Congress or for

the Senate or for the presidency can be very long, complicated, and expensive. Included in the campaign are such activities as speech-making, advertising on radio and television and newspapers, distributing campaign folders, bumper stickers, billboard advertising, registration drives, and drives to get out the vote.

In a broader sense, a campaign includes any effort to achieve a goal. In a sense the word *campaign* is often used with reference to efforts made to raise funds for charity or eliminating litter on the streets or reducing forest fires and the like.

Marcus, 1952. New York Public Library.

THE GAME BEGINS

Canvass   The postelection counting of votes by the designated official for the purpose of determining the victor. The **Secretary of State** canvasses state elections and the county clerk, county elections.

Capital Punishment   The death penalty meted out to one convicted of a major crime. In those states which have capital punishment, death is carried out by hanging, electrocution, or gas. In the military services a firing squad does the deed. Capital punishment is not authorized in Maine, Michigan, Minnesota, North Dakota, Rhode Island, or Wisconsin.

Capitalism An economic system wherein private ownership is the general rule and government ownership is the exception. The United States is a capitalistic nation because most of the productive land, communications and transportation systems, and the means of production and distribution are controlled by private owners. The term has many shades of meaning and has become the target of a great deal of abuse and misunderstanding.

Captive Nations The term applied to those nations which were brought under control of communist governments by the direct or indirect action of the Soviet Union. Though in most cases these non-Russian peoples retain their national name and boundaries, they have, in fact, lost their national independence as was demonstrated by the crushing of the Hungarian revolt in 1956. The nations usually listed as "captive nations" are Poland, Hungary, Lithuania, Czechoslovakia, Latvia, Rumania, Bulgaria, and Estonia.

Carpetbagger An outsider who comes into an area and seeks to gain public office to take advantage of local inhabitants. The term was first applied to itinerant bankers in the Old West who carried their money in bags made from old carpets. It took on unfavorable connotation after the Civil War when it was applied to Northerners who came South with their carpetbags to exploit the South, often from political positions.

Caucus A meeting of the members of a legislative body who belong to the same party. Caucuses are held for various purposes such as the election or nomination of party leaders, the determination of the calendar, and the discussion of party policy. In this sense caucus can be used interchangeably with **conference.** The Republicans in the United States Senate and House of Representatives and the Democrats in the Senate refer formally to such meetings as conferences. House Democrats call their meetings caucuses.

1887. Culver Pictures.

In a more general sense, caucus is a meeting of any group of people interested in politics for purposes of working out a common program or plan for action. Caucuses may be formal or informal; they may be called in accordance with laws governing political party action, or they may be called without any special legal sanction.

Interestingly, this word is derived from an Algonquin Indian word meaning "to urge or to advise."

CCC See **Commodity Credit Corporation.**

C.C.C.P. Russian letters which translate into **U.S.S.R.**

Censure A formal resolution by a legislative body disapproving the action of one of its colleagues or another public official. Censure action is rarely taken in American political life.

Census, Bureau of See **Department of Commerce.**

CENTO See **Central Treaty Organization.**

Central Intelligence Agency (CIA) An agency responsible for the collection and evaluation of intelligence. In the narrow sense "intelligence" includes two things: one, the gathering of information not ordinarily available; and two, the evaluation of this information, together with other information which may be more or less public. The specific activities of the Central Intelligence Agency are a matter of some secrecy. It operates under the direction of the National Security Council, and the Director of the CIA is a regular attendant at the Council's meetings.

Central Treaty Organization (CENTO) An alliance designed to preserve the independence of the Middle East; one of the three organizations, **NATO, CENTO,** and **SEATO,** whose purpose is to contain communist imperialism. The Central Treaty Organization was established in 1959 as the successor of the Baghdad Pact of 1955. It pledges Iran, Pakistan, Turkey, and the United Kingdom to collective defense within the organization. The United States is not a member of CENTO, but has signed bilateral agreements with Iran, Pakistan, and Turkey to protect them against aggression and to furnish assistance

under the **Mutual Security program.** In addition to common military efforts the Baghdad Pact and CENTO both have provided for technical and cultural assistance programs and have been successful in improving economic and educational standards.

Centralization The movement of power and authority toward a single, central point. The term is frequently used in American political debate in an unfavorable sense; it suggests that the federal government is assuming too much power and responsibility. The **Constitution,** it should be noted, was a centralizing instrument and replaced the ineffective and decentralized arrangement existing under the **Articles of Confederation.**

Chamber The room in which a legislative body meets and conducts its business. It is also used to designate the special room outside the courtroom in which judges hold conferences and conduct special inquiries. See also **Floor.**

Chamber of Commerce A national organization of persons and organizations engaged in commerce or business. There are local chambers of commerce, state chambers of commerce, and a United States Chamber of Commerce. These organizations attempt to affect government policies and they make their generally conservative views known on a wide variety of economic matters, including taxes, tariffs, regulation of commerce, and welfare programs.

Chargé d'Affaires A diplomatic officer of lower rank than an ambassador or minister. He receives his credentials from the foreign relations minister of his government rather than from the head of state and deals at the level of the foreign affairs minister or secretary of the country to which he is sent. Ordinarily if the ambassador is away, the chargé d'affaires can fulfil his duties.

Charter The basic law setting forth a city's boundaries, powers, system of government, and method of selecting or electing officials and fixing their duties. Charters are granted by the state legislature and are really statutes. The five common charter systems are:

1. *Special*—each city has its own charter granted by a special act of the legislature.

2. *General*—a charter established for all cities in the state by legislative action.

3. *Classification*—different charters for different classes of cities based generally upon size.

4. *Home rule*—statute permitting inhabitants of each city to draft its own charter.

5. *Optional*—statute incorporating several standard charters and permitting cities to select the one which it approves.

Chauvinism An exaggerated and bellicose patriotism. The term arose when the excessive admiration of Nicolas Chauvin for Napoleon and the days of the First Empire became a source of ridicule. The other veterans who shared his nostalgia for the Napoleonic days came to be known as Chauvins.

Checks and Balances Those various safeguards and devices in the Constitution which protect against too great a concentration of power in any one person or group of persons. The most important "check" is the fact that the national government is composed of three separate branches: the executive (President), the legislative (Congress), and the judicial (the courts). The sharing of power among the three is designed to insure against the concentration and abusive use of power. Interdependence is provided in various ways. The executive branch must appeal to the legislative for appropriations, for example, and the legislature must rely upon the executive to enforce the laws. The courts can always declare laws unconstitutional. A further "check" or "balance" is provided in our government through the division of authority between the central government and the states. See also **Separation of powers.**

Chief of State A person recognized as the one who more than anyone else speaks for the nation. This is one of the many unofficial titles given the President of the United States. It is a title which has symbolic rather than substantive significance. In this role the President resembles most closely the king or queen of a nation like Great Britain or Sweden, rather than a prime minister. The responsibilities of this role involve the President in ceremonial functions, such as lighting the national Christmas tree on the White House lawn, throwing out the first baseball at the opening game of the major league season, and formally receiving visiting heads of other governments.

Child Labor Laws Those laws which relate to the employment of children under a certain age. They generally provide for a minimum health and safety standard of employment and specify those industries or fields of employment in which child labor is either permitted or forbidden. The Public Contracts Labor Act of 1936 outlawed child labor in those industries under contract to the fed- **23**

eral government. The **Fair Labor Standards Act** of 1938 and subsequent amendments to that act forbid the employment of children under sixteen in manufacturing, mining, transportation, and commerce and provide other prohibitions for various age groups. Most states have their own laws in this field.

Church and State In the United States the Constitutional provision dealing directly but somewhat vaguely with the proper relationship between church and state. The First Amendment provides that "Congress shall make no law respecting an establishment of religion, or prohibiting the free exercise thereof." The prohibition against "establishment of religion" has never been clearly and finely determined and is under almost continuous review by the lower courts of the country and also quite regularly by the Supreme Court. From the beginning of our country, for example, the armed forces have had chaplains and religious services. Church property in almost every state has been tax exempt. Most of the controversy about the meaning of the Constitution and its interpretations develops in relation to educational problems, but controversy has extended into such fields as the observation of national holidays —such as Christmas—and also has been raised with regard to tax exemption. See also **Everson v. Board of Education, Illinois ex rel McCollum v. Board of Education,** and **Zorach v. Clauson.**

CIA See **Central Intelligence Agency.**

Circuit Courts (a) See **County Courts for State Circuit.** (b) See **U.S. Court of Appeals.**

24 **Citizen** A member of a nation or

state who has all the civic and political rights and privileges of such members and also the corresponding duties. Citizenship is acquired by birth or by **naturalization.** Nations follow one of two general traditions in determining citizenship by birth, the child receiving his citizenship either from the place he is born or from the nationality of his parents. In the United States a child becomes a citizen by birth in the United States, even though his parents are aliens. However, children of American citizens born while the parents are traveling or living abroad, are citizens. A citizen may renounce citizenship in one country and by certain actions such as residence, registration, payment of taxes, or swearing allegiance become a citizen of another country.

City A municipal corporation of substantial size and population within a state and subject to the laws of the state. The city charter is the basic document describing its powers, system of government, methods of election, and other functions. The principal forms of city government are mayor-council, board of aldermen, or city-manager plan.

City Attorney See **Attorney at law.**

City Commissioners A municipal body usually made up of five elected officials who exercise the legislative and administrative authority in a city which has a commission plan of government. Commissioners are generally elected by the whole city, often without party designation. The mayor usually presides over the commission when it sits as city council, and in some cities he assigns the commissioners to the respective departments after they have been elected.

City Council The governing body of

a city. The city council is generally made up of members who are elected by the people for a specified term of service. Usually the **mayor** is the chief of the council.

City Manager A professional, supposedly nonpolitical, adminstrative head of a city selected by the council to direct the city government. His powers usually include appointing and removing all department heads and key officials within departments; assigning duties of top officials; enforcing city ordinances and applicable state laws; supervising all city administrators; preparing a budget for submission to the council; and general leadership of the city government. City managers are generally trained professional administrators who are expected to be experts in government. Some cities have dropped the city-manager plan because it takes control of the government out of the hands of the electorate and the elected officials.

Civil Aeronautics Board (CAB) An independent regulatory commission composed of five members appointed by the President with the consent of the Senate for six-year, staggered terms. It grants licenses to airlines, regulates the rates which can be charged, determines subsidies paid airlines, passes on all proposed mergers of airlines and route changes, and investigates accidents. See also **Federal Aviation Authority.**

Civil Case A case involving a dispute not covered by criminal law. It may be between private persons or between the government and individuals. Private suits arise in such areas as banking, contracts, torts, copyrights, patents, and workmen's compensation. In about one-third of the civil cases in the federal courts, the government is involved either as plaintiff or defendant; for example, when the government sues for enforcement of contract obligations, or for enforcement of minimum wage laws or antitrust laws. Some cases may involve both criminal and civil law. If a citizen refuses to pay his income tax, for example, the government may institute a criminal suit to penalize him by fine or imprisonment and a civil suit to collect the tax. See also **Criminal case.**

Civil Liberties See **Civil rights.**

Civil Rights Those privileges or prerogatives which are conferred on

Fitzpatrick, St. Louis Post-Dispatch, 1948.

"THERE IS A SERIOUS GAP BETWEEN OUR IDEALS AND SOME OF OUR PRACTICES. THIS GAP MUST BE CLOSED."
—PRESIDENT TRUMAN

a person by law and which he can claim as a citizen. The phrase is sometimes used interchangeably with civil liberties, but actually the terms have **25** slightly different meanings. Civil rights refer to legal rights of a positive kind such as the right to receive equal treatment before the law, the right to vote, and the right to share equally with other citizens in the benefits of organized society—including the use of public schools and public recreational areas. *Civil liberties,* on the other hand, is a term that refers to those things a person is legally free to do without government interference, such as to speak, to assemble, to organize, and to worship. Civil liberties is used generally in opposing government controls or actions, whereas civil rights is related to the efforts to secure full civil rights for Negroes and other groups, and is generally used in relation to programs of positive government action. See also **Natural law.**

Civil Service The service by the non-military employees of the government below the top, policy-making ranks. Usually the term applies only to employees appointed or promoted under the merit system as distinguished from those appointed for political reasons. In this sense there has been some kind of civil service in the government since 1883. An employee is said to be protected by civil service when his continued employment is not dependent upon which political party controls the administration, but depends rather on his record and on his ability to perform his duties.

Civil Service Commission See **United States Civil Service Commission.**

Civil War Amendments The Thirteenth, Fourteenth, and Fifteenth amendments to the federal Constitution, all of which were adopted within a few years after the Civil War and relate to the issues involved in the war and the postwar period. The Thirteenth Amendment provides for the abolition of slavery. The Fourteenth provides for equal protection under the law of all citizens and deals with other questions related quite specifically to the war. The Fifteenth provides that no citizen of the United States shall have his right to vote denied or abridged on account of race, color, or previous condition of servitude and provides that Congress shall have power to enforce this article by appropriate legislation. The Fifteenth Amendment, of course, has been the basis for the recent civil rights debates in the Congress of the United States.

Class, Economic A category of persons whose income or source of income is approximately the same. The simplest system of classification is based on the three traditional distinctions known as "upper class," "middle class," and "lower class." Most Americans regard themselves as being in the middle class. Other distinctions made historically are between land owners and peasants, between the bourgeois and the **proletariat,** and the communist distinction between capitalist and proletariat.

Clayton Act See **Antitrust.**

Classified Material Documents and information a government believes should be available only to certain persons. The federal government has three classifications: classified, secret, and top secret. Military and civilian personnel must undergo "clearance checks" by the Federal Bureau of Investigation to determine their fitness for access to classified material. The checks for top secret clearance are, of course, the most extensive.

"Clear and Present Danger" See **Schenck *v.* United States.**

Clean Bill A bill which corresponds exactly to the final action that is taken by the committee. If the committee sends a bill to the floor of Congress with committee amendments, each of these amendments must be voted on separately by the entire legislative body. Oftentimes difficulty will arise over particular amendments under this procedure. In an effort to avoid such difficulty, a committee member may introduce the committee product as a *clean bill,* which is the same as a new bill. It will then be referred to the committee and reported directly to the floor. See also **Mark up.**

Clerk City or county official, appointed or elected, who serves as a clearing house for city or county business. The clerk to the city council or the county board generally serves as secretary to that body and keeps minutes or proceedings. He may issue various licenses such as liquor, hunting, and fishing and maintains records of chattel mortgages. The city election bureau is under supervision of the city clerk, who directs voter registration and supervises city elections.

Clerk of Court The official who directs all administrative activities of a court. All lawsuits and attendant documents are filed in his office. Notices to jurors and subpoenas to witnesses and other persons having business with the court are sent out from his office. The clerk of court is an officer of the United States Supreme Court, state, county, and municipal courts. In some states the clerks of the state district courts are elected. The United States Supreme Court and most state supreme courts appoint their clerks. In some states the clerk is

assigned additional duties such as issuing marriage and driver licenses, and registering trade names. All court records of verdicts, divorces, and marriages are kept on file by the clerk.

Cloakroom The private room adjacent to a legislative chamber or a committee room used by legislators for consultation and relaxation. It is open only to members of the legislative body and others whom they choose to admit. Cloakrooms are usually informal meeting places where negotiations or conversation can take place in relative privacy. Generally they are provided with outside telephone lines and may have special eating and drinking facilities.

Closed Shop A business or industry which hires only union members. The Labor-Management Relations Act of 1947 forbids the closed shop. See **Taft-Hartley Act.**

Closure See **Filibuster.**

Cloture See **Filibuster.**

Coalition A combination of two or more factions or parties for the purpose of achieving some political goal. The most famous contemporary coalition in American politics is the one between conservative Republicans and conservative Southern Democrats in Congress, although on occasion liberal Democrats and liberal Republicans do unite to advance common objectives.

Coast Guard A branch of the armed forces which operates under the Treasury Department during peacetime and under the Navy in time of war or when the President so directs. Its functions include enforcing maritime law, apprehending stolen or dangerous boats and ships, providing and maintaining navigational aids, per- **27**

forming rescue operations, investigating marine disasters, and providing weather information.

Coast Guard Academy See **Academy, United States Coast Guard.**

Code of Federal Regulations See **Federal Register.**

Code of The United States A systematic collection of all federal statutes in force. The Code contains approximately 50 "titles" or "subject headings" under which are classified all matters which have been the subject of legislation. The Code is brought up-to-date periodically.

Cold War The popular phrase which applies to action short of open military conflict. Elements of the cold war include such things as sabotaging the normal diplomatic means of settling disputes, resorting to threats of military force, using economic grants and concessions to influence neutral nations and even nations friendly to the other side, and the extensive use of propaganda by radio and other means of communication in order to advance one's own interests. Cold-war activities may also include supplying military assistance to revolutionary groups and to underground movements in order to weaken the political, economic, and military power of a government friendly to the opposite side. Cold-war activities often involve violation of international agreements and of world law. See **War.**

Collective Bargaining The negotiations between a labor **union** representing the employees, and representatives of management. Bargaining usually involves such issues as wages, hours, working conditions, and pensions and other benefits. The right of employees to form labor unions and to bargain collectively rather than as individuals is now generally recognized, although it was a right long fought for.

Collective Security The defensive strategy which calls for collective or united action on the part of several nations. Originally, the term implied that almost all of the nations of the world would turn upon any aggressor nation and collectively defeat it. It now has a less comprehensive meaning, referring to the collective action of a limited group of nations to defend themselves against another nation or group of nations. **NATO** and **SEATO** are organized as a means of achieving collective security.

Collectivism A system wherein most or all of the property or means of production is owned by the whole community through some kind of governmental form rather than by individuals or groups of individuals. In the extreme forms of collectivism, the community provides such things as housing, food, and medical care. The term is frequently but inaccurately applied to any measure which extends government regulation to the economy or provides welfare programs by government action.

Colony A territory over which a nation claims the right of possession and the right to exercise political authority and a measure of control of the external and internal affairs of that territory. In the colonies which have existed in the twentieth century, most of the inhabitants have been of a different race and culture from the inhabitants of the mother country. The colonial system has been defended as one which has brought order and economic and cultural advancement, but it has, on the other hand, been criticized as a device for the exploitation of the natural resources and of the colonial people. In the years since World War II, there has been rising opposition to colonialism especially in Africa and in Asia.

Commander-in-Chief The person in charge of a nation's military forces. In the United States, the Constitution assigns this responsibility to the President as one of his most important powers. See the **Presidency.**

Commerce Clause That portion of Article I, Section 8 of the federal Constitution which provides that Congress has the power "to regulate commerce . . . among the several States." This is the constitutional support for much of the regulation of economic affairs of the nation by the federal government. Just how broadly this provision should be construed has always been in dispute, both in the Congress and in the courts. As industry and finance become more complex, the commerce clause has been applied as justifying more comprehensive federal regulation and intervention. See **Gibbons v. Ogden, Hammer v. Dagenhart, U.S. v. Darby.**

Commerce, Department of See **Department of Commerce.**

Commerce, Secretary of See **Department of Commerce.**

Commission on Civil Rights A temporary agency established for two years by the Civil Rights Act of 1957 and twice extended for two more years. It consists of six commissioners appointed by the President with the consent of the Senate. Members of the Commission receive no salary, but are paid on a per day basis for work. The Commission's activities are administered by a staff headed by a staff director who is appointed by the President with the consent of the Senate.

The Commission is charged with investigating specific allegations that citizens are being deprived of the right to vote, with collecting information about denials of equal protection of the laws under the Constitution, with appraising the laws and policies of the federal government in this entire field. It has submitted periodic reports to the Congress and the President.

Committee A body of legislators officially delegated to make studies and report to the parent legislative body on specific problems or legislation. Since most legislatures must deal with a great variety of bills, a division of labor is necessary. The committee system was developed to meet this need. Committee members generally become experts on the subjects within their jurisdiction and come to be relied upon by the rest of the legislative body. See **Standing committee, Select committee, Special committee, Joint committee, Conference committee.**

Committee of the Whole A committee of a legislative body made up of the entire membership of that body. It is usually convened, as in the case of the House of Representatives of the United States, so that the legislative body can carry on its work without meeting all of the ordinary formal requirements of its regular sessions, such as maintaining a **quorum.**

Committee on Committees A committee in a legislative body which makes assignment of its party members to the committees of that body. The Committee on Committees is usually selected by the party members **29**

meeting in caucus or appointed by party leaders. In the United States Senate the Republicans have a Committee on Committees which is elected by the party **conference.** The Democrats assign the task to the **steering committee,** or **policy committee,** which is appointed by the **majority leader** and ratified by the party **conference.** In the House of Representatives the Republican party conference elects a Committee on Committees. The Democratic members of the House **Ways and Means Committee,** a position to which they are elected by the party caucus, act as the Democratic Committee on Committees.

Committee on Rules   A committee of the House of Representatives which exercises great power through its responsibility to determine if, when, and under what conditions bills will be considered by the House of Representatives. Most bills reported to the House by one of the **standing committees** must be cleared for **floor** action by the Committee on Rules. This committee has frequently been criticized for obstructing consideration of legislation which its members oppose, and thereby refusing to allow the full House to express its position. For many years the majority-minority ratio on this committee was 8 to 4. In 1961 it was expanded to 10 to 5.

Commodity Credit Corporation (CCC)   This agency, commonly known as the CCC, is a government corporation within the Department of Agriculture. It provides special assistance to farmers through the mortgaging of crops to the CCC in order that the farmer can receive a price support loan in return. If the market value of the farmer's product goes above the amount of the loan, he can sell the crop, repay the loan, and keep the difference. If the price remains below the loan level, he keeps the money which he has borrowed and the CCC keeps the product. This is essentially the famous "price-support program." When prices drop consistently below the support level, surplus products accumulate in the storage facilities of the CCC.   See also **Department of Agriculture, Parity price.**

Common Law   A body of legal principles developed through the centuries in England and in the United States. It is judge-made law, being based on court decisions rather than on legislative action. Such law can be modified or replaced by legislative action or by judicial decision and therefore varies slightly from state to state.

Common Market See **European Economic Community.**

Community Facilities Administration See **Housing and Home Finance Agency.**

Communism   A set of beliefs and theories as well as an organization which develops from **Marxism.** Communism teaches generally that all history has been a struggle between economic classes and that a final struggle will take place between the **proletariat**—the working classes—and the capitalists, with the former winning and taking control everywhere. This stage is now declared to be in progress and the triumph of communism allegedly is approaching. As elaborated by various communist leaders, communist theory includes such things as support for the violent overthrow of existing noncommunist governments, state ownership of all property excepting a few personal items, organization of a disciplined and loyal political party which will control the government, and primary loyalty to the Soviet Union.

Company Union An organization of the employees in a single firm for the purpose of improving their wages, hours, and working conditions. This type of union is not affiliated with other union organizations such as the AFL-CIO and is often dominated by the employer. Members of international unions do not consider this a real union.

Compromise The act of adjusting conflicting or differing viewpoints on legislation or on other issues. Compromise does not necessarily mean a concession on principle. It may be a concession to reality. Lord Morley in his essay *On Compromise* states that "the interesting question in connection with compromise obviously turns upon the placing of the boundary that divides wise suspense in forming opinions, wise reserve in expressing them, and wise tardiness in trying to realize them, from unavowed disingenuousness and self-illusion, from voluntary dissimulation and from indolence and pusillanimity."

Comptroller See **Controller.**

Conciliation The attempt by a third party to arrange a settlement in a dispute. Conciliation is usually attempted by a person friendly to both sides or by a government official. The term is sometimes used interchangeably with **mediation.** See also **Arbitration.**

Concurrent Resolution See **Resolution.**

Concurring Opinion A judicial opinion written by a justice of a multi-member court, in which he agrees with the conclusion reached by a majority of the members of the court, but differs in his reasoning or in the basis for the decision. It is found most commonly in decisions of supreme courts in the several states and of the United States Supreme Court.

Condemnation **(a)** A sentence or judgment against the accused after he has been found guilty.

(b) The process whereby private property is taken for public use without the consent of the owner, as for a new highway or for the construction of a public building. It involves a forced sale or forced transfer, and the owner is paid reasonable value.

(c) A formal action taken by a legislative body in which it expresses its strong disapproval of the action of one of its colleagues.

Confederacy The group of eleven Southern states which seceded from the United States in 1861 and which fought the Civil War against the established government of the United States.

Confederation A governmental system in which a weak central government derives its power from member states and exercises that power at the sufferance of member states which retain most of their autonomy. The difference between a "federation" and a "confederation" is in a sense only a matter of degree, since authority is divided in both systems. In practice, however, the word *federation* describes a much more strongly centralized government. See also **Articles of Confederation. Constitution,** and **Unitary state.**

Conferee A member of a **conference committee.** He is usually a person of some seniority on the committee from which the legislation being considered in conference originated.

31

Conference A meeting of the members of a legislative body who belong to the same party. In this sense the word is interchangeable with **caucus.** Sometimes the word *conference* is used to apply to a **conference committee.** See **Caucus.**

Conference Committee A committee composed of representatives from each chamber of a legislative body— in the United States Congress, the House and the Senate—and charged with working out differences between bills on the same subject passed by both chambers. Members of the Conference Committee are usually drawn from the committees which drafted the legislation and which handled it in the floor debate in the respective legislative bodies.

Confirmation The action whereby the United States Senate approves, by majority vote, presidential appointments to senior positions in the government.

Confiscation An action whereby private property is taken to protect the public good. Examples of this include such things as government seizures of narcotics, of illegally made alcohol, of unauthorized gambling devices, and illegally held weapons. No compensation is paid to the person whose property is legally confiscated, as he is usually in violation of the law.

Conflict of Interest A situation in which a public official is in a position to decide upon a public matter and the decision may benefit him personally, usually by way of economic advantage. The executive and legislative branches have taken steps to eliminate such conflicts, and possible conflict of interest is one of the principal questions raised during Senate hearings on confirmation of presidential nominees.

Congress The collective name for the United States **House of Representatives** and the United States **Senate.** Congress is the legislative branch of the government. The structure and powers of Congress are set forth in Article I of the **Constitution.**

Congress of Industrial Organizations (CIO) See **American Federation of Labor and Congress of Industrial Organizations.**

Congressional Directory An official government publication containing information about members of Congress and their constituencies, congressional committees, election statistics, administrative agencies, courts, the District of Columbia, international organizations, and press, radio, and television persons in Washington.

Congressional District A geographical and political subdivision of a state. The division is theoretically based upon population, although in many cases there has been great variation in the number of people in a congressional district. Each congressional district is represented by one member of the United States House of Representatives. District lines may be redrawn by the state legislature after each decennial census if the state has gained or lost a representative and reapportionment is required.

Congressional Immunity A special privilege given to United States Senators and members of the House of Representatives by the Constitution of the United States. The Constitution declares that they shall be immune from arrest except in cases of treason, felony, and breach of peace while attending the session of Congress and "in going to and returning from the same." Moreover, it declares that they cannot be "questioned in any other

32

place" for any speech or debate in either house of Congress. The effect of this latter provision is to leave them immune to any libel suit as a result of anything said in the accounts of the official business of the Congress. The Supreme Court has held that this protection covers more than simply floor debate and extends to such things as committee hearings and written reports.

Congressional Quarterly A private publication containing detailed and nonpartisan information regarding the actions of the United States Congress. It is published weekly and also in an annual volume which includes all the weekly publications. It has become, since it was first published in 1945, an important source of information for everyone interested in keeping informed about the actions of Congress.

Congressional Record A complete and official account of debates, votes, and other proceedings of the Congress. The *Record* is a verbatim account of what has taken place, but since members are permitted to revise and extend their remarks after delivering them, the printed record is usually somewhat different from the actual verbal performance. See also **Journal.**

Congressman A member of Congress. Properly applied, the term relates to both representatives in the House and to members of the Senate. In common practice the term is applied to members of the House of Representatives only, and members of the Senate are usually referred to as **Senators.** See **Representative, Senator.**

Connally Amendment The "self-judging" proviso attached by the United States Senate with reference to the right of compulsory jurisdiction of the **International Court of Justice.** The amendment offered by Senator Connally of Texas provides that the Court shall not have jurisdiction in matters essentially within domestic jurisdiction of the United States, the matter which is to be "determined by the United States." See also **International Court of Justice.**

Connecticut Compromise The proposals submitted to the Constitutional Convention by the "Committee of Eleven" which had been charged by the Convention with the responsibility of drafting a compromise. The small states and the large had become deadlocked over representation in the proposed Congress. Because the Connecticut delegation was prominent in the compromise process, the proposals became known as the Connecticut Compromise. This compromise called for a lower house where representation would be based on population and an upper house where the states would be equally represented. See also **Constitutional Convention, New Jersey Plan,** and **Virginia Plan.**

Conscientious Objector One who, for reasons of conscience, objects to military service, and therefore refuses to bear arms. These persons are usually made to perform some form of alternative service, such as working in hospitals or serving in the medical corps.

Conscription The procedure whereby men are called by law to serve in the armed forces either in time of war or peace. The Universal Military Training and Service Act of 1951 requires registration of all men between eighteen and twenty-six years and the induction for 24 months of those between eighteen and a half and twenty- **33**

six, or as many of them within this age group as are required to maintain United States military strength. The program is administered by the Selective Service—an independent agency of the federal government—which operates through local draft boards located in each community.

Conservation The protection and preservation of natural resources. As used in the United States, the term usually relates to policies designed to preserve and develop parks, forests, land, water, wildlife, and minerals.

Conservative One who generally supports the status quo. He is slow to accept change and is generally considered to be opposed to **liberals** and **progressives.**

Constituency The name given the people living in a legislative district or more broadly the population, area, and interests in a legislative district, or in the case of senators—a state.

Constitution A document which sets forth the principles, the processes, and the procedures of the government of a nation, a state, or a society. A constitution may be written or unwritten. It may be a collection of customs and traditions as well as an accumulation of decisions, practices, and precedents; or it may be a precise statement formulated and adopted at a particular time.

The *Constitution of the United States* is a written document which sets forth procedure under law for the United States of America. The Constitution was drafted at the Constitutional Convention in Philadelphia in 1787. The original purpose of that meeting in Philadelphia was to amend the **Articles of Confederation,** but the attempt to amend the Articles was abandoned as a hopeless task. The

Constitutional Convention then proceeded to draft a new constitution which was adopted and signed on September 17, 1787. Representatives of all of the thirteen original states, excepting Rhode Island, signed on that date. By August 1788, the Constitution had been ratified by eleven states and had gone into effect among them.

Amendments one to ten, commonly called the **Bill of Rights,** were ratified by eleven states between November 20, 1789 and December 15, 1791. Since that time, thirteen additional amendments have been adopted.

Constitutional Convention The convention assembled in Philadelphia from May 25 to September 17, 1787, which drew up the basic charter for ratification by the 13 states. Widespread dissatisfaction with the **Articles of Confederation,** which had been used as the basis of government in the newly established government, led Congress to call a convention for the "sole and express purpose of revising the Articles of Confederation." The convention was supposed to report its recommendation to Congress. Instead, meeting behind closed doors, it drew up a new constitution and submitted it to state conventions for ratification, thus violating its instruction in two vital respects. The necessary ninth state ratified the new compact on June 21, 1788. See also **Connecticut Compromise, New Jersey Plan,** and **Virginia Plan.**

Constitutional Courts Courts established under Article III of the Constitution—the article which sets forth the judicial power of the United States. Courts established under other powers granted to Congress are called "legislative courts." Examples of constitutional courts are the District

Courts, Courts of Appeal and, of course, the Supreme Court. Examples of legislative courts are the **Customs Court** and the **Court of Military Appeals.** The chief distinction between the two kinds of courts is that the judges appointed to constitutional courts serve "during good behavior"; that is, for life unless impeached, and judges appointed to legislative courts serve whatever term Congress establishes, which may or may not be for life. See **Judiciary.**

Constitutional Majority See **Majority.**

Constitutional Officers The officials of government named in the constitution of a country or of a state. The constitutions of the states usually name a governor, a lieutenant governor, an attorney general, the secretary of state, the state auditor, and the state treasurer, and describe the executive authority which goes with each of these offices.

Consul An official appointed to attend to the commercial interests of his own country in relationship with other countries. A consul-general is usually stationed in a major city and supervises other consuls in his district. In the United States consuls are part of the foreign service and are appointed through the State Department. Their rights and duties are usually negotiated by treaties.

Contract A legally enforceable promise made between two or more parties. Contracts may be written or oral; they may be expressed or implied; they may be conditional or unconditional, depending upon the terms.

Controller (Comptroller) The public official who audits the accounts of all

other officials charged with the collection or disbursement of funds. He may also issue warrants entitling officials to draw money for authorized expenditures.

Convention A meeting of members of a political party to nominate candidates, adopt a party **platform,** and conduct the general business of the party. Although political conventions are held at local, county, district, and state levels, the most spectacular conventions are, of course, the quadrennial national conventions of the Re-

Morris, 1961. Wide World Photos.
THE RIVAL SHOW MOVES IN

publican and Democratic parties. In many states party conventions are held once a year, but the authority of the convention varies greatly among the states. Some conventions are empowered under state law to place names on the ballot for the general election; others are limited to making endorsements of candidates who must run in a primary if they are opposed.

The word *convention* is also used with reference to assemblies or meet- **35** ings of elected delegates charged with the responsibility of drafting a constitution or deciding on constitutional amendments.

Copyright The exclusive right given to a composer, painter, author, or artist to publish or reproduce his works. This right is protected under the law by the granting of a copyright, in the United States by the Copyright Office in the Library of Congress. A copyright runs for 28 years and includes the right to renew for the same length of time. This protection also covers musical performances in public and the reproduction of them by mechanical devices.

Coroner A county official, usually elected or appointed by a judge or town council, whose duty it is to determine the cause and circumstances of death resulting from violence, accident, or under unusual or suspicious circumstances. The formal hearing is called an inquest. It is conducted by the coroner, sometimes in the presence of a jury.

Corporation A legal person or entity chartered by the state for a particular purpose—generally to carry on some kind of business or professional activity. There are private corporations with limited liability chartered by individuals and also public corporations chartered by governments, such as sanitary districts, school districts, and the like. A corporation can do many things that a person can do. It can sue and be sued, borrow and lend money, sign contracts, and own property. There are also nonprofit corporations such as special charity foundations, religious institutions, and educational institutions which are given privileges under the law such as tax exemption.

Corrupt Practices Act A federal law enacted in 1925 and since amended a number of times. It seeks to eliminate corruption by limiting expenditures by candidates seeking federal office. The law limits expenditures for most candidates to the Senate to $10,000 and most candidates to the House of Representatives to $2,500. Exceptions are made for larger states and larger districts with a limitation of maximum expenditures not to exceed $25,-000 in a Senate race and $5,000 in a campaign for the House of Representatives. These limitations apply only to certain kinds of expenditures by the candidates themselves or their committees. In general the limitations have proved to be unrealistic and ineffective.

The Corrupt Practices Act also requires that every political committee have a chairman and a treasurer. The treasurer must file reports with the Clerk of the House of Representatives listing total contributions and total expenditures. These provisions of the Corrupt Practices Act have been quite easily avoided and often not very seriously enforced. The statute also defines crimes against purity of elections and prohibits under penalty the purchase of votes, bribery, personation or the procurement of personation (an offense against the law which consists in acting under the title and name of another in casting or attempting to cast a vote. under the name of a registered voter), betting on elections, and payment of naturalization fees or taxes by persons other than the voter. Campaign contributions from corporations are forbidden and other acts tending to bring undue influence upon the electorate. Many states also have corrupt practices acts similar in general to the federal law.

Cost-Plus A type of contract entered into by the federal government which guarantees the contractor that he will be paid his costs plus a profit stated in the contract. The profit may be a fixed amount or it may be a percentage of the cost. These contracts were widely used during the war when defense production was needed immediately. A cost-plus contract is usually let without competitive bidding.

Council of Economic Advisers A council made up of three experts in economic affairs who advise the President on matters affecting the economy. This Council was established in the Employment Act of 1946. It analyzes economic and business trends, recommends policy to the President, and assists him in the preparation of such reports as the annual Economic Report to Congress.

Council of State Governments An organization established by all the states for the purpose of facilitating cooperation among the states, and between them and the federal government and units of local government. It is designed to help solve interstate and regional problems, and it serves as a clearing house for information on matters of interest to the states.

County Attorney See **Attorney at law.**

County A political and geographic subdivision of a state. (In Louisiana it is called "a parish.") A county is the largest and the principal unit of government in rural areas. Counties vary greatly in size and population. The governing body of a county is termed a board of county commissioners or board of county supervisors in most states.

County Board The governing body of a county, generally composed of three or more members elected to terms of two or four years. The county board is found in all states excepting Rhode Island which has no counties. These boards are creatures of the state and are concerned more with administrative than legislative or policy questions. Typical functions of the county board are the regulation of zoning, regulation of sale of liquor outside municipalities, levying and collection of taxes for construction of county roads, and conducting welfare activities. County boards are often responsible for the operation of county jails, courthouses, libraries, poorhouses, and hospitals. They administer the election laws by directing voter registration, distributing and counting ballots, and certifying election results. Members usually have other full-time employment as the boards generally meet only once a week and salaries are often low. The growth of suburban areas has added importance to county boards in many areas of the United States.

County Courts Courts of general trial jurisdiction, original and appellate, civil and criminal. They act at a level immediately above police and municipal courts. County courts have county-wide jurisdiction exercised by at least one judge in each county. Some states group several counties together into a judicial district with one district or circuit court for several counties. In 37 states the judges of the county, district or circuit courts are elected—generally for four-year terms. The general requirement for county judges is that they be lawyers.

County Seat The site of the county government. At the county seat are located such things as the county court- **37**

house, the meeting hall of the county board, and offices of the sheriff, clerk, auditor, treasurer, and other officials. Usually the county seat is the largest city or town in the county.

County Surveyor Official charged with measuring boundaries, contours, nature and extent of land, water, and mountains within a county. Generally his responsibilities include construction of county roads and buildings and are often combined with the duties of the county engineer.

Court of Appeals See **Judiciary.**

Court of Claims A court established by Congress in 1855. It has jurisdiction over all contracts and property damage claims against the federal government. The court consists of a chief judge and four judge advocates. The creation of this court was necessary because a sovereign nation cannot be sued without its own consent. Since it would be burdensome for Congress to decide the merits of each case involving the federal government, it was deemed necessary to set up the Court of Claims in which claims against the government could be processed.

Court of Customs and Patent Appeals This court hears appeals from the Customs Court and from the Patent Office, which makes decisions on patents and trademarks. The court consists of a chief judge and four associate judges.

Court of Military Appeals The highest court in the military court system of the United States. Since persons in the military service are tried under military law by court martial, that is, by courts made up of military personnel rather than by ordinary civil courts, this separate court system has

been established. The United States Court of Military Appeals is required to review all decisions involving admirals or generals, death sentences within the armed services, and certain other cases. It also has discretionary authority to hear other cases such as those wherein a person has received a bad conduct discharge. Its decisions are reviewable by the Supreme Court, but this rarely happens. The Court is made up of three civilian judges appointed for 15-year terms.

Courts of Arbitration Special courts established in some cities. Parties in disagreement may submit their disagreements and disputes to the Court of Arbitration. They must agree in advance to abide by the decision of the arbitrator who presides over this court. His decision is enforceable as are the decisions of the regular courts.

Courts of Conciliation Special courts established in some cities to assist disputing parties to adjust their differences without resorting to a formal law suit. A conciliator presides over this court, but his decisions are not enforceable in another court if one party refuses to abide by a decision of the Court of Conciliation.

A common kind of conciliation court is a small claims court. It is presided over by a judge whose decisions are enforceable, but the jurisdiction of the court is usually limited to claims of $100 or less.

Criminal Case A court case involving an alleged violation of criminal law, that is, an offense against the state. There are three categories of crimes: felonies, misdemeanors and petty offenses. A *felony* is an offense for which the penalty is death or more than one year in prison. A *misdemeanor* is an offense for which the penalty is not more than one year or less than six months in jail. A *petty offense* is one which carries a penalty of less than six months. Typical examples of criminal cases which are considered in the federal courts involve automobile theft across state lines, avoidance of taxes on liquor, violation of immigration laws, and laws relating to narcotics. See also **Civil case.**

Cross-filing A system or practice which allows a candidate for political office to run in the primary election for the nomination of more than one party. In its extreme form cross-filing does not require a candidate to identify his own party or party preference on the ballot. This was the practice in California until recently. Cross-filing is still permitted, but it is required that the candidate declare his own party affiliation. The practice of cross-filing is generally considered to be particularly advantageous to incumbents whose names are well known, and it is considered destructive of party responsibility.

Currency Coin or paper money, such as government or bank notes, which is accepted as a medium of exchange.

Customs Court This court has responsibility for reviewing disputed appraisals and duties on imported goods. It is made up of one chief judge and eight associate judges; these nine are divided into three tribunals of three judges each which hear cases in New York and other ports of entry.

Dark Horse A person who is given a slight chance of winning a nomina-

tion or an election. A dark horse is usually looked upon as a possible compromise who would be acceptable in the event that no one of the **front runners** can win.

D.C. See **District of Columbia.**

Deal An agreement between two or more persons to do certain things supposedly of advantage to the participants and to all concerned. Usually the term is used in a derogatory sense, and political deals are usually frowned upon by the public and are denounced by those who feel they were left out. To the extent that compromise is a necessary part of politics, some agreements may be necessary and defensible. An example of the kind of thing labeled a political deal would be one in which a possible candidate for the presidential nomination would agree to throw his support to another in return for the vice presidential nomination.

Debt Ceiling See **National debt.**

Declaration of Independence The formal announcement by the Second Continental Congress on July 4, 1776, that the thirteen British colonies there represented "are, and of right ought to be, free and independent states." The Declaration was primarily the work of Thomas Jefferson and contains some of the most eloquent and influential phrases ever written by an American. It is not actually a part of American law but it has exerted a great influence on political thought both here and abroad. See **Appendix** for text.

Declaratory Judgments Decisions of a court which clarify a point of law upon motion of a petitioner before the beginning of a lawsuit. This process, now a part of the law in most **39**

THE DECLARATION OF INDEPENDENCE

states, keeps many disputes off the court calendar and contributes to a speedier trial and settlement of other lawsuits.

De Facto In fact or in reality. The phrase is usually used to describe a situation which is different from what it appears to be or what it legally is supposed to be. For example, the United States government realizes that communist regimes are *de facto* in control of such areas as Eastern Germany and mainland China, but it refuses to grant them formal recognition because it does not accept their legality. See also **De jure.**

Defendant See **Suit.**

Defense, Department of See **Department of Defense.**

Defense, Secretary of See **Department of Defense.**

De Jure According to law or legally. It is often used in connection with a situation which is different in fact from what it legally is supposed to be. For example, the United States government recognizes the Nationalist Chinese government, currently on Formosa, as the *de jure* government of all of China. In fact, however, it is not. See also **De facto.**

Delegate (a) A person selected or elected to represent a **constituency** at a **convention.** Delegates to political conventions are chosen in a variety of ways in accordance with the laws or practices of the states involved. In some cases delegates are appointed by party leaders; in others they are selected by conventions within the state; others may be elected in primary elections.

(b) In some states the word *delegate* is the name used to designate a member of the branch of the legislature.

Delegation A group of official representatives or delegates from a given area or organization. For example, a state party sends a delegation to the national political convention.

Demagogue One who stirs up the people for wrong reasons or through the use of improper methods. A person who appeals to the emotional and irrational instincts of large numbers of people and manipulates them for his own purposes. The line between a demagogue and a stirring orator is sometimes hard to draw, but the term *demagogue* has unfavorable overtones, implying that the person has little respect for truth and is primarily concerned with extending his own influence and power. A demagogue is a threat to orderly democratic government, which depends on a certain measure of tolerance and on reason.

Demobilization The process of changing from a nation at war to a nation at peace. It involves such things as drastically reducing the size of the armed forces and changing from the manufacture of war material to the production of civilian goods.

Democracy A philosophy of social and political organization which gives to individuals a maximum of freedom and a maximum of responsibility. Generally democracy requires institutions through which individuals are at least periodically given an opportunity to exercise their choice with regard to leaders and political policies and programs.

Democratic Party One of the two major political parties in the United States. It had its origin in the very early years of the republic and is today the oldest political party in the world. Over its long history it has embraced a great diversity of viewpoints and has included the advocates of many and varying interests. The composition and policies of the Democratic party today were heavily influenced by the administrations of President Franklin D. Roosevelt (1933–45). In briefest sketch, the major elements of the party today are the South, the working class—including large segments of organized labor—racial and ethnic minority groups, and most intellectuals. Its general policy position is liberal, supporting international programs and showing greater willingness to use the power of government to bring about economic and social changes. Compare with **Republican party.**

Department of Agriculture A department of the federal government established in 1862 and raised to cabinet status in 1889. It was originally concerned with research and with educating the farmers of America in the best agricultural techniques. Since the depression of the thirties, however, it has assumed many new responsibilities which have made the department an extremely important influence in the economic life of the nation.

The broad scope of the activities of the department includes the work of various bureaus engaged in research covering such matters as prevention and control of plant and animal diseases, improvement of animal breeding, increased yield and quality of crops, agricultural marketing methods, and soil conservation methods.

Following are a few of the more important agencies of the department: the **Commodity Credit Corporation, Rural Electrification Administration, Federal Extension Service,**

Forest Service, Soil Conservation Service, and **Farmers Home Administration.**

Department of Air Force See **Department of Defense.**

Department of Commerce A cabinet-level department of the federal government established in 1903 as the Department of Commerce and Labor and designated as the Department of Commerce in 1913 when a separate Department of Labor was established. The principal purpose of this department is that of fostering, encouraging, and aiding American business. Its services include the publication of commercial statistics, weather information, promotion of foreign trade, administration of a subsidy program for the Merchant Marine, and the issuance of patents and registration of *trademarks.*

Its *Bureau of the Census* analyzes and publishes the national census.

The *Bureau of Public Roads* administers the expanding federal highway construction.

The *National Bureau of Standards* is charged with maintenance of uniform weights, measures and standards, and also investigates claims for commercial products when asked to do so by such agencies as the **Federal Trade Commission** or the **Department of Justice.**

Department of Defense A cabinet-level department of the federal government established in 1949. It is the successor to the "National Military Establishment" which was created in 1947 by the first Unification Act. Before 1947, military affairs were conducted by two departments: the Department of War and the Department of the Navy. Both of these departments lost their cabinet status in 1947 and were combined with the new Department of the Air Force into the Department of Defense. These three subordinated departments now make up most of the Defense Department, with one other administrative agency, the Office of the Secretary of Defense. Each of the three departments is headed by a Secretary. These are the only departments of the government that have secretaries below cabinet rank.

The Department of Defense is by far the largest executive agency. It employs over one million civilian workers in addition to approximately 2.5 million members of the armed forces. Its primary responsibility is the development and maintenance of an effective military establishment. Its headquarters is the Pentagon.

The Secretary of Defense carries great responsibilities. He must pass upon and sometimes resolve for the President disputes and disagreements among the three branches of the armed services, if these disputes are not resolved by the Joint Chiefs of Staffs. He must make decisions, or at least give direction with regard to decisions, involving billions of dollars in budget requests and expenditures. He is responsible also for the administration of our overseas military aid program. He is expected to work with the President and the Secretary of State in coordinating military and nonmilitary policies relating to international affairs.

Department of Health, Education, and Welfare (HEW) Established in 1953, the newest cabinet-level department of the federal government. The Secretary of HEW presides over a department with a broad range of problems, many of them problems that only recently have come under the

jurisdiction of the federal government. In the department there are numerous agencies and services.

The *Public Health Service* conducts medical research, administers aid to the states for certain health programs, provides medical services for merchant seamen and for Indians, and endeavors to prevent introduction of communicable diseases into the United States.

The *Food and Drug Administration* enforces federal laws designed to promote purity and honest labeling of food and drugs.

The *Office of Education,* primarily an information agency, in recent years has been charged with the administration of many federal grants to the states.

The *Social Security Administration* is responsible for the administration of the general laws dealing with social security. These include the old-age, survivors' and disability insurance program, the grants to the states for old age assistance, aid to dependent children, aid to the blind, aid to the totally and permanently disabled, and a number of other smaller programs such as grants to the states for maternal and child health services.

Department of the Interior A cabinet-level department of the federal government established in 1849. Its primary responsibility is the conservation of the nation's resources. Under its jurisdiction are 750 million acres of federally owned land. It also has responsibility for the conservation, protection, growth and control of fish and wildlife, supervision of reclamation projects, and management of the federally owned hydroelectric power systems. It also administers the decreasing number of United States territories. **43**

Its *National Park Service* administers national parks and monuments. This service was created in 1916 and by law is directed to "conserve the scenery and the natural historic objects and the wildlife therein and to provide for the enjoyment of the same in such manner and by such means as will leave them unimpaired for the enjoyment of future generations."

The *Bureau of Indian Affairs* carries out the federal responsibility, or attempts to carry out this responsibility, for the Indians of the United States. It acts as trustee with respect to Indian lands and moneys held in trust by the United States government, provides public services such as education and welfare aid under certain conditions to the Indians, and assists those Indians who wish to leave reservations. In addition it performs other advisory services.

The *Bureau of Mines* endeavors to conserve and develop the nation's mineral resources and to promote safe and healthful working conditions in the mines. One of the most difficult areas of decision for the Secretary of Interior results from the fact that he and his department are responsible for the leasing of mineral deposits and public grazing lands for private use.

Department of Justice A cabinet-level department of the federal government established in 1870 and headed by the Attorney General. The office of Attorney General was established in 1789 and its occupant has been a member of the cabinet since that time. This department is charged with responsibility for the enforcement of federal laws. It also has under its jurisdiction the protection of civil rights, the investigation and prosecution of tax laws, antitrust legislation

and narcotics cases, the administration of the Immigration and Naturalization Service, and the supervision of federal prisons. The Attorney General administers the work of the department which includes the activities of the United States District Attorneys across the country. He makes broad policy determinations as to who and what shall be investigated and prosecuted and is the cabinet officer who generally advises the President on matters of law and on the constitutionality of legislative proposals.

The *Solicitor General* is the chief prosecuting officer of the federal government and usually represents the government in cases before the Supreme Court.

The agency in the Justice Department which is best known is the *Federal Bureau of Investigation,* the FBI. This agency conducts investigations of all alleged violations of federal law excepting those specifically assigned to other agencies. This jurisdiction includes such things as espionage, sabotage, treason, kidnapping, thefts in interstate commerce—stolen aircraft and stolen automobiles.

Department of Labor A cabinet-level department of the federal government established in 1913. Its primary purpose is to promote the welfare of wage earners. This department administers and enforces federal laws relating to fair labor standards, including minimum wages, maximum hours, and child labor. It also has responsibility for administering the various labor relations laws that have been adopted.

Its *Bureau of Employment Security* administers those federal laws under which state programs of unemployment insurance and employment service receive federal financial assistance or use taxes collected under federal law.

The *Women's Bureau* attempts to promote the welfare of wage-earning women by making studies and offering proposals with respect to such matters as minimum wages, maximum hours, and equal pay for women.

The *Bureau of Labor Statistics* collects public information on the number of employed and unemployed workers as well as on strikes, accidents, wages, and the cost of living. The famous "cost-of-living" index, which receives a great deal of public attention, particularly in the course of political campaigns, and which is the basis for escalator clauses in some wage contracts, is the monthly report of this bureau.

Department of State The first-ranking cabinet-level department of the federal government. It was established in 1789. Its primary responsbilities are to assist in the formulation of American foreign policy and in the execution of those policies. The Secretary of State is expected to be the President's chief foreign policy adviser as well as the administrator of the Department of State. Through ambassadors, ministers, and foreign service personnel, the department represents this government in foreign capitals in most countries throughout most of the world. Through the State Department negotiations are conducted with foreign governments, and information about all the countries of the world is collected. The State Department also issues passports and visas and provides special services for Americans overseas. The Secretary of State is often an extremely controversial member of the cabinet. He is often blamed for things over which he has little or no control, and in cases of mistaken judgment, he is commonly expected to shoulder the blame which otherwise might be placed upon the President himself.

Department of the Treasury A cabinet-level department of the federal government established in 1789. The primary responsibilities of the Department of the Treasury are managing the national debt and controlling the currency of the United States. It also acts as a bank for the government and is the government's borrowing agency. The United States Secret Service, commonly known as T-Men, is a part of the Department of the Treasury as is the Coast Guard.

The Secretary of the Treasury is usually an influential member of the cabinet, serving not only as the administrator of his own department, but also as a financial adviser to the President. Recommendations of the Treasury Department have a strong influence upon the tax policy of the Congress. The interest rates on national securities are also the direct concern of the department since these rates affect the interest rates of the entire economy.

The *United States Secret Service* is especially responsible for the protection of the country against counterfeiting and against narcotics traffic. It is also responsible for the physical safety of the President, the Vice President, the President-elect, and their families. The Vice Presidents-elect must for the most part look out for themselves.

In addition to the Secretary of the Treasury, there is the *Treasurer of the United States* who heads an office in the Treasury Department. He acts as the official custodian of the government's money. The name of the Treasurer of the United States appears on **45** the paper money issued by the federal government.

The *Internal Revenue Service,* also a part of the Treasury Department, is the agency of the government responsible for the collection of taxes.

Deportation   The expulsion of a person by a country because he is politically dangerous and undesirable or is a habitual criminal. It happens most frequently to aliens who enter a country illegally. Usually deportation includes loss of property and civil rights.

Depression   A very serious economic disorder, marked by high unemployment, declining prices, bank failure,

Kirby, 1930. Museum of the City of New York.
LABOR DAY

lower production and sales, and other evidences of a breakdown in the economic system. Depression was once regarded as an inevitable phase of the business cycle in capitalistic societies. Current views of government and of the economy hold that depres-

46

sions can be avoided.   See also **Recession.**

Development Loan Fund   A corporate agency of the United States established in 1957 to assist the less developed free nations. Its purpose is to stimulate their economic growth. It supplies investment capital at very favorable interest rates and on convenient repayment schedules to private enterprise in other nations or to their governments. It can also guarantee private loans made by United States investors in enterprises in other lands. The agency was brought within the **Agency for International Development** in 1961.   See also **Mutual Security Program.**

Dictatorship   A system of government wherein one person, the dictator, wields virtually all political power. The people, therefore, enjoy few or no civil rights or liberties. The chief mark of a dictatorship is the complete suppression of political opposition or the tolerance of it within very restricted limits. The most shocking dictatorships in modern history have been those of Germany under Hitler, Italy under Mussolini, and China and Russia under the communist party leaders.

Diplomacy   The art of conducting official negotiations and maintaining relationships between two states or governments. Historically, diplomacy has required outward dignity, courteous forms, and respect for status, even on matters which were in almost total disagreement. In recent years diplomatic exchanges have come to be more like political campaigns. In a more popular sense diplomacy refers to skill in negotiations in the interest of one's own nation or country.

Diplomat   An official accredited to

World copyright by arrangement with Mr. David Low.
Photo by London Daily Express.

"EASTERN EUROPEAN SAUSAGE MACHINE"

represent his government in another country or state on political matters and negotiations. A diplomat is also charged with responsibility for protecting the rights of citizens of his own country who are living or traveling in the country to which he is assigned. A ranking diplomat enjoys a number of immunities under international law. He can transmit information to his government without censorship. He is immune from arrest, though he may be expelled. His residence and papers are exempt from search or seizure. He is permitted freedom of worship and enjoys freedom from taxation and from civil suit. These privileges are shared generally by his family and his staff. A diplomat is under the direction of the Foreign Office of his government (Department of State in the United States). See **Ambassador, Minister, Attaché, Chargé d'affaires, Consul.**

Diplomatic Corps The comprehensive name given to all the ranking diplomatic officials of the various states who are assigned to the same capital of a nation. **Protocol** determines their rank at state affairs.

Direct Democracy See **Town meeting.**

Disarmament A policy of seeking agreements by major powers to reduce armaments and to limit the capacity to wage aggressive war. Efforts to bring about disarmament are based on the assumption that an arms race

47

is the cause of war or that if the effort and resources that go into the production of arms were turned to peaceful uses, war could be avoided. Disarmament has had strong support in international conferences and agreements throughout the twentieth century. As a practical matter, however, these efforts and the agreements which have resulted from them have broken down in the face of action by powerful nations. The problem of disarmament and of arms control has become especially urgent with the development of nuclear weapons and missiles. See **Arms control.**

Lions Along the Way

Carmack, The Christian Science Monitor, 1960.

Disenfranchisement See **Voting qualifications.**

Dishonorable Discharge Release or separation from military service as a result of conviction by a court martial for a crime, for bad moral character, or for some other reason requiring

separation from the service. Dishonorable discharge entails loss of certain benefits such as pension, bonus, reenlistment rights and benefits, and rights to be treated in a Veterans Administration hospital.

Displaced Persons (DP's) The popular name for refugees applied following World War II. These were people who were moved from their homeland into forced labor camps or displaced persons camps. The realignment of national boundaries after the war and the establishment of communist governments in several nations made it impossible or dangerous for them to return to their homes. Many nations modified and liberalized their immigration policies in order to assist in the resettlement of displaced persons, and the State of Israel was set up as a principal means for providing a homeland for the Jewish people. The *International Refugee Organization* was established under the United Nations to care for displaced persons and to facilitate their resettlement. See also **Refugees.**

District Attorney See **Attorney at law.**

District of Columbia An area located between Maryland and Virginia to which the federal government moved from Philadelphia in 1800. The city of Washington, D.C., occupies exactly the same area as does the District of Columbia. The District of Columbia was originally made up of 100 square miles of land ceded to the federal government by Maryland and Virginia. In 1846, almost all of the Virginia land was returned to that state. Now the District is made up almost entirely of the territory ceded by Maryland. The people of the District of Columbia are the only people in the United

States who do not have full citizenship as they do not have representation in Congress nor do they vote for local officials. With the ratification of the Twenty-third Amendment in 1961, District citizens finally have the right to vote for President and Vice President.

Division Vote A vote of a legislative body by which members favoring a measure first stand to be counted and then members opposed stand to be counted. Under this procedure a total vote count is secured, but it is difficult to know who voted for a measure and who voted against it. In the Congress any member of either the House or the Senate may demand a division vote instead of a **voice vote,** and if such a demand is made at the proper time the presiding officer must conduct a vote. See also **Teller vote, Roll call vote.**

Dixiecrat A member of the **Dixiecrat party** of 1948. More loosely it is

Morris, 1957. Wide World Photos.

the term applied to any Southerner who rejects the position of the majority of Democrats, yet does not publicly endorse the Republican party

and who favors a third party to represent the South.

Dixiecrat Party A party made up of Southern Democrats who disapproved of the Democratic platform and candidates in 1948. They held their own convention and nominated Strom Thurmond of South Carolina for the presidency. Mr. Thurmond polled over a million votes, carrying four states: Alabama, Louisiana, Mississippi, and South Carolina—and won 39 votes in the electoral college. The battle cry of the party was "states' rights," but its fundamental appeal was to white supremacy.

Doctrinaire A person who holds rigidly to a set of abstract theories or propositions—or doctrines—with little regard to their practical effect. It is also a quality ascribed to persons or ideas of being rigid and inflexible irrespective of practical consequences.

Dole The distribution by government of money, food or other necessities to the poor and needy.

Dollar Diplomacy A term of criticism implying that the aim of our foreign policy is primarily to protect and increase American investments in other nations. It suggests a willingness to control other governments and to exploit their people in the interest of private profit. The term originated at the turn of the century to describe American foreign policy toward Latin America and China.

Domestic Affairs In politics, those affairs which are primarily internal and the concern of one nation, as distinguished from international affairs. It is increasingly difficult to draw a line between international and domestic affairs, but the distinction is widely used and recognized in the operations of the **United Nations.** For example, **49**

Algeria is declared by the French to be a domestic affair and therefore not subject to UN action, although some members of the UN obviously think that the Algerian affair is really an international problem.

Double Jeopardy Trial for the same act or crime on two separate occasions. There is both a common law and a constitutional prohibition in the United States against this procedure. Once a person has been tried for a crime, he cannot be tried again, whether he be found innocent or guilty.

Draft A procedure by which young men are selected and called to military service.

Dred Scott v. Sandford (1857) A case in which the Supreme Court held that no slave was a citizen with power to sue in the federal courts, and that no Negro, whether slave or free, enjoyed any rights or protections under the Constitution. Dred Scott was a Negro slave who sued for freedom in the federal courts on the grounds that because his master had taken him on a trip into territory where slavery was forbidden by federal law, he had become a free man. This decision contributed to the flood of events leading to the Civil War.

Dry An advocate of legislation or other measures forbidding the sale or use of intoxicating beverages. The term was applied to persons who campaigned for passage of the Eighteenth Amendment to the United States Constitution and who opposed its repeal. Today drys are most active in advancing efforts to exercise **local option** against the sale of liquor and in advocating such things as prohibition of the sale of liquor on airplanes or the forbidding of liquor advertising.

Due Process of Law See **Palko v. Connecticut.**

Duty The obligation to conform actions to the conditions set forth by law. **(a)** In United States law, duty is most commonly used to describe the obligations of an official to perform designated functions. **(b)** In the field of commerce, a duty is a tax due a government for the right to import or export goods. **(c)** In a wider sense, civil rights imply a duty in others to respect those rights.

Dynamic Conservatism This is another name for **modern Republican** which suggests the respectability of the conservative with the addition of twentieth century energy. The term has no necessary relationship to progress or to truly progressive achievement, but establishes only that there is great activity.

Economic and Social Council One of the principal organs of the **United Nations.** It operates under the **General Assembly** to carry out programs relating to improvement of international economic, social, cultural, health, educational, and other standards. It undertakes research and drafts recommendations for raising standards and securing the cooperation of member nations to achieve its goals. The Economic and Social Council has 18 members elected by the General Assembly for a three-year term. A number of regional economic commissions are organized under the Council as are several functional commissions such as those on population, human rights, status of women, and statistics.

Economic Report of the President An annual message from the President to Congress which must be submitted by January 20. This report contains detailed information about the condition of the nation's economy. See also **Employment Act of 1946.**

Education (State and Local) A responsibility which has increasingly been accepted by various levels of government. The primary responsibility for education rests with the states. The public schools, except state universities and colleges, are usually run by school districts or by municipalities. It is customary for the state to enact laws establishing a state school system, to set standards for teachers, curricula, textbooks, school construction, and pupil health. Generally the states provide funds to assist local school districts in financing and meeting the cost of education, and commonly establish supervisory control through a state department of education and operate schools for the blind, the deaf, the feebleminded, and others who are severely handicapped.

At the local level, cities and school districts carry much of the burden of education. They sell bonds, levy taxes, and otherwise administer major details of the entire education program, subject only to broad statutory requirements. See also **Department of Health, Education, and Welfare.**

Eighteenth Amendment An Amendment which prohibited the manufacture, transportation and sale, and importation and exportation of intoxicating liquors in the United States. This Amendment was adopted in 1919 and was repealed by the Twenty-first Amendment in 1933. This is the only Amendment to the Constitution which has been repealed by a subsequent amendment.

Elastic Clause The concluding portion of Article I, Section 8 of the federal Constitution which grants to Congress power "to make all laws which shall be necessary and proper for carrying into execution . . . all . . . powers vested by this Constitution in the government of the United States. . . ." This has been called the "elastic clause" because it can be interpreted in a variety of ways and can be "stretched," or has been stretched, in keeping with the judgment of individuals and with changing times. This clause is the principal base upon which the doctrine of **implied powers** has been developed.

The doctrine of implied powers holds that congressional power is not to be narrowly construed and that the powers of the federal government actually go beyond those specifically listed in the Constitution. In the early history of our nation, there was great difference of opinion whether a narrow or loose interpretation of the Constitution should be followed. The argument still persists in various forms and over various issues, but for the most part the liberal construction is widely accepted.

Electoral College The name given to those persons elected from each state to cast the electoral votes of that state for the President and the Vice President. Each state has electoral votes equal to its total number of senators and representatives in Congress. The men who drafted the Constitution expected that the electoral college would be made up of eminent men who would gather in their state and deliberate over the question of who should be President of the United

Nathaniel Currier, 1852. Library of Congress.

A CONTESTED SEAT

States. The system has never worked out in this manner.

Today the electors are chosen for their publicly expressed positions in support of presidential and vice presidential candidates of a political party. The law, however, does not clearly require that in every state the electors vote for the candidate of the party with which the electors are identified.

The electoral college is often called unrepresentative, old-fashioned, and dangerous. The major complaint expressed against it is that it does not accurately reflect the popular vote for presidential candidates and that it can, as it did in 1876 and again in 1888, elect a man who received fewer votes than his opponent. Under this system, State X, with a population of 10 million persons, may give Candidate A a 2,000 vote margin, and State Y, with a population of 10 million, give Candidate B a 300,000 vote margin. The electoral vote, however, would be a draw, even though the one candidate had polled 290,000 more votes than the other. The electoral college also fails to reflect the popular vote to some degree because each state, no matter how small it may be, has at least three electors.

Electorate Persons who are eligible to vote.

Eligibility (for office) Those requirements set forth in the Constitution or by statute fixing requirements for candidates or holders of various posts in government. Requirements are usually nominal, including age, residence, and citizenship.

Embassy The official residence of an ambassador in the capital city of another nation. The word embassy is also used to designate the staff and functions associated with the office of an ambassador. See also **Legation, Ambassador.**

Eminent Domain The power of a state to take property for its own use, as for a highway or public housing project, after paying the owner the fair market value.

Employment Act of 1946 An act of Congress which declared that it is the policy of the federal government "to promote maximum employment, production, and purchasing power." Despite various qualifications and limitations in this declaration of policy, the law was a precedent-making affirmation of government responsibility for the economic well-being of the country. The law requires the President to submit an annual **Economic Report** to Congress by January 20 of each year. This report must contain the following information: levels of employment, of production, and of purchasing power in the nation; levels of production needed to achieve the goals set forth in the declaration of policy; current and foreseeable trends in those levels; a review of the economic program of the federal government; and a program containing legislative recommendations for achieving these goals. To assist and to advise the President in drawing this report, the law created a **Council of Economic Advisers.** In order that Congress may evaluate the report properly, the law also established a **Joint Economic Committee,** composed of seven senators and seven members of the House of Representatives. This committee is charged with conducting a continuing study of matters relating to the Economic Report

and submitting periodic reports to the Congress itself.

Enabling Act A legislative act which permits an administration official or a subordinate unit of government to take a specific kind of action. For example, an act of a state legislature which permits local housing authorities to enter into agreements with the federal government for a public housing project is an enabling act.

Enacting Clause The leading phrase in a legislative proposal, usually following the title and statement of purpose which reads generally as follows: "Be it enacted by the Senate and the House of Representatives of the United States in Congress assembled. . . ." Frequently a legislator will move to strike out the enacting clause. If this amendment is adopted, the bill is defeated.

Engrossed Bill An official copy of a bill as passed by one legislative body. An employee of that body is responsible for the engrossment, or copying of the bill, which must incorporate any changes or amendments enacted during floor debate. The demand for an engrossed, handwritten copy, rather than the usual printed form, is not often made. When it is made, it usually has the purpose of delaying final action on the legislation.

Enrolled Bill The final official copy of a bill as approved by a legislature. The enrolled bill is written or printed in permanent form ready for executive signature.

Entente A general understanding or agreement reached between two or more nations.

E Pluribus Unum Latin phrase meaning "one from many." It appears on United States currency and on one **53**

side of the Great Seal of the United States. It expresses the unity of the United States made up as it is out of people of many races, nationalities, and religions. It also suggests the union of the states into the United States of America.

Equal Protection of the Law See **Brown** *v.* **Board of Education.**

Equal Time A phrase taken from the laws relating to the use of radio and television in political campaigns. Under equal time provisions, a radio or television station which provides time to one candidate or one party can be required to provide equal time to spokesmen who are opposed to the issue or who represent the opposing political party. See also **Federal Communications Commission.**

Equity Law A body of legal principles and rules developed through the proceedings at equity or chancery courts. These are designed to apply to cases not covered by the common law. Equity law originated in the twelfth or thirteenth century in England because of inflexibilities in the common law which, for example, made it impossible to get court action in advance of an expected violation of property rights. Like the common law, it is judge-made; it is subject to change by legislative action. Equity law had been developed before the American Revolution, and it was largely taken over by the new states following the Revolution. Equity courts formerly were a separate court system. Today equity and common law are usually handled by the same court.

European Economic Community A group of European nations made up of Belgium, France, Italy, the Netherlands, West Germany, and Luxembourg. These nations in 1957 agreed

to conduct trade and economic exchange within a common agreement or a common market. This group of nations, called the Inner Six, is pledged to eliminate, over a period of years, tariff barriers, facilitate the movement of workers and capital across their borders, and cooperate in a number of other economic efforts. The treaty establishing the Community also provides for a limited common political authority. The common market is a form of customs union. Its members are not only attempting to reduce tariffs among themselves, but will also develop a common trade policy with reference to trade with other nations. The establishment of the common market has caused other European nations to be concerned about their trade opportunities and practices with members of the common market, and it has brought about a movement to organize other European nations, called the Outer Seven. In 1961 Great Britain applied for membership in the European Economic Community. If Britain and other nations join the EEC, the effects upon the Western World's economic life no doubt will be profound. See also **European Free Trade Association.**

European Free Trade Association A free trade area of European nations established in 1959, partly to offset the effects of the common market established by the **European Economic Community.** The member nations, called the Outer Seven in distinction to the Inner Six of the common market, are Great Britain, Sweden, Austria, Denmark, Norway, Switzerland, and Portugal. The members of the European Free Trade Association agree to eliminate tariffs on imported goods in a series of steps. Each nation is free to maintain tariffs on goods imported from outside the free trade area. The program of the European Free Trade Association is less comprehensive than that of the common market and does not involve the same degree of planning and of cooperation. See also **European Economic Community.**

Everson v. Board of Education (1947)
A case in which the Supreme Court upheld the right of the State of New Jersey to reimburse parents for what they had paid in bus fares to transport their children to private or parochial schools. The Court held, five to four, that this was no violation of the First Amendment because it was aid to the children and not to a religion. See also **Church and State.**

Excess Profits Tax A tax imposed on profits which exceed a legislatively determined standard for "normal" profits. The excess profits tax is imposed on that portion of the profit which is above the so-called normal rate. In the United States an excess profits tax is generally imposed in wartime.

Excise Tax A tax on the production, distribution, or use of a commodity or service within the country. The common forms of excise taxes are taxes on theatre admissions, gasoline, tobacco, alcohol, automobiles, tires, radios, cameras, and household appliances.

Executive Agreement An agreement between heads of government to establish certain reciprocal privileges and responsibilities. In the United States the President may enter into these contracts without going through the treaty process or securing congressional approval. An example is an accord reached with foreign nations where American military troops are stationed covering such matters as the respective jurisdictions of the foreign and the United States military courts, access to the military bases, financial arrangements, and so forth. An executive agreement usually concerns administrative matters, but it can reflect an important policy decision as when President Roosevelt in 1940 transferred 50 destroyers to Great Britain in return for leases on naval and air bases in Newfoundland and other British possessions.

Executive Branch See **Presidency.**

Executive Office of the President A group of agencies operating directly under the President. The President as chief executive officer has authority over all regular administrative departments, agencies, and bureaus. In addition the presidency itself, as distinguished from the executive branch as a whole, has become a large institution in recent years. In response to this, the Executive Office of the President was established in 1939, bringing together various agencies already in existence. It has been expanded since then and now consists of six-major divisions: the **White House Office,** the **Bureau of the Budget,** the **National Security Council,** the **Central Intelligence Agency,** the **Council of Economic Advisers,** and the **Office of Civil and Defense Mobilization.**

Executive Order A directive from the President or someone acting under his authority based on power granted to the President by Congress or the Constitution. Such an order may apply only within the executive branch or it may affect the population at large. In recent years Congress has delegated extensive authority to the President to implement the laws, and hence the **55**

number and importance of executive orders has grown. Executive orders have the force of law.

Executive Privilege   The right of the executive branch—a right oftentimes disputed—to withhold information from the legislature. This right is not clearly specified in the Constitution or the laws of the United States, but is defended as an inherent right of the executive branch of the government. Although it is sometimes vital to the nation's security that some information be kept secret, Congress has the right to information necessary for passing judgment upon activities of the executive branch of the government and in forming reasonable judgments about legislation and appropriations.

Executive Session   Originally a meeting of a legislative body in order to deal with executive business such as recommendations for appointments or proposed ratification of treaties. Because these sessions in the Senate were usually held in secret, the phrase has since come to be applied to any session of a committee or legislative body held behind closed doors. Committees may hold such meetings in order to hear testimony of a confidential or secret nature from officials of the executive branch of the government, or to work out compromises and prepare a final draft of a bill. A final committee vote, too, may be taken in executive session.

Ex Officio   By virtue of the office held. A person who is an *ex officio* member of a board or committee is not a regularly appointed member but is a member because the office he holds entitles him to such membership. For example, the chairman of a full committee in Congress is fre-

quently an *ex officio* member of his committee's subcommittee.

Ex Parte   A proceeding in which there is no adverse side to be heard. It refers also to a hearing at which only one side is heard without the opposite party receiving notice.

Expatriate   A person who has voluntarily abandoned allegiance to his country or has been expelled from it, and who has become a subject of another nation.

Export-Import Bank   An independent agency of the federal government set up to finance and to facilitate exports and imports between the United States and foreign governments or their nationals. The Bank makes loans for operations which will stimulate trade, and it also guarantees private loans for this purpose. It was authorized in 1934 and made an independent agency in 1945. Its five-member Board of Directors is appointed by the President with the consent of the Senate.

Ex Post Facto Law   A law which makes an act illegal after the act has been performed. Such a law provides a penalty for a past action not a crime at the time it was performed. The Constitution prohibits both Congress and the states from enacting such laws.

Extradition   The surrender by one jurisdiction or country to another of an individual accused or convicted of a crime in the second country, or jurisdiction.

Extraterritoriality   The principle of the immunity of diplomatic officials from the laws of nations in which they are stationed. In effect it permits diplomats to live under the authority of the laws of their own nation. The host country may request the diplomat's own government to request the recall of those who break the law regularly or in serious matters. See also **Diplomat.**

FAA See **Federal Aviation Agency.**

Faction A group of persons or a **bloc** in a legislature or a political party who act together in pursuit of some special interest or position. A faction is generally in opposition to the majority in a legislature or a party. This is not always the case. In one-party states, for example, there are frequently many factions competing for the party's nomination, each supporting a particular candidate.

Fair Deal A label applied by President Truman and others to his domestic policies, especially those recommended to Congress in 1949. The slogan was a variation on President Franklin D. Roosevelt's **New Deal.**

Fair Employment Practices Commission (FEPC) Commissions established in 16 states and over 40 cities to enforce laws which require that racial or religious discrimination not affect the employment practices of business or labor. There have been some attempts to pass an FEPC law at the national level to apply to interstate commerce, but none has ever been successful.

Fair Labor Standards Act (1938) Established for the first time minimum wages and maximum working hours for employees working for firms engaged in interstate commerce, with some exceptions.

Farm Bureau See **American Farm Bureau Federation.**

Farm Credit Administration An independent agency whose major policy decisions are made by a 13-member Farm Credit Board and administered by an official known as the Governor of the Farm Credit Administration. It supervises the cooperative credit system which provides long- and short-term loans to farmers and certain kinds of cooperatives established by farmers. The magnitude of its operations can be seen from the fact that in a recent typical year, farmers and their cooperatives borrowed four billion dollars from the banks and associations operating under the supervision of the Farm Credit Administration.

Farmer-Labor Party See **Third party.**

Farmers Home Administration (FHA) An agency operating within the Department of Agriculture with the responsibility of providing loans to farmers. It makes money available for such purposes as purchasing farms, meeting operating expenses, establishing sound soil and water conservation projects, building decent farm homes, and providing emergency economic aid in the event of natural disasters.

Farmers Union See **National Farmers Union.**

Fascist A supporter of the dictator Benito Mussolini, who ruled Italy from 1922 to 1943. The term is also applied to any person who holds very strong, authoritarian views about government and who believes that the elite should rule without such democratic institutions as elections, representative legislatures, and individual freedom.

Fat Cat A wealthy person who gives money to support a political party or

Rogers, 1907. The Bettmann Archive.

FIRST YOU SET THEM UP, AND THEN—

candidate. It is a slang term which suggests that the person's money rather than his ability is important in politics.

Favorite Son A candidate for the presidency proposed at a national convention whose support is exclusively or largely from his home state's delegation. Often the state will delegate a governor or a senator as an honorary gesture, although sometimes the favorite son is proposed as a serious candidate. Usually, however, the term implies that the candidate is not likely to receive the nomination of the convention or the party.

FBI See **Department of Justice.**

FCC See **Federal Communications Commission.**

Featherbedding The forced hiring of unneeded workmen, or limiting the output per man below a reasonable level, in order to insure full employment of union members. The term is also used to describe any unnecessary positions created or maintained to provide jobs for favored persons.

Federal Aviation Agency An independent agency headed by an Administrator appointed by the President with the consent of the Senate. Its primary concern is the safety of air travel. It controls the use of airspace in the United States for both civilian and military aircraft and issues and enforces safety regulations ranging from the manufacture and construction of aircraft to the operation of the aircraft. It carries on research in air safety, installs and maintains aids to air transportation, and administers grants for the development of public airports. See also **Civil Aeronautics Board.**

Federal Bureau of Investigation See **Department of Justice.**

Federal Communications Commission (FCC) An independent regulatory commission established in 1935. It is made up of a chairman and six other commissioners appointed by the President with the consent of the Senate for seven-year staggered terms. One of the FCC's main tasks is granting and renewing licenses for radio and television stations. It is charged by law with determining whether those to whom licenses are granted will operate the station in accord with "public interest, convenience, or necessity." It also has power to review the conduct of licensees. Licenses are in effect for three years, and almost all of them are renewed since the Commission has been unable to develop any clear standards by which it determines "public interest, convenience, or necessity."

The FCC has been the center of a great deal of controversy in recent years, particularly because of the TV quiz show scandals and because of alleged improper influence in the allocation of licenses of television and radio stations. Efforts to strengthen the Commission's regulatory activities have run into difficulty: on the one hand because of those who have been interested in avoiding such regulation, and on the other because of the proper fear that regulation might become censorship, thereby jeopardizing freedom of speech. The Commission also endeavors to enforce the statutory requirement that stations granting time—free or with charge—

for political purposes must also make available equal time to all political candidates for the same office. This requirement was suspended in 1960 for the presidential candidates in order to permit the debates between the two major presidential candidates. A second major responsibility of the FCC is the regulation of interstate telephone and telegraph communication. It is empowered to fix rates, control expansion, curtailment, and mergers relating to these services.

Federal Deposit Insurance Corporation (FDIC) A government corporation established in 1933, managed by a board of directors of three members serving six-year staggered terms and appointed by the President with the consent of the Senate. The primary responsibility of this Corporation is to insure deposits in eligible banks. Under the law deposits of individuals up to $10,000 may be insured. The Corporation was established in the early days of the New Deal in the midst of a banking crisis. In addition to carrying out the insurance function, the FDIC also examines banks to determine their insurability, approves mergers between insured banks, and acts as receiver for all national banks placed in receivership. Its activities are financed by assessments on the insured banks and on investments.

Federal Extension Service An agency within the Department of Agriculture. Its task is to cooperate with state officers and county agricultural agents to make available the results of the latest research into agricultural matters. Its influence at the local level has been a great contribution to the progress made in scientific farm production during the last thirty-five years. **59**

Federal Government In the United States, the central or national government.

Federal Housing Administration (FHA) See **Housing and Home Finance Agency.**

Federal Mediation and Conciliation Service A service established in 1947. This service has no law enforcement authority but is available for mediation and conciliation in labor disputes whenever in its judgment a substantial interruption of interstate commerce is threatened. Its mediators are located in seven regional offices, spread throughout the country, and in major industrial cities.

Federal National Mortgage Association See **Housing and Home Finance Agency.**

Federal Power Commission (FPC) An independent regulatory commission established in 1930 as the successor to a cabinet-level commission which had been established within the executive branch in 1920. The FPC is composed of five commissioners appointed by the President with the consent of the Senate. Their terms are staggered and each one runs for five years. The Commission has the authority to investigate the water power resources of the nation and to issue licenses to nonfederal public agencies and private businesses which wish to build hydroelectric dams. It can obtain and publish information regarding electrical energy in the United States and regulates the interstate rates and services of public and private suppliers. It also has broad regulatory power over natural gas companies operating in interstate commerce. Its activity or lack of activity has been the subject of much political controversy and discussion within recent years.

Federal Register A daily publication of the federal government which contains presidential proclamations, executive orders, and administrative regulations and notices. The *Code of Federal Regulations* codifies all these documents.

Federal Reserve System A banking institution established by federal law in 1915. The system includes 12 quasi-public banks located in Boston, New York, Philadelphia, Richmond, Atlanta, Dallas, Cleveland, Chicago, St. Louis, Minneapolis, Kansas City, and San Francisco.

These banks operate under the general supervision of the Board of Governors of the Federal Reserve System, whose seven members are appointed by the President with the consent of the Senate. Each member of the Board is appointed for a 14-year term. A Federal Reserve bank is generally referred to as a "banker's bank" because each Federal Reserve bank is owned by the banks which are members of the system. All national banks are required to be members; banks incorporated under state laws are permitted to join if they meet certain requirements.

The purpose of establishing the Federal Reserve System was to provide a more effective monetary and banking system for the United States. Some of the most important functions of the Federal Reserve Board are the following:

1. To determine within limits set by the Congress the proportion of a member bank's total deposits which that bank must deposit in its Federal Reserve bank as a reserve against its own deposits.

2. To engage through the Federal Open-Market Committee in such open-market operations as the pur-

chase and sale of government bonds and certain other commercial securities.

3. To raise or lower the interest rate which member banks must pay to the Federal Reserve bank on loans from that bank.

4. To regulate the amount of credit which may be extended for the purchase of securities registered on the National Securities Exchange.

Federal Reserve banks deal directly with individual banks and have very few dealings with the general public. They rediscount commercial paper for banks and hold reserves for member banks. They assist in the transfer of funds, issue notes, act as fiscal agencies for the government, and hold government funds on deposit.

The question of the degree of control which the government should exercise over the Federal Reserve System is regularly raised in congressional debate and sometimes becomes an issue in presidential campaigns. Usually the controversy revolves around the interest policies of the Federal Reserve banks, as well as their open-market activities. It has been observed that the injection of the Federal Reserve into a campaign is not really significant since, to make a new application of Mr. Dooley's famous statement about the Supreme Court, it has been noted that the Federal Reserve, too, follows the election returns.

Federal Trade Commission (FTC) An independent regulatory commission of the federal government established in 1914. It is made up of five members appointed by the President with the consent of the Senate. Members serve for seven-year, staggered terms. Its basic purpose is the preservation of competitive business enterprise. It is empowered to issue, after proper investigation and hearings, "cease and desist" orders to prevent certain illegal practices. Some examples of the latter are price-fixing agreements, combinations in restraint of trade, the use of false or deceptive advertising—especially of such products as food, drugs, and cosmetics— and the interstate marketing of dangerously flammable wearing apparel and the like. The FTC frequently negotiates an agreement with a company without actually issuing a formal complaint.

Federalist Papers A series of essays in defense of the proposed new Constitution. These appeared in New York newspapers in the winters of 1787 and 1788. They were part of a great debate which was carried on after the Constitution was submitted to the states for ratification. They were written by Alexander Hamilton, James Madison, and John Jay and were published under the name of "Publius." These essays have survived not only as authoritative commentaries on the Constitution, but also as brilliant political tracts in their own right.

Federalist Party The first national political party in the United States. It had its beginning in the split between Alexander Hamilton and Thomas Jefferson when they were members of President George Washington's cabinet. Hamilton and the Federalists were the conservatives of their time. They favored a strong central government capable of protecting the interests of property and capital. The administrations of Washington and John Adams were dominated by Federalists and Federalist policies. Jefferson's election to the presidency in 1800 marked the beginning of the **61**

decline of the Federalists and they were never again a strong political force. The Federalist movement, however, left a lasting imprint on American history. In addition to Hamilton and Adams, it counted among its supporters such eminent persons as John Jay, John Marshall, and for a time, James Madison.

Federalism   See **Federation.**

Federation   A governmental system wherein authority is divided between a strong central government and divisional government. For example, in the United States the division of authority is between the federal government and the states. This theory of government and the systems developed under this theory are called *federalist*. A federation is a compromise system lying between a **unitary state** and a **confederation** in which each separate unit retains its own sovereignty. Authority is generally less centralized in a federation than it is in a unitary state, but more centralized than it is in a confederation.

Fellow Traveler   A person who follows somewhat closely a particular party line, although not actually a member of that party. The word is generally applied to those who support the position of the Communist party, although they either are not members or do not admit to membership. It is sometimes used with reference to those who support other political parties without identifying themselves directly with them.

Felony   See **Criminal case.**

Fence Mending   See **Mending fences.**

FHA (Federal Housing Administration)   See **Housing and Home Finance Agency.**

Fifteenth Amendment   See **Civil War amendments.**

Fifth Amendment   The **due process** amendment to the Constitution. It provides that no one should be held to answer for a capital or infamous crime, except under conditions of war or other unusual conditions, unless he is indicted by a grand jury. It provides that no person shall twice be put in jeopardy of life or limb for the same offense, or compelled in a criminal case to bear witness against himself; that no one shall be deprived of life, liberty, or property without due process of law; and that private property cannot be taken for public use without just compensation. "Taking the fifth" has become a common phrase because many witnesses before televised congressional committee investigations have refused to answer questions about their records and activities on the grounds that such answers might incriminate them.

Filibuster   The practice in a legislative body of talking and debating a bill at great length in an effort to modify the bill significantly or prevent it from being acted upon finally. This tactic can be carried out with success only in a legislative body like the United States Senate, where the rules permit almost unlimited debate. In the Senate the only way in which a determined filibuster can be defeated and a vote on a measure actually taken is by imposing *cloture,* or *closure,* that is, the closing off of debate. Under current Senate rules this requires the approval of two-thirds of the senators present and voting. In practice filibusters in the Senate seldom drag on for extended periods of time because it usually becomes clear whether the filibuster will be successful. Senate filibuster or the threat of one is often sufficient to insure that the bill will not be considered before significant modifications, acceptable to the minority, are made. Today the chief target of filibusters, either real or threatened, is civil rights legislation, although there has been prolonged debate in the Senate on such measures as atomic energy.

Seaman, ILGWU Justice.

Finance Committee   A standing Senate Committee of 17 members, which considers all measures dealing with taxes, customs, duties and tariffs, social security, veterans affairs and pensions, and similar bills.

Fireside Chats   The frequent and informal radio addresses of President Franklin D. Roosevelt when he discussed problems of interest to the nation. The term is now used for any informal presidential address to the nation.

First Amendment   One of the ten amendments that make up the Bill of Rights of the United States Constitution. It forbids Congress to make any law: respecting an establishment of religion; prohibiting the free exercise of religion; or limiting the freedom of speech or the press, or the right of people to assemble or to petition the government for redress of grievances. The safeguards provided by this Amendment protect the individual citizen against invasion of his rights by both federal and state governments.   See also **Palko v. Connecticut, Schenck v. United States,** and **Church and state.**

First Reading   See **Readings of bills.**

Fiscal Year   The 12-month period in the federal government beginning July 1 and ending June 30 of the next year. This constitutes a financial year for bookkeeping purposes. The fiscal year bears the date of the calendar year in which it ends; that is, the fiscal year 1961 ends on June 30, 1961. It, of course, covers part of the year 1960. Businesses often use other 12-month periods for their fiscal years.

Fishing Expedition   A slang term for a legislative investigation conducted for no specific purpose, but rather with the hope that some evidence will turn up which can be used for partisan or personal political purposes.

Floater   A person who illegally votes in several different places under assumed names or a person whose vote can be bought.

Floor   The main room of a legislative chamber; the area in which the members present themselves and participate in debate and in voting. The floor is usually restricted to members or former members and special employees of the legislative body.   See also **Chamber.**

Food and Agriculture Organization (FAO)   A specialized agency of the **United Nations** established in 1945 to secure improvement in the production and distribution of food, to raise   **63**

levels of nutrition, and to better the conditions of rural peoples. There are 81 member nations (1960), and the central office is located in Rome, Italy. The FAO operates through a Conference (held at least once every two years and at which each member has one vote) and an Executive Council made up of representatives of 24 member governments. The Director General is appointed by the Conference. The FAO maintains a department of technical assistance which has been of great value, and it has developed several programs to secure international cooperation in solving food and agricultural problems.

Food and Drug Administration (FDA)
See **Department of Health, Education, and Welfare.**

Foreign Aid See **Marshall Plan, Mutual Security Program.**

Foreign Policy The general character and direction of a government's actions in its relationships with other nations. Foreign policy reflects a government's principles and objectives in its foreign affairs and is designed to implement them.

In the United States the negotiation of foreign policy is the exclusive right of the federal government and chiefly of the executive branch. Only the President can deal with representatives of other nations, appoint and receive ambassadors, extend or withhold recognition of other governments, and state the official attitude of the United States toward policies in other nations, in the United Nations, and in similar international organizations and alliances. The Congress, however, can exert considerable influence through its power of appropriations, joint resolutions, committee hearings, and floor debates. The Sen-

ate has additional authority through its powers of confirming officials and ratifying treaties. In the long run public opinion is also a strong factor in determining foreign policy. Until recent times foreign policy was considered quite distinct from domestic policy, but since World War II foreign and domestic policies have moved closer together and frequently overlap and influence one another. At the same time the scope of foreign policy has been broadened to include direct economic, social, and cultural relationships as well as traditional diplomatic exchanges and military alliances. Likewise, the military phase of foreign policy has seen the development of intricate mutual defense programs such as **NATO.** See **American foreign policy.**

Foreign Service The employees of the State Department who are eligible for assignment both in this country and abroad. The foreign service is a special kind of government service for which separate entrance examinations are given. Its task is to represent the United States in embassies and consulates abroad, to supply and evaluate information about foreign nations, and to perform various administrative tasks for Americans abroad.

Forest Service An agency responsible for the conservation and rehabilitation of the nation's forests. It is an agency within the Department of Agriculture. Since the nation's forests constitute one-third of the total land area of the United States, and since there are 151 national forests, the work of this agency is of great economic importance.

Four Freedoms The statement of the principal objectives of the United States and her allies in World War II

Message From President Roosevelt

1941

In the future days, which we seek to make secure, we look forward to a world founded upon four essential human freedoms.

The first is freedom of speech and expression — everywhere in the world.

The second is freedom of every person to worship God in his own way — everywhere in the world.

The third is freedom from want — which, translated into world terms, means economic understandings which will secure to every nation a healthy peace time life for its inhabitants — everywhere in the world.

The fourth is freedom from fear — which, translated into world terms, means a world-wide reduction of armaments to such a point and in such a thorough fashion that no nation will be in a position to commit an act of physical aggression against any neighbor — anywhere in the world.

That is no vision of a distant millennium. It is a definite basis for a kind of world attainable in our own time and generation. That kind of world is the very antithesis of the so-called new order of tyranny which the dictators seek to create with the crash of a bomb.

To that new order we oppose the greater conception — the moral order. A good society is able to face schemes of world domination and foreign revolutions alike without fear.

Since the beginning of our American history we have been engaged in change — in a perpetual peaceful revolution — a revolution which goes on steadily, quietly adjusting itself to changing conditions — without the concentration camp or the quick-lime in the ditch. The world order which we seek is the cooperation of free countries, working together in a friendly, civilized society.

This nation has placed its destiny in the hands and heads and hearts of its millions of free men and women; and its faith in freedom under the guidance of God. Freedom means the supremacy of human rights everywhere. Our support goes to those who struggle to gain those rights or keep them. Our strength is in our unity of purpose.

To that high concept there can be no end save victory.

Franklin D. Roosevelt

THE WHITE HOUSE,
January 6, 1941.

United Nations.

AT THE CLOSE OF HIS MESSAGE TO CONGRESS, ON JANUARY 6, 1941, THE LATE PRESIDENT ROOSEVELT GAVE TO MANKIND HIS VISION OF A FUTURE WHERE FOUR FREEDOMS—FREEDOM OF SPEECH, FREEDOM OF WORSHIP, FREEDOM FROM WANT, AND FREEDOM FROM FEAR—WOULD BE THE BIRTHRIGHT OF EVERY HUMAN BEING.

as expressed by President Franklin D. Roosevelt in his message to Congress, January 6, 1942. The basic human freedoms, he stated, are: freedom of speech, freedom of each person to worship God, freedom from want, and freedom from fear.

Fourteenth Amendment An amendment adopted in 1868. It has become one of the most important and controversial of all the amendments to the Constitution. It contains five provisions, all of which related to issues involved in the Civil War. Section One, the most significant, provides that "no state shall deprive any person of life, liberty, or property, without due process of law; nor deny to any person within its jurisdiction the equal protection of the laws." Whereas the first ten amendments, the Bill of Rights, restrict the power of the federal government, the Fourteenth Amendment, in effect, extends much of the Bill of Rights and other provisions of the Constitution to the states. See also **Brown** *v.* **Board of Education** and **Palko** *v.* **Connecticut.**

FPC See **Federal Power Commission.**

Franking Privilege The right of members of Congress and the executive branch to use the United States postal service for the official conduct of business without payment of any postal charges.

Freedom The opportunity for individuals and voluntary groups to make their own decisions in the pursuit of their legitimate objectives. The primary and most difficult problem in democracy is that of reconciling freedom and authority, of maintaining a balance between the natural and civil rights of individuals and groups and the restraints required by government

to protect the common good. Government has responsibility to promote procedures and institutions which enable citizens to develop and exercise freedom as well as the negative function of preventing interference by others in the freedom of citizens. In American government the Constitution sets forth the powers of the Congress and the other branches while the **Bill of Rights** sets limits on the areas in which government can act. There always remains, however, a kind of no man's land in which some confusion and conflict exist about the claims for freedom and those for regulation. In the tradition of Western civilization a free society is based not only on external procedures but also upon the virtue of citizens. It rests, too, on the direction given by religious, educational, and civic groups in society and upon respect for the individual.

See also **Civil Rights, Natural Law.**

Free Enterprise See **Private enterprise.**

Free Trade A policy of eliminating national tariffs and quotas to permit the free exchange of goods in international trade. As an economic theory it is based on the belief that if each nation produces goods for which it is best equipped, all people and nations will benefit. The United States has never had a free trade policy, but since 1933 its policy has been in that direciton rather than toward **mercantilism.** Factors peculiar to each nation —such as fiscal stability, kinds of natural resources, interests of national defense, different wage rates and standards of living—limit the adoption of an unrestricted free trade policy. See **Tariff.**

Front Runner A person who appears to be far ahead in a race for a nomination, or the ultimate winner of an election.   See also **Dark horse.**

FTC   See **Federal Trade Commission.**

Full Faith and Credit Clause   A constitutional provision requiring all states to honor duly authenticated transactions of government and commerce occurring in another state. These transactions include business contracts, court decisions, and the acts of corporations. The "full faith and credit" clause has never been fully extended to personal relationships. For example, Nevada divorce decrees are not honored in all other states.

Fusion Ticket   A slate of candidates made up of members of more than one party and supported by members of the parties from which the candidates were drawn. Probably the most common fusion tickets are in New York City where the minority Republicans sometimes join with the **Liberal party** in an effort to defeat the Democratic party.

Gag Rule   A rule in a legislative body which restricts the time available for debate. All legislative bodies have some provisions for limiting debate; therefore the term *gag rule* is usually used by opponents of a given measure who do not wish to see it brought to a vote, but sometimes with justification against a majority which arbitrarily and too quickly cuts off debate.   See also **Filibuster.**

GAO   See **General Accounting Office.**

GATT   See **General Agreement on Tariffs and Trade.**

General Accounting Office (GAO)   An agency of the federal government directly responsible to the Congress. It was established to provide for the independent auditing of the financial operations of the executive branch of the government. It is sometimes referred to as a "congressional watchdog" agency because it has authority to look into spending by all executive agencies. The head of this agency is the *Comptroller General of the United States* who is appointed by the President with the consent of the Senate. His term runs for 15 years and he cannot be reappointed. His independence of the President and the executive branch is further safeguarded by a provision in the law that he cannot be removed except for specific cause and then by joint resolution of the Congress rather than by the President.

General Agreement on Tariffs and Trade (GATT)   An international contract for reducing tariff barriers agreed upon by 23 nations at a conference in Geneva in 1947. A series of negotiations since that time has resulted in multilateral lowering of tariffs on hundreds of items and in agreements on national quotas. The General Agreement on Tariffs and Trade has become an important procedure for promoting international trade. Although not formally an agency of the **United Nations,** GATT has for practical purposes taken the place of the proposed International Trade Organization. Negotiations by the United States under GATT have been by way of executive agreement rather than treaty. Thirty-eight countries are now a party to negotiations under GATT. The secretariat of GATT is located at Geneva, Switzerland.

General Assembly The deliberative body of the **United Nations.** It includes representatives of all of the member nations. Each nation has one vote, and on important questions a two-thirds majority of members voting is required for action. The General Assembly meets each year, and it may take up any issue within the scope of the Charter except issues reserved for the **Security Council.** At the time of the Korean conflict the General Assembly asserted its right to recommend collective action when the Security Council failed to act because of the inability of the permanent members to agree upon a course of action. In general the Assembly has served as a forum for discussion on points of conflict and tension. On a number of important issues the votes have reflected the differences in the beliefs of the Western and democratic bloc as opposed to the Soviet bloc or as distinguished from the position of the neutral nations.

General Assistance State or local programs designed to give financial aid to needy persons who do not qualify under an ordinary state public assistance program. The help may take the form of cash payments to those in need, or medical assistance, food certificates, or other forms of aid.

General Election A regularly scheduled election which finally determines who shall occupy a public position. It differs from a **primary election,** wherein party candidates are selected; and it differs from a **by-election,** which is not regularly scheduled.

General Pair See **Pair.**

General Services Administration (GSA) A federal agency established in 1949 by the merging of several existing agencies. It is responsible to the

President and is headed by the General Services Administrator, who is appointed by the President with the consent of the Senate. It performs three basic functions for agencies outside of the military establishment: it regulates or actually does the purchasing of supplies; it designs, constructs, and maintains federally owned or leased buildings; and it promotes improved management of current records and the selection, preservation, and availability of permanently valuable noncurrent records. It is sometimes referred to as the President's housekeeping agency.

General Welfare Clause That section of the Constitution which stipulates that Congress may tax to provide for "the general welfare of the United States." This is contained in Article I, Section 8. There has always been an argument whether or not this is a broad grant of power to tax for the general welfare or whether the phrase "general welfare" was meant only to serve as shorthand for the specific grants of power listed in the rest of Article I, Section 8. The broader and more comprehensive interpretation prevails today and has been sustained by the courts. This clause has been the constitutional source of the great extension of governmental power. See also **Commerce clause** and the **Elastic clause.**

Gerrymander The practice of arranging legislative districts, either state or congressional, in such a way as to give advantage to a party or special-interest group. Since state legislatures determine boundaries for districts, many times the rural legislators are reluctant to redistrict their state despite the rapid shift of population from the rural to the urban areas. This results in districts with wide variation in population which often provide an advantage for a political party or for rural interests against urban interests.

The term is said to have arisen when an artist drew a picture of a sprawling district created in Massachusetts in 1812 which he made to resemble a salamander with claws, wings, and teeth. An editor changed the title to "Gerrymander" because the governor at that time was Elbridge Gerry.

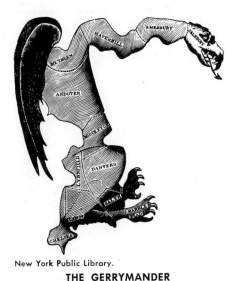

New York Public Library.
THE GERRYMANDER

Gibbons v. Ogden (1824)   This was the case in which for the first time the **commerce clause** of the Constitution was interpreted by the Supreme Court. The controversy in the case was over whether certain steamboats operating under a federal license could be barred from operating between New York and New Jersey because exclusive right to New York waterways had been granted to another steamboat company by the State of New York. The Court held that the New York law must yield to the law passed by the national Congress. The decision did not eliminate the authority of the states over commerce conducted within a state, but it established a divided authority over commerce—partly state (intrastate) and partly federal (interstate). This line has never been clearly drawn and has been the source of controversy and litigation ever since this decision in 1824.   See also **Hammer v. Dagenhart, United States v. Darby,** and **NLRB v. Jones and Laughlin.**

GNP   See **Gross national product.**

Good Neighbor Policy   The slogan used to describe the Latin American policies of the United States initiated by President Franklin D. Roosevelt.

Good Offices   Position or influence. One is often asked to use his good offices to accomplish a particular end.

GOP   Abbreviation for Grand Old Party, an affectionate name for the Republican party.

Government Corporation   An organization incorporated under federal law and owned by the federal government. Government corporations were little used until World War I when they became a popular device for achieving quick independent action for certain types of programs. Many government corporations are set up to lend money or to secure credit—for example, the **Export-Import Bank,** the **Commodity Credit Corporation,** and the **Federal Deposit Insurance Corporation.** Others have been set up to administer extensive programs such as the **Tennessee Valley Authority** and the **St. Lawrence Seaway Development Corporation.** These corporations vary greatly in their measure of independence, their degree of direct government control and dependence on   **69**

appropriations from the Congress. Basically, of course, all are under the control of the government.

Government Printing Office The government office in Washington, D.C., which does all of the printing for Congress including the **Congressional Record,** all executive departments and agencies, and for the judiciary with the exception of the United States Supreme Court.

Governor The governor is the chief executive officer in each of the fifty states. He is usually elected for a term of two or four years. In some states he is not allowed to succeed himself, and in some states cannot run for reelection even though some other person has served since his last term. The powers vary from state to state, but generally include the power to appoint department heads in the state government, to appoint judges, and to veto legislation.

Governors' Conference An annual meeting of the governors of all the states and territories of the United States. Its express purpose is to facilitate cooperation among the states, to improve state-local and state-federal relationships by an exchange of views and experience. The group meets annually, usually in a resort area, and seeks to focus national attention on state problems and sometimes on state governors.

GPO See **Government Printing Office.**

Graduated Income Tax A tax on income, either personal or corporate, which increases in proportion as the income rises. For example, an income of $5,000 might be taxed at a rate of 20 per cent and an income of $10,000 might be taxed at a rate of 33 per cent. The income tax of the United States government is a graduated one, as are most state income taxes. Such taxes are based upon the principle of the "ability to pay," which holds that a person who has a higher income can afford to pay a higher rate of taxation.

Graft The illegal or immoral use of public funds for private benefit. Graft includes such things as outright theft and the awarding of contracts at inflated prices to friends of persons in power. It also describes taking of bribes by officials in power. See also **Honest graft.**

Grand Jury A group of persons, usually numbering between 12 and 23, assigned the responsibility of hearing witnesses and determining whether sufficient evidence exists to return an indictment against someone who is accused of violating a law. Occasionally a grand jury conducts a broad-scale investigation into a general problem for the purpose of obtaining information for public use rather than as a probe of a specific action. Grand juries have come under heavy criticism over the years and about half of the states have abandoned them in less serious cases in favor of a system whereby the prosecuting attorney is empowered to initiate a trial simply by filing an information affidavit declaring that he has sufficient evidence to warrant a trial. The Constitution requires that in federal cases "no person shall be brought to answer for a capital, or otherwise infamous crime, unless on the presentment of indictment of a grand jury."

Grand Old Party The **GOP.**

Grange See **National Grange.**

Grant-In-Aid A grant from the federal government to a state government, or from a state government to a local government in order to spur action in a specific area, such as education or public works. Such a grant is often made with the proviso that the recipient body expend some funds of its own to help get the job done. Grants-in-aid have become widespread in recent years.

Grass Roots   The local area and its people. A politician goes to the grass roots when he returns home to find out what the individual voter is thinking about.

Great Seal of the United States   The official emblem of the United States. It has an eagle on one side holding an olive branch in one claw and arrows in the other. The reverse side has a pyramid, an eye, and an inscription which reads as follows: *"Novus ordo seclorum"* (New order of the ages). This seal is symbolic of the authority of the United States government. It is displayed on the one dollar bill, on official federal documents and publications.

Gross National Product   The total amount of goods and services produced in a country in one year stated in terms of dollar value.

GSA   See **General Services Administration.**

Habeas Corpus   A court order—a writ—requiring a jailer, or other official who is detaining someone, to bring the prisoner before the court and to state the time and cause of his arrest. The judge then determines whether the detention violates the prisoner's rights. The Constitution provides that "the privilege of the writ of habeas corpus shall not be suspended unless when in cases of rebellion or invasion the public safety may require it." This right, which is taken for granted in the United States, is extremely important. In many countries detention for long periods of time without formal charges or trial is a common practice and a real danger to freedom.

Habitual Offender Laws   Statutes which require a judge to impose a much heavier sentence, oftentimes life imprisonment, on a person who has been convicted of a crime a number of times. These laws also generally foreclose parole to the offender. The general rule seems to be to impose a sentence of life imprisonment after a person has been convicted of crime for the fourth time. The theory is that such a person is a grave danger to society because he is incorrigible.

Hague Conferences   A series of international conferences held at the Hague in the Netherlands. The first was held in 1899 and a second in 1907 at which 44 states were represented. The purpose of the Hague Conferences was to secure peace and disarmament by agreement among nations. One of the major achievements was the establishment of the Permanent Court of Arbitration at the Hague in 1899. This Court provides the means for the arbitration of international disputes. Other important conventions agreed upon through the Hague Conferences relate to maritime neutrality, the laws of the sea, and the laws of warfare with their emphasis upon limiting war and restricting its methods to those which are more humane.

Hammer *v.* Dagenhart (1918)   A case in which the Supreme Court de-   **71**

clared that a law passed by Congress in 1916 prohibiting the transportation in interstate commerce of goods made by, or with the help of, child labor was unconstitutional. The Court held that this law interfered with the reserved powers of the states under the **Tenth Amendment.** This decision was in keeping with the very strict interpretation of the **commerce clause** which prevailed from 1916 to 1920, but the decision was reversed and modified later by the Supreme Court. See also **United States** *v.* **Darby** and **Gibbons** *v.* **Ogden.**

Hard Money Money which maintains its value. It is generally desirable that the money of a country maintain a constant value in relation to economic goods for which it can be exchanged or in relationship to the currencies of other countries. Maintaining the value of money is a complicated process. It involves the amount of money in circulation, the nature of the reserves behind the money, balance of payment with other countries, and the general level of economic activity.

Hatch Act This Act passed in 1939 was designed primarily to protect government employees from exploitation through partisan political pressure. It provides that, with certain exceptions (heads of departments and other high-ranking officials appointed by the President with the consent of the Senate), no officer in the executive branch of the government "shall take any active part in political management or in political campaigns." This prohibition applies to many state employees whose salaries are paid in part by the federal government. The law also prohibits the intimidation of voters in federal elections and the solicitation of campaign contributions from

employees on federal relief projects.

In its broader aspects, the law deals with campaign contributions, prohibiting contributions of more than $5,000 from any one person during any single year to a national political party or to a candidate for federal office or to a committee supporting such a candidate. This limitation is not particularly effective, however, since contributors can give money in the names of their wives and children and can also give through state and local committees. In addition to providing some protection to civil service employees, the Hatch Act also has the effect of limiting their political activities.   See also **Corrupt Practices Act.**

Berryman, 1939. Library of Congress.

Hat In The Ring A popular expression to indicate that a politician has formally announced his candidacy for an office. Throwing some personal item to the ground is an ancient symbol of challenge and a pledge to battle, and in some areas of the American frontier a volunteer threw his hat into the ring to show his willingness to wrestle or box. The political use of the term was popularized by ex-President Theodore Roosevelt when he opened his campaign for the Republican nomination in 1912 by announcing: "My hat is in the ring."

Health Department Exists at almost every level of government—federal, state, county, city, and other municipalities. Functions of health departments include such things as: preserving vital statistics; operating state, city, or county hospitals and nursing services; supervising health of school children by providing for such things as vaccinations for common diseases and examination of eyes and teeth; and conducting educational programs to promote the health of the citizens. A state department of health usually regulates and licenses the practice of medicine, dentistry, pharmacy, and medical education. It collects and publishes birth, sickness, and death statistics, carries on various programs for the control of communicable diseases, and guards the purity of milk, water, and food. Health departments at various levels of government may have special responsibilities such as maternal and child care and the direction of special programs such as heart and cancer programs.

Health, Education, and Welfare, Department of See **Department of Health, Education, and Welfare.**

Health, Education, and Welfare, Secretary of See **Department of Health, Education, and Welfare.**

Hearings A formal session of a legislative committee in which witnesses present testimony on matters under consideration by the committee. Congressional committees may hold hearings for many purposes. All hearings are supposed to be concerned with gathering information which will be a guide in determining whether new legislation should be introduced or passed, or whether the existing legislation is effectively achieving the purposes for which it was enacted. The courts of the United States have been very liberal when asked to define the limits of the matters which may come before congressional committees. Most congressional hearings are rather quiet and receive little publicity. Some, however, dealing with crime or subversion or foreign policy receive much publicity and attention.

HEW See **Department of Health, Education, and Wefare.**

HHFA See **Housing and Home Finance Agency.**

Highways (a) Local—those roads which are primarily the responsibility of counties, townships, towns, cities, and villages. These are usually supported in part by contributions by the federal and state governments. At the state level the revenue for road construction and maintenance is usually derived from gasoline and automobile license taxes. A portion of these state funds is then passed on to the cities, counties, and other local units of government for the support of their road programs.

(b) State—the major system of hard road surfaces within a state, usually linking the principal cities within that state, or cities within one state with major highways running into neighboring states. Construction and maintenance is usually directed by a state highway department in cooperation with the Bureau of Public Roads in the United States Department of Commerce. The federal government contributes at least a portion of the funds for state highways and it provides 90 per cent of the funds for the *Interstate*

Highway system, a 40,000 mile network of superhighways to link all the state capitals and principal cities of the nation.

Holidays Days designated by law to commemorate special persons or occasions and customarily observed by freedom from the regular work schedule. Technically, there are no national holidays, but the President and the Congress designate holidays to be observed in the District of Columbia and by federal employees throughout the nation. These days are usually observed by the states and the people. The legal public holidays are: New Year's Day, Washington's birthday, Memorial Day, Independence Day, Labor Day, Veterans' Day, Thanksgiving and Christmas. Each state is free to designate the holidays it will observe and states frequently add to the list of federal holidays. In the United States Sunday is the only national holiday recognized by common law, and statutes requiring citizens to refrain from certain activities on Sunday have been upheld by the courts.

Home Rule A charter for city government which has been drafted by local officials. All local governmental units are created by authority of state law, and a home rule charter is the most flexible system and permits the greatest degree of local initiative. At one time or another more than half the states have authorized home rule charters. See also **Charter.**

Honest Graft A phrase made famous by George Washington Plunkett, a Tammany leader during the early years of the twentieth century. It was represented, in this view expressed by Plunkett, that he could not understand those who ate of the forbidden fruit

of the tree of penal code when there were so many other trees in the garden to which no such penalty was attached.

Hoover Commission The name given two commissions on reorganization of the executive branch of the government. One was established in 1947 and the other in 1953, and both were headed by former President Herbert Hoover. Each commission had 12 members: four named by the Speaker of the House of Representatives, two of whom were congressmen; four named by the president of the Senate, two of whom were senators; and four named by the President.

The first Hoover Commission was primarily concerned with the organization and efficiency of the executive branch, and its recommendations were generally approved. The second Hoover Commission had a broader mandate and looked into the merits of programs and policies. The latter commission's recommendations were not so widely hailed or generally approved. Many of the recommendations made by the Hoover Commission were adopted either by executive order or by act of Congress. It is generally believed by people close to government, however, that the claims of economy and efficiency made for its recommendations by the Commission itself were somewhat inflated.

House of Representatives The popular branch of the United States government. The term is also used for the similar branch in bicameral state legislatures. It was the intention of the men who drafted the Constitution that this should be the predominant force in the government of the United States. It still remains a most important body, although the passage of time, the change and emphasis upon issues, and the amendment to the Constitution which provides for popular election of senators has had the effect of making the two bodies of relatively equal strength. The number of members from each state in the House of Representatives is based upon population. The size of the House has varied with the growth of the nation until in 1929 the number was set by law at 435.

Housing and Home Finance Agency (HHFA) An independent agency established in 1947 by merging several federal agencies having responsibility for various housing programs. The administrator, appointed by the President with the consent of the Senate, supervises the activities of agencies administering a variety of programs designed to provide better housing and related facilities. The HHFA includes the *Public Housing Administration* (PHA) which carries out the federal responsibility for low-rent public housing projects; the *Federal Housing Administration* (FHA) which administers a system of insurance for institutions that provide loans for the purchase of homes, for property improvement, and for the construction of cooperative and rental housing projects; the *Urban Renewal Administration* (URA) which administers the federal programs of slum clearance, urban renewal, and urban planning; the *Community Facilities Administration* (CFA) which administers loans for college housing, loans to hospitals for housing for nurses and interns, and loans to state and local governments for certain public works projects; and the *Federal National Mortgage Association* (FNMA, also called Fannie Mae) which performs various services designed to assist in the financing of home mortgages.

ICC See **Interstate Commerce Commission.**

Idealism The political philosophy which holds that politics and life generally can be arranged on the basis of noble ideals and aspirations. An idealist is a person who wants to change existing conditions in politics, either at home or abroad, according to a set of ideas, and who believes quite optimistically that these objectives can certainly be achieved.

Ideology A set of political, economic, and social views or ideas; the more or less total view of a person or of a movement. Thus we speak of the "communist ideology" as we did of the "fascist ideology" or the "Nazi ideology." The "democratic ideology" includes the ideas or concepts of individual rights and freedom, popular election, restrictions on the power and authority of the government, the free enterprise system, and the like.

The word *ideology* is more accurately applied, however, to communism or Marxism because this is a more thoroughly systematic and dogmatic set of ideas and much of its appeal rests upon its overly simplified and unified approach to the explanation of history, to the determination of values, and to the establishment of a program. Fundamental to the philosophical basis of democratic society is the acceptance of pluralism which rejects a rigid set of dogmas and the belief that one set of ideas should be imposed upon all members of society.

Illinois *ex rel* McCollum v. Board of Education (1948) A case in which the Supreme Court, by an eight to one vote, declared unconstitutional a program which permitted privately chosen instructors to teach religion during school hours to stu- **75**

dents whose parents had approved such instruction. The Court held that this particular version of "released time," during school hours and involving the use of school rooms, violated the First Amendment. See also **Zorach v. Clauson, Church and state.**

Immigration and Naturalization Service A branch of the United States Department of Justice which administers the laws relating to immigration and naturalization; regulates the admission, exclusion, or deportation of aliens; and patrols Mexican and Canadian borders to prevent unlawful entry into the United States. It also supervises naturalization work in the various courts.

Immigration Laws Those laws which regulate the entrance into a nation of persons from other nations or countries. For nearly a century millions of Europeans were permitted to come into the United States without any restrictions, and millions of them did come and became citizens of our country. In 1882 Congress passed legislation to bar paupers and convicts and also to exclude Chinese. After 1882 additions were made to those who were excluded, but strict controls were not imposed until after World War I. The Immigration Act of 1924 established a permanent quota system based on "national origins" of the immigrants. The chief purpose of this restriction was to favor immigrants from northwestern European countries and to limit sharply those from southern and eastern Europe. The 1924 Act also excluded most Oriental peoples, but immigrants from Canada and Latin American countries were still allowed to come in without limit as to number, although they were subject to certain

"qualitative" restrictions. In 1952 the McCarran-Walter Act removed to some degree the stigma of racial exclusions by permitting a token quota of 100 immigrants annually from nearly every nation, but the national origins quota system was retained as a basic standard. The number of immigrants allowed to come in each year from all countries, except Canada and Latin America, is about 154,000. See also **National origins.**

Impeachment A formal accusation against a public official by a legislative body. The Constitution of the United States provides that the House of Representatives shall have the power by a majority vote to impeach the President, the Vice President, and all civil officers of the United States on the grounds of treason, bribery, or other high crimes and misdemeanors. After the House has acted, the Senate tries the person who has been impeached. A vote of two-thirds of the members of the Senate present is required for conviction.

In the history of our country, impeachment proceedings have been brought against only eleven persons; only four have been convicted. The most famous of these cases was the impeachment of President Andrew Johnson in 1868. He was not convicted in the Senate, however, where those opposed to him failed by one vote to obtain the votes of the necessary two-thirds of the members of the Senate.

Implied Powers The doctrine based upon interpretations of the Constitution by the Supreme Court that the federal government has powers which are implied by the Constitution as well as those which are specifically listed. See also **McCulloch v. Maryland, Elastic clause.**

Import To bring into this country goods manufactured or produced abroad or those things that are brought into a country.

Inauguration The formal act of installing the President of the United States or the governor of a state in office. It is usually the occasion for extensive ceremonies, the central point of which is the taking of an oath by the chief executive officer and his delivery of the inaugural address. The President of the United States is required by the Constitution to take the following oath of affirmation:

I do solemnly swear (or affirm) that I will faithfully execute the Office of President of the United States, and will to the best of my ability, preserve, protect and defend the Constitution of the United States.

Income Tax A tax imposed on the income of individuals and corporations. The Sixteenth Amendment to the United States Constitution authorizing the income tax was ratified in 1913.

Incorporation The formal procedure of creating a private or public corporation. The Articles of Incorporation must be drawn to legal specification, officers chosen, stock issued, and the articles filed with the proper state authority.

Incumbent One who holds office. In some states the term is allowed on a ballot in order to identify the candidates and prevent confusion.

Independent A person who is not identified with either political party. The difference between a party man and an independent may in many cases be hard to define. Some persons who call themselves independent actually vote consistently for one party, while others who claim a party preference sometimes vote quite independently. An independent is likely to say that party differences are too slight to be meaningful, and therefore he "votes for the man, not the party."

S. J. Ray, The Kansas City Star.

FISHING FOR THE BIG FELLOW THAT TIPS THE SCALES

Indian Affairs, Bureau of See **Department of Interior.**

Independent Agency An agency in the executive branch of the government which is not a part of any one of the ten major cabinet-level departments. Its officials are appointed by the President with the consent of the Senate and can be removed by the President. Decisions by independent agencies are subject to presidential approval. The "independence" of the agency refers to its existence outside the regular departments. Important agencies classified as "independent" are the **Veterans Administration** and the **Small Business Administration.** Compare with **Independent regulatory commission.**

Independent Regulatory Commission A board which has specified powers over industries or activities in a particular field. Regulatory commissions usually are bipartisan. Their function is partly legislative, when they establish general regulations which have the force of law; partly executive, when they investigate charges of unfair practices against a company; and partly judicial, when they render decisions on controversial cases and problems in dispute. The members of a regulatory commission, usually three or more, are appointed by the President with the consent of the Senate for staggered terms, usually running from five to seven years. Members of a regulatory commission cannot be removed by the President except for reasons set forth in the law. Decisions of the commission are sometimes reviewable in court, but they are not subject to presidential approval or disapproval. Regulatory commissions are therefore technically "independent" of the President and of the Congress, and independent also of the heads of the cabinet-level departments. Examples are the **Federal Communications Commission** and the **Interstate Commerce Commission.**

Indictment A formal, written accusation, presented by a prosecuting officer, for instance, a county attorney, charging a person or persons with violation of a criminal law. See also **True bill.**

Individualism Ideas which stress the value and importance of the individual person and of individual initiative

and decision, as opposed to community or governmental programs. To the extent that individualism emphasizes the importance of the responsibility of the individual, it is an essential concept in democratic society. Insofar as it argues against necessary government action, it is subject to question.

"Rugged individualism," a phrase frequently used in American political debate, refers to the pattern of behavior of American pioneers; speakers often suggest that this spirit needs revival and application in the modern world.

Inflation A change in the relationship between monetary units and purchasing power whereby more units of money are required to purchase a constant quantity of goods or materials. This change may occur as the result of an increase in the available supply of money without a corresponding increase in available goods, or it may occur when the volume of money remains relatively constant and the available supply of goods decreases. In the United States the expression "not worth a Continental" developed from an inflationary period in which the printed money of the Continental Congress became practically worthless. The South had a similar experience with the Confederate currency during the Civil War. In modern times the worst experience of inflation occurred in European countries following World War I.

Initiative A procedure whereby a specified percentage of voters can formally propose a constitutional amendment or a law. It is a method for bypassing the legislature and was adopted in many states early in this century, along with the **referendum** and the **recall,** in an effort to give the public a more direct voice in governing. Twenty states now make provision for the initiative procedure. Some initiatives go first to the legislature, if rejected or amended, then they must go on the ballot for public acceptance or disapproval. Other initiatives go directly to the voters. The initiative has not been used as extensively as its sponsors originally hoped, but the possibility of its use sometimes serves as a prod to state legislatures.

Injunction A court order prohibiting or requiring some specified action. Injunctions were the cause of great controversy in the early part of this century as they became a powerful instrument in the struggle between labor and management. Their use has since been more carefully defined and restricted. The use of the injunction continues to be a subject of controversy whenever labor-management relations legislation is under consideration.

Insurgent A person or group seeking a radical change in the policies of an organization. In American political usage, the term usually applies to a group within a party or a legislature seeking to gain control or greater influence.

Insurrection Rebellion against an established political authority.

Interest Group A group which attempts to influence public policy in such a way as to serve its own interests or purposes. In American political life, there are interest groups concerned about nearly every subject, including taxes, tariffs, foreign policy, military policy, labor-management relations, conservation, agriculture, urban affairs, education, highways, and professional athletics. Interest groups are often represented by **lobbyists,** and

they endeavor to make their views acceptable to the legislature, the executive branch, and/or the courts.

Intergovernmental Maritime Consultative Organization See **United Nations Specialized Agencies.**

Interim Commission Established by a legislature to study a particular, special, or limited problem between sessions of the legislature with instructions to report findings to the next legislative session. Usually an interim commission is made up of a number of legislators together with other public officials or private citizens. It has a staff of professional or technical experts. The use of the interim commission at every level of government has increased within recent years.

Interior, Department of See **Department of the Interior.**

Interior, Secretary of See **Department of the Interior.**

Internal Revenue Service See **Department of the Treasury.**

International Atomic Energy Agency See **United Nations Specialized Agencies.**

International Bank for Reconstruction and Development (World Bank) Established in 1945 as a specialized agency of the **United Nations** to assist in the postwar reconstruction and in the economic development of member nations. Since 1948 the Bank's loans and technical assistance have been primarily for underdeveloped nations. When private capital is not available the Bank makes loans for productive purposes to member governments and, if guaranteed by member governments, to their agencies and to private groups in the country. Loans have been made for the devel- **79**

opment of transportation, communication, agriculture, electric power, and industrial expansion. The Bank provides technical assistance for specific projects and also for planning long-range programs of economic development. There are 68 member nations (1960). Each is represented on the Board of Governors in which all the powers of the Bank are vested and voting is proportionate to the amount of capital subscribed by a nation. The headquarters of the Bank are located in Washington, D.C.

International Civil Aviation Organization See **United Nations Specialized Agencies.**

International Cooperation Administration (ICA) A semi-autonomous agency established in 1955 within the State Department. It has the responsibility for coordinating the foreign assistance programs and for administering most of the nonmilitary phases of the **Mutual Security program.** ICA gives special attention to technical assistance programs designed to share United States experience and skills in furthering the economic development and in raising the standard of living of peoples in the less developed nations. It also provides defense support through economic assistance programs and special programs for the promotion of political and economic stability. In most of the participating countries, the ICA maintains a United States Operations Mission which cooperates with the local government in development and execution of programs. See **Agency for International Development.**

International Court of Justice Established by the United Nations charter in 1945 as the successor to the **Permanent Court of International Justice.**

Its jurisdiction is limited to interpretation of treaties, questions of international law, and the existence of facts which, if established, would constitute a breach of international obligation. The 15-judge tribunal is elected by the **General Assembly** and **Security Council** and has its headquarters at the Hague. All members of the United Nations are parties to the statute, but no member is required to accept compulsory jurisdiction by the Court without filing a specific declaration of willingness to accept such jurisdiction. The Court has not had influence comparable to that of other major branches of the United Nations. In the first 15 years of its existence it handled fewer than 20 cases. Enforcement of its decisions depends upon voluntary compliance, and a majority of nations either have not granted the Court compulsory jurisdiction or, like the United States through the **Connally amendment,** have qualified the grant by declaring its own right to determine in each case whether the issue is a domestic matter or one subject to the Court.

International Finance Corporation (IFC) Established in 1956 as a specialized agency of the **United Nations** to encourage the growth of productive private enterprise. It is closely associated with the **International Bank for Reconstruction and Development,** but it is legally distinct and its funds are separate. The Board of Governors of the IFC is composed of the governors of the International Bank whose nations are also members of the IFC. The IFC has 58 members (1960), and it is located in Washington, D.C. The IFC is an investing rather than a lending corporation. It invests only in private enterprise and deals directly with private business-men, not with their governments. The IFC does not compete with private capital; rather, its investment in an enterprise is intended to encourage private capital to invest in the new or expanded industrial project.

International Labor Organization (ILO) An international organization to improve labor conditions and to raise standards of living throughout the world. It was created as a part of the **League of Nations** in 1919 and became one of the **United Nations Specialized Agencies** following World War II. The ILO has a membership of 97 nations (1960) and has its headquarters at Geneva, Switzerland. An International Labor Conference is held annually at which standards are developed to guide member nations in developing an international labor code regarding hours of work, employment conditions, freedom of association, workmen's compensation, and similar matters. No nation is obligated to ratify these standards. The ILO operates a program of technical assistance to assist governments in economic development, and it makes and publishes reports on special topics related to labor.

International Monetary Fund One of the proposals of the Bretton Woods Conference in 1944 to promote international monetary cooperation and established as a specialized agency of the **United Nations** in 1945. The Fund serves somewhat the same purpose as the gold standard once did, but it is more flexible. It aims at facilitating international trade through creation of a multilateral system of payments as regards current trade transactions and at eliminating foreign exchange restrictions. The Fund extends short-term credit to a nation

with an unfavorable balance of trade so it can maintain the par value of its currency used in foreign exchange. The Fund can also permit a member nation to depreciate its currency and exchange rate to some degree in order to restore equilibrium in trade. Authority is vested in a Board of Governors with one governor representing each member nation and with voting weighted by the size of the quota that a nation subscribes to the Fund. The International Monetary Fund has 68 members (1960) and is located in Washington, D.C.

International Refugee Organization See **Displaced persons.**

International Telecommunication Union See **United Nations Specialized Agencies.**

Internationalism A policy of cooperation with other nations and a lively interest in the relationships between one's own nation and other nations. Internationalism is generally reflected in a favorable attitude toward active United States participation in international organizations, alliances, and agreements. See also **Nationalism.**

Interposition See **Nullification.**

Interregnum The rule applied to the period of the Eisenhower Administration when Sherman Adams supposedly was the most forceful member of the Administration and had taken to himself many of the responsibilities of the presidency.

Interstate Commerce The movement of goods, persons, or energy from one state to another or among the several states. In recent court decisions the term has been expanded to include nearly all transportation and business transactions in nearly every business activity which affects directly or in-   **81**

directly commerce in other states. The federal government under the Constitution has exclusive authority in the field of interstate commerce.

Interstate Commerce Commission (ICC) The oldest independent regulatory commission of the federal government. It was established in 1887 and is composed of eleven members appointed by the President with the consent of the Senate. Each member serves for seven-year staggered terms. The ICC originally had very limited regulatory authority over discriminatory and unfair railroad practices, and it was quite ineffective. In 1906, it was granted the authority to set rates, and its authority has been broadened considerably since then. In 1935, interstate trucking was brought under its jurisdiction, and in 1940 coastal and inland water transportation was also added. Besides the all-important power to fix "just and reasonable" rates which the carriers may charge, the ICC also establishes requirements for minimum standards of service, safety and insurance coverage, accounting procedures, mergers, the issuance of securities, and determination of mail rates.

Interstate Highways See **Highways.**

Intrastate Commerce That business activity which is wholly within the borders of a state and does not affect interstate commerce. Very little commerce within the United States is considered as being purely intrastate, since court decisions generally apply the interstate commerce clause very broadly.

Investigation See **Hearing.**

Isolationism The philosophy that the United States should avoid political or military commitments to foreign nations or any involvement with those nations. Historically the United States was largely an isolated power and remained outside the troubles of Europe and Asia until 1917 when we entered World War I and again when we became involved in World War II. Isolationism is not as strong a force as it once was. It is obvious to most people that we can no longer escape involvement in international affairs and in international problems. See **Internationalism.**

Kirby, The New York World, 1923.

"I SYMPATHIZE DEEPLY WITH YOU, MADAME, BUT I CANNOT ASSOCIATE WITH YOU."

Item Veto See **Veto.**

Jail A place of confinement for persons who are being held pending judicial trial or who are held as a result of a judicial sentence for a minor offense. A county jail is usually under the jurisdiction of the county board and is run by the sheriff. A city jail is commonly operated by the Department of Public Safety, or a similar department. See also **Prison.**

Jim Crow A slang term applied to the Negro, derived from the title of a minstrel song popularized by T. D. Rice about 1835: "Wheel about and turn about and jump, Jim Crow." In modern usage it identifies a law or practice which discriminates against Negroes or requires their segregation.

Jim Crow Laws Laws passed in many Southern states soon after the Civil War which required the segregation of the races. These laws have been under increasing attack and are slowly being modified and eliminated. See **Brown v. Board of Education.**

Morris, Wide World Photos.

OPEN SEASON

Jingoism A policy of aggressive and belligerent action to promote national interest abroad. Jingo was the nickname for supporters of Disraeli's pol-

icy of intervening in the Russo-Turkish War of 1877–78 and of sending the British fleet into Turkish waters; it came from the chorus of a popular song: "We don't want to fight, But by jingo if we do—We've got the ships, We've got the men, We've got the money, too."

John Birch Society A semi-secret society organized to advance an extremely reactionary political point of view. It is generally isolationist. It has irresponsibly accused many Democratic and Republican leaders of communist sympathies.

Eng, Newspaper Enterprises Association, 1961.

KNIGHT IN SHINING ARMOR

Joint Chiefs of Staff The official title given to the four highest military officers: the Chief of Staff of the Army, the Chief of Naval Operations, the Chief of Staff of the Air Force, and the Chairman appointed by the President. The first three of these serve under the civilian secretaries and are responsible for the Army, the Navy, and the Air Force. At the same time, as members of the Joint Chiefs of **83**

Staff, together with the Chairman, it is their responsibility to formulate over all military strategy for the nation. They are the chief military advisers to the Secretary of Defense, the National Security Council, and the President.

Joint Committee A committee made up of members of both legislative bodies. In the United States Congress there are two important joint committees: the Joint Committee on Atomic Energy and the Joint Economic Committee.

Joint Committee on Atomic Energy. See **Atomic Energy Commission.**

Joint Economic Committee See **Employment Act of 1946.**

Joint Resolution See **Resolution.**

Joint Session A session wherein both houses of a legislature come together for a meeting. In Congress joint sessions are held to hear the President's State of the Union address, to listen to visiting foreign officials, and to consider the President's request for a declaration of war.

Jonah A person in office or in a party who is believed to be a great handicap or hindrance to the success of the party. The word is, of course, drawn from the biblical story of Jonah who was thrown overboard in the hope that this action would save the ship from sinking.

Journal A summary outline of the daily proceedings of Congress. The Constitution requires that "each House shall keep a Journal of its proceedings, and from time to time publish the same, excepting such Parts as may in their Judgment require Secrecy. . . ." See also **Congressional Record.**

84 Judge of Probate The judicial official who presides over the county court which hears official proof of the validity of a decedent's last will and testament. The judge, upon being satisfied that the will is valid, orders it to be executed and thereafter decrees the distribution of decedent's property as stipulated in the will. Probate judges also preside over hearings to determine whether individuals brought before the court on petition should be committed to mental institutions, and in many states probate judges deal with cases of juvenile delinquents.

Judicial Review A doctrine and practice by which the courts have authority to declare legislative acts unconstitutional, that is, in violation of the Constitution and therefore null and void. The Constitution did not explicitly grant this power to the courts, but it has long been generally accepted as part of our constitutional system. This doctrine is currently under attack by those who disagree with the federal court decisions affecting segregation. There is little likelihood of such attacks gaining much support or that the doctrine of judicial review is in danger of being overthrown. See also **Marbury v. Madison.**

Judiciary The Constitution provides that "the judicial power of the United States shall be vested in one Supreme Court and in such inferior courts as the Congress may, from time to time, ordain and establish." This system, provided by the Constitution and added to by Congress is called the judiciary; the term is sometimes also applied to judges as a group. The national judiciary consists of the *Supreme Court,* eleven *Courts of Appeals,* 86 *District Courts,* a **Court of Claims,** a **Court of Customs and Patent Appeals,**

a **Customs Court,** a **Tax Court,** and courts in the District of Columbia and in the territories and dependencies of the United States.

In the states there is always a Supreme Court, sometimes called the Court of Appeals or the Court of Errors and Appeals. Most states have intermediate courts below their supreme court, such as county courts, special criminal courts, probate courts, domestic relations courts, children and juvenile courts, and so on. At the base of this judicial pyramid are the minor courts presided over by justices of the peace or magistrates.

Cases brought before federal courts are usually initiated at the *District Court* or the "trial courts" as they are sometimes called. It is here that most federal law suits begin and end. Usually cases are heard by a single judge with a jury participating when required. When an injunction is sought against enforcement of a federal or a state law, however, on the ground that that law is unconstitutional, a three-judge court must be convened. There are today 86 District Courts in the 50 states (plus one each in the District of Columbia and Puerto Rico) and 226 judges.

Cases may be appealed from the District Court to the *Court of Appeals.* The primary purpose of this level of courts is to relieve the Supreme Court from having to hear appeals from the District Court and from federal administrative boards and commissions. Certain cases may be taken directly from the District Court to the Supreme Court.

The *Supreme Court* is the highest court of the land, and it has original jurisdiction in certain cases: for example, when a state is a party in the controversy. But its primary importance is as a final court of appeals.

The procedure by which a case is brought before the Supreme Court generally follows this pattern: an appellant petitions for a *writ of certiorari.* Such a writ directs the lower court, state or federal, to send up the record of the case for review. This gives the Supreme Court control over the flow of cases coming before it and allows it to direct its time and energy to the resolution of important matters. After examining the record, the Supreme Court decides to hear the case, not to hear the case, to review the case, or to remand it to a lower court.

The size of the Supreme Court is not specified in the Constitution. The number of justices can be determined by Congress. President Roosevelt's attempt to increase the size of the Supreme Court, called "court packing" by critics of the move, was neither unconstitutional nor without precedent in the history of the country. In the early years of our national existence, the number of Supreme Court justices varied until in 1869 it was set at nine, a number which has continued until the present time. The Court meets each year from September to June.

The judges on the Supreme Court are called justices. They are appointed by the President for life, with the consent of the Senate. They serve "during good behavior" and can be removed only by their own resignation, death, or impeachment.

The actions of the Supreme Court have throughout its history been subject to much criticism. This has been particularly true in recent years, especially in the case of those decisions dealing with civil rights. Mr. Dooley's famous statement that the Supreme Court follows the elections does not quite describe the relationship within recent years in that there are those who say that the Court has anticipated the election and set the pattern for political controversy.

Junket   An excursion or pleasure trip taken by legislators or other officials at public expense under the pretext of making a study. The term comes from the Italian word for cream cheese, extended to mean a sweetmeat or any delicate food and hence a feast.

Juridical   A general term meaning performed or done according to law or by a judge. It relates primarily to the administration of justice.

Jurisdiction   A term referring to authority of a court to hear certain kinds of cases in a given locality. Federal courts have a jurisdiction which is different, in part, from that of state courts.

Original jurisdiction refers to the authority of a trial court to hear a certain kind of case originally.

Appellate jurisdiction refers to the authority to hear appeals, that is, to review decisions reached in a lower court. The Supreme Court, for example, hears only a few kinds of cases as a trial court; it is primarily an appellate court.

The term *jurisdiction* is used also in controversies among labor unions as to which union should do a specific job, for example, whether the plasterers or the lathers should install prefabricated wallboard. The term is also used with regard to the authority or the right of various committees of Congress to hold hearings and to take action in certain legislative fields as, for example, whether a question relating to foreign trade properly belongs to the Finance Committee or to a committee in charge of foreign relations.

86   Jurisprudence   The study of law and legal systems. In its broadest sense it is the study of the origins of law and its relationship to society at large. A student of jurisprudence is primarily interested in knowing such things as what the laws of a country are, how they become laws, what role they play in the society, how they compare with laws in other countries, and what kind of a court system has been established to deal with the laws.

Jury   See **Grand jury** and **Petit jury.**

Justice   A relationship in which each citizen or group receives due respect and return. The problems of justice arise from the relationships between individuals, between individuals and groups, among groups, and also between all of these and government. The Preamble of the Constitution includes to "establish justice" as one of the basic purposes of our government. The claims of justice are based on the common law regarding natural rights of man and contracts, upon statutes and procedural rights such as those guaranteed in the **Bill of Rights.** In practice the question of determining what is just, along with regard for other constitutional purposes such as providing for the common defense and the general welfare, presents the Congress and the judicial and executive branches with a continuous test of judgment.

Justice of the Peace   A local official usually elected for a two- or four-year term. He tries minor civil and criminal cases and conducts preliminary hearings in some more serious cases. He may also fix bail. His jurisdiction usually extends throughout a county and he is usually empowered to conduct marriages and to notarize papers, although his jurisdiction may be more restricted.

Keynote Speech An address at a convention designed to arouse the delegates' enthusiasm and to promote a sense of loyalty and unity to one's party. The keynote address is usually given early in the proceedings of the convention. Sometimes it has a decisive impact on the convention and also on the campaign, either in setting the general tone for the party effort, in arousing enthusiasm for major candidates, or in actually developing a candidate.

In 1948 when the Democrats met at their national convention, they were disunited and with little hope for success in the November election. Senator Alben Barkley, one of the "grand old men" of the party, delivered a stirring keynote speech which dramatically raised the spirits of the delegates and also set the stage for his nomination as Vice President. The somewhat unexpected victory of the Democrats in November was in a measure traceable to this effective keynote speech.

Kitchen Cabinet An informal group of persons upon whom a President may rely for advice. This term was coined during Andrew Jackson's presidency and was applied to a small group of his close personal friends who supposedly were more important than the regular cabinet advising him on decisions of policy.

Ku-Klux-Klan A secret political organization founded to establish white supremacy in the South after the Civil War. The Klansmen, disguised in white masks and robes, used violence and terror to keep Negroes from voting. Under the authority of the Force Bill of 1871, the federal government took steps to suppress secret conspiracies and the Klan soon declined. In 1915 the Klan was revived as a national organization to oppose foreigners, Catholics, and Jews as well as Negroes. It attained considerable political influence in the twenties, but again faded. The name is derived from the Greek, *kyklos,* meaning circle.

Labor, Department of See **Department of Labor.**

Labor Legislation That whole body of laws which seeks to protect the health and safety of workers, establish fair working conditions, wages and hours, compensation in the event of injury, and care of workers and their families in case of disability or unemployment. Employment services are also maintained to assist the unemployed in their efforts to find work. Many states provide mediation services to prevent or to assist in the settlement of labor-management disagreements, and some states also have **fair employment practices commissions** which seek to insure equal job opportunities without discrimination because of race, creed, or color. Under the **New Deal,** labor legislation became a greater concern of the federal government through the application of the **commerce clause** of the Constitution. In more recent times the term has been broadened to include laws which regulate union activities.

Labor-Management Relations Act See **Taft-Hartley Act.**

Labor, Secretary of See **Department of Labor.**

Labor Statistics, Bureau of See **Department of Labor.**

Labor Union See **Union.**

Laissez Faire An economic theory which holds that there should be little or no governmental interference in the economy. It is based on the assumption that if everyone seeks his own advantage that all will benefit.

Lame Duck A person or legislature or administration which has been defeated in an election but still holds office for a period of time. Until the ratification of the Twentieth Amendment in 1933, outgoing Congresses met in December following the November elections and were not replaced until March. This situation was changed by the Twentieth Amendment which provided that congressional sessions begin in January, at which time the newly elected Congress is installed. Similar changes were applied to presidential terms.

Despite the amendment, there is still a "lame duck" interval for Congress from November to January every two years, and also for the presidency whenever administrations change. Since Congress is ordinarily not in session at this time, this gap is more important for presidential changes, when the defeated or retiring President stays in office for over two months after the election of his successor. These are difficult intervals since the new President cannot assume power and the outgoing President is somewhat weakened by the attention being focused on his successor.

Landslide An election result which is not close. The term is designed to convey the impression of a massive and irresistible event.

League of Nations The first worldwide attempt to establish a permanent international organization designed to prevent war and to promote coopera-tion among nations. The Treaty of Versailles ending World War I provided for the League, and it was established in 1920 with headquarters at Geneva, Switzerland. Its Covenant provided for a permanent Secretariat, an Assembly which met annually and in which each member nation had one vote, and a Council of nine nations, later expanded to fourteen, which had the responsibility of settling international disputes. A number of other international organizations were also associated with the League. More than 60 nations eventually joined, the United States being the only great power which failed to join the League. It provided a forum for discussion of international problems and made several contributions, but in its major tests it lacked effective structure and authority. It failed, for example, to do anything about the Japanese attacks on China in 1931 and 1937, about the Italian invasion of Ethiopia in 1935, and about Hitler when he proceeded to violate the Versailles Treaty and rearm Germany. It was officially dissolved in 1946.

Leak A breach in the normal pattern of giving out news by government officials or agencies. Usually a "leak" is used when information is given to only one or a few reporters rather than to the press as a whole. An authorized leak is intentional and is approved by appropriate authorities. Its usual purpose is to serve as a kind of *trial balloon* or to prepare the way for more detailed, more comprehensive or more serious news. It is often used as a means of testing public response to a new idea or to a new policy before it is officially announced.

An unauthorized leak is one not approved by appropriate authorities. It occurs when an official or employee

unintentionally divulges information, or intentionally leaks news in order to embarrass his superiors or to justify his own position or because he disapproves of a policy and wishes to draw attention to it, or for other reasons. The leak often occurs in the executive branch, but leaks do occur in legislatures as well, especially with the actions taken by committees in **ex-executive session.**
See also **Background Conference.**

Left Wing   The term applied to persons or ideas which aim to change existing laws or governmental practices, especially if they seem to increase government's influence. If these persons or ideas tend to be extreme, they may be described as **radical;** if somewhat less extreme, they may be described as "moderate." Some people even equate **liberal** with left wing. Terms of this kind are never used very precisely in political debate in the United States and therefore take on a wide variety of meanings. It is difficult to fit either persons or ideas very clearly into categories such as left wing, center, or **right wing.**

Legal Tender   That money which the government declares must be accepted by creditors in payment of debt, and which a debtor must offer in payment if his offer is to have legal standing. State banks issue notes as currency, but only gold and silver coin can be made legal tender according to the United States Constitution. Federal notes, however, are certificates redeemable in "lawful money" and are therefore also legal tender.

Legation   A diplomatic minister and his associates. A nation may send a legation to another nation or to an international assembly for some specific purpose. The term is also used with reference to a diplomatic corps representing a state in another nation of lesser importance where it does not choose to maintain an embassy. In this application, legation may also be used to refer to the buildings and grounds of the diplomatic corps.   See also **Embassy, Minister.**

Legislation   The laws passed by duly constituted legislatures or parliaments.

Canfield, 1955. Culver Pictures.
"THERE'S WORK TO BE DONE"

Legislative Body   The legislative branch of the government. In the case of a **unicameral** legislature, the legislative body would, of course, refer to the entire legislature.

Legislative Branch   See **Congress.**

Legislative Counsel   A lawyer employed by a legislative body to assist members in the complicated task of drafting bills. Both houses of Congress have large legislative counsel staffs.

Legislative Courts   See **Constitutional courts.**

Legislative Day   A formal period of time which begins at the meeting of a legislative body and ends at adjournment. The rules of procedure for any such body usually provide that certain   **89**

Daumier. New York Public Library.

things such as offering prayer and allowing time for brief routine speeches and announcements must be done each legislative day. If the legislative body wants to avoid such matters or for some other technical reasons wishes to prolong a legislative day, it may recess overnight rather than adjourn. When this practice is followed, the legislative day may run through many calendar days.

Legislative Reference Service A special service of the **Library of Con-** **gress** which does research for members of Congress. It has divisions staffed by specialists in American Law, Economics, Education and Public Welfare, Foreign Affairs, History and Government, Natural Resources. In addition there are other specialists who carry out research upon request from members of Congress.

Legislature A body of elected persons who are empowered to pass laws binding on the population which it represents.

90

Levy **(a)** The seizure of property under a court order for the purpose of selling it and obtaining the sum of money contained in an order.

(b) The rate of taxation, as in "a three-mill levy."

Liberal The term generally applied to those in American politics who advocate a rather advanced position on both foreign and domestic issues. Liberalism in the United States must be distinguished from the traditional liberalism of Europe in that American liberalism does not follow a set ideology. It is nondoctrinaire. The American liberal is generally optimistic and progressive in politics, concerned over the protection of individual liberties and civil rights, tolerant of the views of others, and is somewhat more willing to use government as an agency for advancing the common good than are those who oppose him.

Liberal Party A third political party in New York. It is probably the only effective third party in the country today. Its membership is made up largely of labor union members—especially from the Ladies Garment Workers—and of professional people and intellectuals. The party has been able to affect local, state, and even national politics by endorsing the candidates of one or the other of the major parties. It usually manages to receive between 5 and 10 per cent of the statewide vote and hence it can often determine the winner by its endorsement. It ordinarily backs Democrats.

Liberty See **Freedom, Civil Rights, Natural Law.**

Library of Congress A national library established by Congress in 1800. It is located in Washington, D.C., and was originally established to serve the Congress. It still does perform this function, but it has become one of the great libraries of the world, serving the public. See also **Legislative Reference Service.**

License A formal permission, usually embodied in a certificate, issued by a government to an individual or to a group or organization authorizing some act, such as marriage, fishing, driving a car, operating a bus or truck company, radio station, or other business. Some are granted as a matter of course, others after lengthy protracted hearings, as in the case of radio or television stations.

Lien A claim or charge against property in order to assure the payment of a debt or the performance of an act. An example is a mechanic's lien filed against a house by the contractor who built it, but whose bill is unpaid.

Lieutenant Governor In 39 states the elected official whose principal function is to preside over the state senate and to succeed the governor in the event of the latter's death, disability, removal, or resignation. The lieutenant governor's term of office usually coincides with that of the governor. He may assume the duties of the governor during the latter's absence from the state under certain circumstances. There are eleven states which do not provide for a lieutenant governor.

Life Tenure The appointment of a person to an office for life. In the United States such appointments are limited to the judicial branch of the government. A life term is designed to protect the independence of the appointee from political or other pressures.

91

Lily Whites   A political group that excludes Negroes. The term has particular reference to a faction of the Republican party in the South, flourishing from the 1890's to the 1930's, which excluded Negroes and developed as a strong rival to the regular party organization. Patronage was frequently distributed through the lily white group by the national party, and this practice was one of the factors that cost the national party the solid support of Negroes.

Limited War   The political and military policy of attempting to confine war to "conventional" weapons and to a limited area or issue. The concern for developing some technique for limiting war has become particularly great since the development of weapons of mass destruction. The Korean conflict of 1950–53 was an example of limited war in that nuclear weapons were not used and the military action was confined to a restricted area of the globe. See **War, Total war.**

Literacy Test   A procedure by which a citizen establishes his ability to read and write as a qualification for voting. The first literacy test requirements were adopted by Connecticut in 1855, and the test was later used by many Eastern seaboard states to keep immigrants from voting. After 1890 it was copied by several Southern states to exclude Negroes from voting and variations were sometimes introduced such as a requirement to read and give a reasonable interpretation of the state constitution. About 16 states still retain some form of literacy test. See **Voting qualifications.**

Live Pair   See **Pair.**

Lobby   A person or a number of persons who try to influence government action in either a legislature or

an executive branch. The lobby usually speaks through lobbyists who may be volunteers or hired agents. The term grew out of the fact that occasionally legislators or administrators would be met in the lobby or hallway by persons interested in expressing their views or in influencing the officeholder. Some interest groups maintain year-round lobbies and other groups or persons may hire a lobbyist, or set up a lobby, for a limited purpose or for a single objective. Lobbies are frequently accused of exercising undue influence over legislative programs or government policies. It is often argued that well-financed and well-organized lobbies have an unfair advantage over unorganized persons or institutions within the country. The activities of lobbyists have been subjected to legislation in the United States Congress and in many states, and it is common to require lobbyists to register and to report the expenditures incurred in lobbying activities.

Lobbyist   See **Lobby.**

Local Option   The principle in law permitting counties, cities, or other units of government to do or not to do something. It is more commonly used with reference to permitting the sale of alcoholic beverages.

Lochner *v.* New York (1905)   A case in which the Supreme Court held by a five to four vote that there were no special health hazards in being a baker and that general legislative control of hours of industry was a violation of the rights of both employers and employees. The case grew out of legislation enacted in the State of New York which prohibited persons from working in a bakery more than ten hours a day or sixty hours a week. The law was declared unconstitutional, thereby temporarily blocking state efforts to regulate industry. The rigid doctrine in this case was overturned by the decision in the case of **Bunting v. Oregon** in 1917.

Lockout   The action by an employer of locking employees out of the plant and refusing to let them work because of their refusal to agree to his terms in a labor dispute, or because they went on **strike** or joined a **union.**

Log Rolling   The practice sometimes followed in legislative bodies of agreeing to vote for someone else's projects in return for support for one's own. Public works bills are supposed to be passed in Congress largely because of effective log rolling, although in fact it has very minor effect upon the approval of most projects. If a city congressman agrees to vote for farm price supports in return for a vote favoring an urban redevelopment program, this exchange would be described as log rolling.

Long Ballot   See **Ballot, long.**

Loophole   A provision or lack of provision in the tax code, as a result of which some persons or some companies obtain unusual, unexpected, and unanticipated tax advantages. Not every extreme tax advantage is a loophole, since some are written into the code by design.

Loose   Construction   See   **Elastic clause.**

Lower House   See **Upper house.**

Loyal Opposition   Somewhat euphemistic title given to those who oppose the political party in power or the policies of an incumbent administration or majority in the legislature. The phrase originated in England as a description of those members of Par-

liament who were opposed to policies of the King but were loyal to him. It means that the opposition is limited in character and not revolutionary. In the United States the question of loyal opposition is seldom raised.

Carmack, The Christian Science Monitor, 1960.
"CAN'T AFFORD TO HAVE HOLES IN MY POCKETS"

Lunatic Fringe   In politics a name applied to those who remain just within the bounds of political party activity, but are inclined to take extreme stands on issues that are of common concern or to raise issues which are only remotely related to the field of political action.

Machine   A political organization which is relatively efficient and has a successful record of winning public office for its candidates. The distinguishing characteristic of a machine is its high degree of organization and

93

effectiveness. All political candidates and all political parties do have some organization behind them. The title of machine, however, is earned only through repeated successes. Frequently the word *machine* is used in a derogatory sense, implying corruption, but this is not necessarily the case. Machines are ordinarily associated with large cities, but it is possible to have an effective machine covering an entire state. Newspapers refer to the machine politics of Chicago and New York, but also refer to the Byrd machine, a statewide organization in Virginia.

The leader of a city machine is usually called a **boss.** The machine attracts and holds supporters in a wide variety of ways: through **patronage,** dispensing charity to the poor, providing satisfactory government services, and sometimes, of course, through corrupt activity such as providing police protection for illegal activities and by buying votes. Machines are less prominent in political life today than thirty or forty years ago.

Magistrate In the broad sense, a person clothed with power as a civil officer. Popularly the term is used to designate minor judicial officers such as police court judges, or justices of the peace.

Magistrates Courts See **Police courts.**

Majority (a) The number of votes or persons which constitutes one more than half of the total. A *constitutional majority* or an *absolute majority* constitutes more than half of the total membership of a legislative body. A *simple majority* constitutes more than half of those present and voting.

(b) The difference between the number constituting a majority and the number constituting a minority. For example, if a candidate received 50,000 votes and his opponent received 40,000, when there are only two in a contest the winner's majority is 10,000. See also **Plurality.**

Majority Leader A member of a legislative body chosen by the members of the majority party in that body as their spokesman. In the United States Senate the majority leader is usually a most influential member. In the House of Representatives the majority leader is second in command after the Speaker of the House. The majority leader in Congress or in state legislatures usually controls or carries great weight in determining such important matters as what bills shall come before the legislature, when they shall be brought up, who shall serve on committees, and in setting party policy. The power of the majority leader depends upon many things, including his own personality, the size of his party's majority, his skill as a parliamentarian, the popularity of his views, the particular political conditions existing while he holds office, and his relationship with the President and with the minority party, as well as with the leadership and the members of the other house of Congress.

Majority Report In legislative committees, the formal report on a bill which is being reported out to the full chamber. A majority report contains a brief statement about the bill and a somewhat detailed analysis of its contents with arguments for its adoption.

Mandate A direction or command, either explicit or implicit, to take a certain course of action, given from one person or persons to another. The term is frequently used in connection with presidential elections when analysts endeavor to discover whether the returns indicate a clear pattern of voter sentiment. There is invariably an argument after every major election as to what mandate, if any, the electorate gave to the elected officials.

Manifesto (a) A declaration of policy by a person or organization. Manifestoes are often written in flamboyant and unrestrained language to attract attention and appeal to widespread fears or emotions. The term is not often used in American political life, in part because it is often associated with the most famous of all manifestoes, the *Communist Manifesto* of 1848, which outlined the theory and goals of communism.

(b) A statement signed by most members of Congress from the Southern states dealing with the issue of states' rights and segregation was issued in 1957. It has been called the "Southern Manifesto."

Marbury *v.* Madison (1803) Probably the most famous case in the history of the Supreme Court. Chief Justice John Marshall and his associates on the Court declared a section of the Judiciary Act of 1789 to be in violation of the Constitution and hence null and void. This was the first demonstration of the doctrine of **judicial review.** The Constitution did not explicitly grant to the Supreme Court the power to declare laws unconstitutional. Since *Marbury v. Madison* this power has been recognized and accepted.

Mark-Up Putting in final form a legislative proposal. After a committee has held hearings on a proposal and decided to recommend it to the full legislative body, it usually meets privately, or in what is called *executive session,* to work out necessary compromises and technical language. This *marked-up* bill is usually different from any bill actually introduced and represents what a majority of the committee believes should be considered by the whole legislative body. See also **Clean bill.**

Marshall Plan The extensive United States program for relief and rehabilitation of European nations following World War II, first proposed by Secretary of State George Marshall in 1947. The Marshall Plan (or European Recovery Program) has been given major credit for the remarkable economic recovery of European nations following the war and indirectly for diminishing the strength of the communist parties in several nations.

In 1948 the Congress established the Economic Cooperation Administration and in the next few years appropriated over $13 billion for economic aid. In turn the 16 cooperating nations formed the **Organization for European Economic Cooperation** to implement the program by pooling resources, breaking down tariff barriers, and by similar joint actions. The Soviet Union was originally invited to join but denounced the program as an "imperialist plot" and along with her six satellite nations remained outside OEEC. The features of the Marshall Plan eventually became part of broader programs for **Mutual Security.**

Martial Law That law administered by the National Guard or other military organization when it is called upon to replace civil authority in time of emergency or national disaster. When a situation occurs, such as a flood, riot, or strike with violence, a governor of a state calls upon Na- **95**

tional Guard troops to maintain law and order and declares martial law to be in effect. The soldiers replace the police.

Marshal, United States See **United States Marshal.**

Marxism A set of economic, political, and philosophical theories drawn from the writings of Karl Marx (1818–83); the term is sometimes used interchangeably with **communism.** Marx was born in Germany but spent most of his adult life in exile and wrote his most important books and pamphlets in England. He was a **revolutionary** who despised the capitalist system and developed a complex theory Marxists believe explains the past, provides a program for the present, and accurately prophesies the future. The basic idea is that of economic determinism, which means that economic factors determine the character of everything in society, including politics, art, and religion; whoever controls the ownership and distribution of property controls the society. All of history can be explained, Marx thought, in terms of the struggle and warfare between economic classes. The last great struggle, which Marxists believe is now going on, is between capitalists and the proletariat, the working class. The proletariat will win, and the communist new era will begin. The influence of Marx does not rest merely on his abstract analysis of society. Marx attacked not only exploitation but the whole system. Communists "openly declare that their ends can be attained only by the forcible overthrow of all existing social conditions," Marx wrote in the *Communist Manifesto,* and he promised the world to those who joined in the effort. Marxism has few followers in the United States. It is, of course, the official doctrine of all communist nations. Many types of socialism also are based in part on Marxist doctrine. See also **Communism.**

Mass Media Forms of communication which reach great numbers of people, such as newspapers, magazines, television, and radio. The mass media play a very important role in American political life; therefore, the public and the men who hold public office have a considerable stake in how they perform their task of informing the people. Newspapers and magazines are almost entirely free of governmental controls. Since radio and television use licensed frequency channels, the federal government does have a legal claim to exercise some control. In practice, however, these latter mass media are as free as newspapers and magazines.

Mayflower Compact An agreement drawn up by the Pilgrims on board the ship Mayflower before landing in the New World in 1620. It was the basis of the legal system in the colony until 1691. The Mayflower Compact is a landmark in the history of establishing democratic institutions, and it is an unusual example of the formation of a government by popular consent through a social contract. The Pilgrims agreed before God to form a civil body politic and by virture of their covenant to "enacte, constitute, and frame such just and equal Lawes, Ordinances, Acts, Constitutions and Offices, from time to time, as shall be thought most meete & convenient for ye Generall Good of ye Colonie, unto which we promise all due submission and obedience."

Mayor Chief executive official of a municipality elected by the voters. He performs all ceremonial functions for the city such as greeting visitors and opening supermarkets. The mayor's duties are varied and include presiding over the city council, appointment of many officials, representing the city in its dealings with other governmental units, and coordinating all municipal activities.

Mayors are called *strong* if their appointments do not require council approval, if they have the veto power, and if they have control over city departments and city administration generally. Mayors are called *weak* if they must submit all appointments to the council for approval and have little or no veto power, and when administrative duties are taken out of their hands. Heads of city departments are appointed by the mayor in a *strong*-mayor type government and elected by the voters in a *weak*-mayor type.

McCarran-Walter Act See **Immigration laws.**

McCulloch *v.* Maryland (1819) This case clarified two questions about the Constitution: one, that of implied powers, and second, that of national supremacy. In the case itself the Supreme Court struck down a tax which the State of Maryland was attempting to levy on the Baltimore branch of the Bank of the United States. Since the Constitution did not specifically give to the federal government the power to establish a national bank, the question arose whether the federal government had any powers beyond those specifically listed in the Constitution. The Supreme Court held that the federal government had implied powers as well as expressed powers.

The second question involved in the case was whether federal or state authority should prevail in cases of conflict between the two jurisdictions. The decision of the Court was that the federal law had priority, and the doctrine of **national supremacy,** as it has been called, was established. See also **Elastic clause, National supremacy.**

Mediation The attempt by a third party at the invitation of one or both parties to a dispute to settle it. The term is sometimes used interchangeably with **conciliation.** See also **Arbitration.**

Mending Fences The political activity of an elected official to smooth the way for his renomination and reelection. It is characterized by special attention to requests by constituents and by efforts to cement the factions in the party for a united effort in behalf of the candidate as well as by frequent or extended visits to one's district or state.

Mercantilism An economic theory that to be strong a nation should export more than it imports. The mercantilists advocated the use of government to impose high protective tariffs and where necessary to subsidize domestic industry and to facilitate exports. The mercantilist theory was widely promoted in the seventeenth and eighteenth centuries and it reappeared in the twentieth century in the attempts of many modern states to achieve a high degree of economic self-sufficiency. As a theory it has few defenders among modern economists.

Merchant Marine The commercial shipping industry of a nation. The term is generally applied to the ships and to their personnel. To help maintain the United States merchant marine the federal government grants financial subsidies to private shipping companies for the construction of vessels, hauling of cargo, and similar purposes. The government operates the Merchant Marine Academy at King's Point, New York, to train officers for commercial ships. It also subsidizes four state-operated marine schools. See **Academy, United States Merchant Marine.**

Merchant Marine Academy See **Academy, United States Merchant Marine.**

Merit System A system within the **civil service** whereby persons are appointed and promoted on the basis of merit, or worth, and not because of political patronage.

Metropolitan Area Center of concentrated population, often including a number of local units of government and sometimes even crossing state lines. Commonly used to refer to a large city with its suburbs.

Militarism A set of beliefs and attitudes which glorify war and military affairs. Since very few people today believe that a nuclear war would be desirable, the term is often used loosely for ideas which allegedly stress military preparedness at the expense of efforts to negotiate disarmament agreements or the peaceful resolution of international tensions.

Militia An organization of nonprofessional, citizen soldiers. In the early days of the republic, this "citizens' army" was an important part of the national defense. The revolutionary army under George Washington was largely composed of militia from the various states.

Minimum Wage Legislation Those federal and state laws which establish the minimum wage which an employer must pay an employee in specified occupations or industries.

Minister (a) The head of a department in the cabinet of the national government. The term is not in usage in the United States but it is common in parliamentary systems, as in the British government where members of the House of Commons take posts in the cabinet and are called ministers while retaining their position in the legislature.

(b) In international relations, the minister is the official who ranks next after an ambassador. A minister receives his appointment from the head of state and generally performs the work of an ambassador, but lacks official status. See also **Diplomat.**

Minister Plenipotentiary See **Ambassador.**

Minister Resident See **Ambassador.**

Minority Leader The member of a legislative body chosen by the minority party in that body as their spokesman and leader. He is usually an experienced member of the legislature who will be able to unify the minority party in an effort to affect legislation and provide his party with issues and publicity for the next campaign. He is generally selected as one who can also work effectively with the majority party. In the Congress, both the House of Representatives and the Senate have minority leaders. See **Majority leader.**

Minority Report Generally, any statement issued by persons representing the minority viewpoint on a given issue.

In legislative committees, the formal report issued by a minority which sets forth its disagreements with the majority report and declares its own position on the matter under consideration.

Minutes The formal written record of a meeting of a city council, town board, or of a private corporation or group. Generally the minutes are kept by a designated official and certified to as to accuracy. Usually the members of the body have the right to review and correct errors at a subsequent meeting of the group.

Misdemeanor See **Criminal case.**

Moat Filling Expression usually uttered by those who feel that they have been bypassed or used for political purposes without being properly rewarded. The term is drawn from the maneuver in medieval warfare in which soldiers marched, fell, and died until they had filled the moat, allowing other soldiers to march over their bodies to capture the castle.

Mobilization All those activities undertaken in an effort to prepare a nation to conduct a war. It includes mobilization of men to expand the armed forces, accumulation of large reserves of needed raw materials, and conversion of the economy to military production.

Modern Republican The term applied to Republicans who have separated themselves somewhat from the Republican tradition. Generally it is accepted by those to whom it is applied as a political asset, since identification with strict Republicanism has proven in most parts of the United States to be something of a handicap.

Modus Vivendi Literally, a way of living. Two nations are said to have arrived at a *modus vivendi* when they at least temporarily agree to put aside their quarrels.

Monarchy A system of government headed by a king or queen. In an absolute monarchy the king has unlimited powers; in a limited or constitutional monarchy his powers are restricted. He may serve as little more than a symbol of a nation. The British monarchy is of the latter type while the Ethiopian monarchy concentrates great power in the king.

From Herblock's Special for Today (Simon & Schuster, 1958).

"WHAT *IS* 'MODERN,' ANYHOW?"

Monetary System A set of practices by which a country attempts to regulate the supply of money and credit, interest rates, and other financial forces bearing on its economy. In the United States the federal government under the Constitution has the responsibility for controlling the currency. This responsibility is carried out primarily through the United States Treasury and through the Board of Governors of the **Federal Reserve System,** which by changing interest rates and reserve requirements of banks can affect credit directly and the monetary supply of the country indirectly.

Money Bill See **Appropriation.**

Monopoly An exclusive privilege or power vested in one person or organization to carry on a business, to manufacture an article, or to control the sale of a commodity, and thus its price. The privilege may be a legal one or it may be a power which has been accumulated or gathered outside the law.

Monroe Doctrine A declaration of principle of United States foreign policy, set forth by President James Monroe in 1823, by which we virtually assumed responsibility for the defense of the American hemisphere. By 1822 the colonies of Spain and Portugal had won their independence, but their status was insecure. Russia was also pressing claims on the Oregon coast. The Monroe Doctrine declared that European nations must no longer colonize in the Americas, that they must not interfere with the independence of the existing Latin American nations, and that the United States would not interfere in the internal affairs of Europe. The doctrine was not seriously tested until the Civil War when France established Maximilian as emperor of Mexico. After the war the United States applied pressure and in 1867 France withdrew her support. This meant the end of Maximilian's regime and French interference in Mexico.

The "Roosevelt Corollary" of 1904 enlarged the Monroe Doctrine by implying the right of the United States to intervene in the political affairs of Latin American governments guilty of "chronic wrongdoing" or unable to maintain stability. Too frequently this meant intervention to protect business investments. The Latin American nations, pleased with our protection from European nations, resented

100

what they saw as "Yankee imperialism."

From the time of the Hoover administration the United States has greatly modified its position. Under President Franklin Roosevelt and the **Good Neighbor policy,** the approach has been that of mutual sharing by all the American states in hemispheric defense. Now the rise of communism has further complicated the application of this doctrine, because the force of communism is often applied secretly rather than by physical invasion.

Rogers, 1902. Culver Pictures.

UNCLE SAM—THAT'S A LIVE WIRE, GENTLEMEN!

Morning Hour A period at the beginning of a legislative day which is used for such routine matters as introducing bills, filing reports, and making short speeches.

Motion A formal proposition placed before a legislature or some other organized group.

Muckraking The exposure of illegal or immoral activities on the part of government or government officials. President Theodore Roosevelt coined the term *muckraker,* applying it to journalists, novelists, historians, and others who in the early years of the twentieth century published shocking and sometimes exaggerated accounts of such things as illegal and brutal practices followed by some large corporations, unhealthy conditions in factories, mines and packing houses, and corruption in government. The word, originally intended to have unfavorable application, has now assumed some respectability with reference to legitimate exposure of illegal or antisocial activities or conditions.

Rogers, 1924. Library of Congress.

WHITHER, OLD WOMAN, WHITHER SO HIGH—
TO RAKE THE COBWEBS FROM THE SKY?

Mugwump   A person associated with one political party but who often votes for another party. The term was first applied to Republicans who refused to support the party in 1884.

Municipal   **(a)** Having to do with city or town activities. Municipal elections, for example, are elections to local positions such as mayor and councilman.

(b) In international law, the word *municipal* refers to affairs within a nation; that is, internal affairs as distinguished from affairs between or among nations.

Municipal Courts   Courts of minor to intermediate ($1,000) jurisdiction in civil and criminal cases. They are presided over by elected or appointed judges with or without legal training. In some municipal courts, parties to the action may demand a jury trial. The jurisdiction is confined to the municipality.

Municipality   A city, town, village, borough, or other place incorporated to carry out municipal government. A municipality usually enjoys a measure of self government. The term is generally applied to larger and more heavily populated units of government, often the suburban area adjacent to a large city.

Mutual Security Program   The general term applied to a number of government programs of the United States intended to stabilize and strengthen the economies of the countries of the free world and to provide military aid for their collective defense. It has been operated primarily through grants of aid to other nations for two types of programs: one of military assistance, and the other of technical and economic assistance. Since 1957 loans have also been included under the program through the **Development Loan Fund.** A special contingency fund is also provided to be used at the discretion of the President to respond to emergency requests from other nations.   See also **International Cooperation Administration.**

NAACP   See **National Association for the Advancement of Colored People.**

NAM   See **National Association of Manufacturers.**

NASA See **National Aeronautics and Space Administration.**

National A person regarded as a member of a particular nation. Sometimes a person can be a national without being a citizen, as for example, the residents of Samoa who are regarded as American nationals but are not American citizens. See also **Nationality.**

National Aeronautics and Space Administration (NASA) An independent agency of the federal government established in 1958 to administer the nation's civilian space program. The administrator is appointed by the President with the consent of the Senate. This agency conducts advanced research into many fields relating to space exploration—the development of launching vehicles, the perfection of satellites capable of relaying weather information and communicating signals, and the development of machines to carry human beings into space.

National Aeronautics and Space Council (NASC) A council formed to advise the President on all matters relating to outer space. The Council is headed by the Vice President and also includes the Secretaries of State and Defense and the chairman of the Atomic Energy Commission. It is directed by law to develop a comprehensive program for space and to coordinate the activities of the various military and civilian agencies concerned with the problems of space.

National Anthem Patriotic song of a country usually sung on national holidays and at public meetings of national significance. *The Star Spangled Banner,* composed by Francis Scott Key, is the national anthem of the United States.

National Archives and Records Service. An agency located in Washington, D.C., which is responsible to the General Services Administrator for preserving or disposing of federal records, making them available to the general public, publishing laws, constitutional amendments, presidential documents, administrative regulations, and for preserving, publishing, and administering materials in presidential libraries. The agency publishes the **Federal Register,** the *Code of Federal Regulations, United States Government Organization Manual,* and the Public Papers of the President of the United States. Many of the historical documents are now put on microfilm for use by scholars.

National Association for the Advancement of Colored People (NAACP) An organization of approximately 325,000 persons which endeavors to improve the economic and political status of Negro Americans. It has come into special prominence in recent years because of its representation of Negroes in historic court cases involving civil rights, such as **Brown v. Board of Education.** It has also been active in the campaigns to enact civil rights legislation in Congress.

National Association of Manufacturers (NAM) A conservative business organization which represents approximately 22,000 manufacturers and others engaged in related activities. The NAM is prominent in political affairs, and it employs all of the traditional techniques of an effective interest group or lobby. It testifies before congressional committees, keeps its members appraised of political developments, and influences public opinion through advertising and the distribution of literature supporting its point of view. The NAM opposes most federal spending programs and consistently calls for lower tax rates.

National Bureau of Standards See **Department of Commerce.**

National Committee A party committee usually composed of two representatives from each state—a man and a woman—which acts as the governing body for a political party between national conventions. It selects its own officers, including the national chairman. The national committee of the party which does not control the presidency is often more important than the national committee of the President's party since the President is the chief spokesman for his party. National committees and national chairmen tend to represent the "presidential wing" of the party and are sometimes not in sympathy with the congressional leaders of their own party.

National Debt That part of the public debt owed by the federal government. When revenue from taxes or other sources are not adequate to meet the current expenses of government, the government must borrow money. When the federal government must borrow, the Treasury Department sells securities to banks, insurance companies, or other investors. Or it may sell bonds to individual citizens; usually these are called savings bonds.

The national debt has increased as government activities have expanded and as the national economy has expanded. In 1900, the national debt was $1.2 billion. After World War I, it was $25.4 billion. It was reduced to $16.1 billion by 1930, but after the depression it was up to $40.4 billion. By 1946, because of World War II principally, it had risen to $269.4 bil-

lion. The debt was slightly reduced in the next few years, but by 1960 it had again climbed to approximately $288 billion.

'AFTER ME, DEARIE'

CONGRESSIONAL REDUCING SALON

NATIONAL DEBT

TAXES

White, 1956. Culver Pictures.

Interest paid on the public debt now constitutes an important part of the federal expenditures. In 1960 it amounted to over $7.5 billion or nearly 10 per cent of the total federal expenditures. Congress has by law established a debt ceiling for the federal government by passing a law which makes it illegal to borrow in excess of the stated limit. This legislation has not effectively stopped the increase in federal debt; quite regularly Congress is called upon to raise

103

the debt ceiling either on a permanent or on a temporary basis.

National Farmers Union One of the three major farm organizations. It has approximately 300,000 members. The Farmers Union, as it is usually called, began as a radical expression of farm discontent and remains the most liberal of the farm groups, vigorously supporting government programs for agriculture. Its organization and influence is concentrated in the Great Plains states and such states as Wisconsin, Minnesota, and Colorado. It strongly endorses co-ops and promotes them and tends to get along more easily with organized labor than the other farm organizations. Compare with the **American Farm Bureau Federation** and the **National Grange.**

National Grange The oldest of the three major farm organizations, consisting of approximately 800,000 members. Its organization and influence are concentrated in New England, New York, Ohio, Pennsylvania, Washington, and Oregon. The Grange, as it is usually called, was founded in 1867 as a fraternal organization of farm families which concerned itself with all aspects of rural life: economic, educational, political, and spiritual. It still retains some of these early characteristics, but it is no longer a militant protest group. It is organized as a lodge and tends to take a rather conservative or moderate view of the government's responsibilities for agriculture, usually standing somewhere between the **Farm Bureau** and the **Farmers Union.**

National Guard The organized militia in each state. It is ordinarily subject to the orders of the governor or the President when called into federal service in time of war or national emergency. Members of the Guard are paid by the states by funds given them by the federal government. To be eligible for federal funds, the Guard units must meet federal standards with regard to training, efficiency, and equipment. Most members of the Guard are also members of the United States Army, Navy, or Air Force Reserve.

National Labor Relations Act (Wagner Act; 1935) Frequently referred to as "Labor's Magna Carta." It declared that employees working for firms engaged in interstate commerce, with some exceptions, had the right to organize into unions and to bargain collectively with their employer. It defined the types of employer practices which thereafter would be regarded as unfair and illegal, and it established the ground rules for deciding the contests between competing unions and between employees and employers over who, if anyone, would represent employees in a given industry. It established the **National Labor Relations Board.** See also **National Labor Relations Board *v.* Jones and Laughlin.**

National Labor Relations Board (NLRB) An independent regulatory commission established in 1935. It consists of five members appointed by the President with the consent of the Senate, serving five-year, staggered terms. The Board was provided for in the **National Labor Relations Act**—popularly known as the Wagner Act —one of the most important statutes enacted during the New Deal. The Act established the right of workers to organize into unions and to bargain collectively with their employers. The NLRB is empowered to protect these and certain other rights against abuse by either employers or by labor organizations. For example, it can issue orders requiring employers or labor organizations to "cease and desist" from "unfair practices"; it designates the union organizations which can legally represent a group of employees in collective bargaining with the management of companies; and it supervises and certifies the results of secret ballots held for the purpose of determining the employees' choice of their bargaining representative.

The National Labor Relations Board (NLRB) *v.* **Jones and Laughlin (1937)** In this case the Supreme Court upheld the provisions of the National Labor Relations Act, the Wagner Act, passed in 1935. The Court divided five to four in support of the National Labor Relations Board and its right to take action to protect the right of employees to organize into unions and to bargain collectively. This decision marked a significant turning point in constitutional interpretation of the **commerce clause.** It established that the power of Congress to regulate the economy is a very broad power and that it can be applied in many areas which had in the past been regarded as exclusively within the jurisdiction of the states. See also **Gibbons** *v.* **Ogden** and **United States** *v.* **Darby.**

National Origins The basis for the **quota** system established by the Immigration Act of 1924. The quota for each of the European nations of the 154,000 immigrants to be admitted annually is allotted in proportion to the contribution of each nation by birth or descent to the United States population in 1920. Since the great majority of early immigrants came from countries in Northwest Europe, those nations received the largest quotas, while the areas of later immigration from Southern and Central Europe were discriminated against. Under the national origins quota system about 82,000 immigrants can be admitted annually from Great Britain and Ireland and 25,000 from Germany while Italy, for example, is limited to about 5,600. See also **Immigration laws.**

National Park Service See **Department of Interior.**

National Recovery Administration (NRA) See **Schecter Poultry Corporation** *v.* **United States.**

National Science Foundation An agency of the federal government established in 1950 to promote the progress of science. Its over-all policy is set by the National Science Board, a body of 24 members competent in the basic sciences: medical science, engineering, agriculture, education, and public affairs. Members are appointed by the President with the consent of the Senate. A director, also appointed by the President with the consent of the Senate, and his staff are responsible for the administration of the various programs. The Foundation offers grants and scholarships for basic scientific research in such fields as mathematics, the physical sciences, the biological sciences, medicine, and engineering. In cooperation with the Department of Defense, it supports research projects specifically related to the national defense. It also endeavors to coordinate the various scientific information activities within the federal government and to serve as a clearinghouse for information concerning all scientific and technical personnel in the entire United States.

National Security Agency (NSA) A top-secret agency administered by military personnel which performs highly technical intelligence functions such

105

as cryptanalysis, the attempt to read the secret codes of other nations, and cryptography, the development of codes and instruments for sending messages for our own country. It also deals in other intelligence activities.

National Security Council (NSC) A body of top presidential advisers. The NSC was established in 1947. Its primary purpose is to advise the President on matters relating to the defense and security of the United States. The National Security Council, of course, is not limited to considering purely military matters, but is concerned with the broad concept of national security. It includes the President, the Vice President, the Secretary of State, the Secretary of Defense, and the Director of Civil and Defense Mobilization. It is common for the President to ask other officials to join in weekly meetings, depending somewhat on the nature of the subject under discussion. Among those often asked to participate are the Chairman of the Joint Chiefs of Staff, the Director of the Central Intelligence Agency, the Director of the Bureau of the Budget, and the Secretary of the Treasury. This Council is sometimes referred to as the "super" cabinet.

National Supremacy The doctrine which holds that when there is a conflict between federal and state authority, the federal authority shall prevail. The first important decision dealing with this controversy was that of **McCulloch v. Maryland.**

Nationalism An attitude of loyalty and pride in one's own nation. In colonial areas it is one of the driving forces for independence and self determination. The term is sometimes used in defining attitudes and policies which are opposed to international involvement or international cooperation. See also **Internationalism.**

Nationality The common attribute of a group of persons who have a common language and common customs and who either reside in or whose ancestors came from a particular geographical area. In the United States the term usually refers to the place of origin of a person's ancestors as, for example, a descendant of German immigrants who says that his nationality is German. This usage is becoming obsolete as more and more citizens of the United States ignore the racial or ethnic background of their ancestors and declare their nationality to be American.

Nativism The belief that native or old stock citizens are superior to others and deserve treatment and recognition different from that given immigrants or persons from ethnic groups who have become established in the country more recently. Nativism has at times been a powerful force in American political life but is manifest today in somewhat limited form.

NATO See **North Atlantic Treaty Organization.**

Natural Law A term generally applied to those rights and standards of conduct which can be derived by the application of reason to the study of the nature of man. The Declaration of Independence declares that "all men are created equal, that they are endowed by their Creator with certain inalienable Rights, that among these are Life, Liberty and the pursuit of Happiness." These rights might be said to be derived from nature and therefore in accordance with natural law. Laws against stealing, taking the lives of other men and similar offenses are generally also justified as being based upon the natural law.

Natural Resources Those material and physical realities that are provided by nature. They include forests, land, wildlife, oil, gas, minerals, and water.

Naturalization The process whereby a person born in one country becomes a citizen in another. In the United States, the process consists of: first, immigrating to the United States for the purpose of becoming a citizen; second, declaring an intention to become a citizen, followed by five years' residence in the United States; third, passing a test on citizenship, renouncing the country of one's birth, and taking an oath of allegiance to the United States.

Naturalized Citizen A person born in another country who takes the citizenship of his adopted country according to the procedure prescribed by law. In the United States new citizenship can be taken away again if it is later discovered it was obtained by fraud, through certain misrepresentations at the time of the taking of citizenship.

Navy, Department of See **Department of Defense.**

Nazi A member of the National Socialist Party in Germany which seized power in 1933 and ruled until the end of World War II. The Nazis were led by Adolph Hitler, whose totalitarian regime was among the most tyrannical and brutal of all time.

More loosely, any advocate of a totalitarian regime. Occasionally a group of fanatics in the United States forms an organization and calls itself a Nazi party.

"Necessary and Proper" Clause See **Elastic clause.**

Negotiated Contract An agreement entered into between the government and a contractor on the basis of a discussion of the government's needs and the contractor's ability to provide for these needs. Usually the discussion takes into account the past performance of the contractor and his special knowledge, skills, and available personnel.

Nepotism The practice of employing one's relatives, especially members of one's immediate family. Nepotism in government is frequently regarded with suspicion by the public because it is assumed that relatives are put on the payroll solely for the purpose of increasing the income of the office-holder. Relatives working for public officials may, in fact, be hard working and extremely valuable, but the practice is generally frowned upon by the public and is considered a risky practice by politicians.

Fischetti, Newspaper Enterprises Association, 1961.
"WHAT'S THE MATTER—CAN'T YOU READ?"

Neutral The diplomatic position of a nation which refuses to become involved in a war and which, in anticipation of possible war, declares that it intends to stand apart, giving no aid or assistance to either side.

Neutralism A term applied to describe the attitude of those nations who in the period following World War II remain uncommitted to either the Western or the Soviet blocs. It also refers to the position of those nations and persons who oppose further armament and oppose, also, participation in alliances which might involve their nations in military conflict.

New Deal The label usually given the administration and policies of President Franklin D. Roosevelt. It had its origins in the 1932 presidential campaign when candidate Roosevelt promised "a new deal for the American people." This campaign took place during the worst economic depression in American history and

the phrase stuck. As a slogan, it had the flavor of Theodore Roosevelt's "Square Deal" and Woodrow Wilson's "New Freedom."

The New Deal period ended, certainly by the time we entered World War II, but some define it more narrowly as covering 1933 through 1938. Its basic ingredients were a considerably increased governmental regulation of economic affairs and the establishment of greatly expanded national social welfare programs. As such, it has a distinctly partisan and controversial character, since it represents a Democratic Administration. Some of the most important pieces of legislation which were passed during the New Deal period are the **National Labor Relations Act, Fair Labor Standards Act, Social Security Act, Tennessee Valley Authority Act,** and **Agricultural Adjustment Act.** These laws are merely representative of what the New Deal did and tried to do. They were bitterly, but unsuccessfully, opposed at the time. Most of

Berryman, 1934. Library of Congress.

these major changes have now been accepted by most Americans.

New Jersey Plan A set of resolutions presented in series to the Constitutional Convention by William Paterson of New Jersey. These resolutions set forth the views of the smaller states. They proposed generally a weak central government, a unicameral legislature in which all states would have an equal vote. Significantly, the resolutions were simply amendments to the **Articles of Confederation.** See also **Connecticut Compromise, Constitutional Convention,** and **Virginia Plan.**

NLRB See **National Labor Relations Board.**

Nomination A political party's formal designation of its candidate for a public office. Nominations are made in conventions or by primary elections. A campaign for a nomination can be as vigorous and expensive as the regular campaign. This is especially true in one-party states or districts where the nomination of a particular party is almost a guarantee of election; it is also frequently true of the presidential nomination of a major party.

Nonpartisan (a) Describes an attitude which shows no favor for any particular political party. A newspaper which generally maintains strict neutrality about the parties is said to be nonpartisan.

(b) An action which does not involve political parties. Many local and some state elections are at least technically nonpartisan in that no party affiliation is shown on the ballot, and the candidates generally refrain from identifying themselves with a particular party. Many such elections are really partisan in fact as the party identification and support of the candidates is generally known. See also **Bipartisan.**

Normalcy A condition of internal and external affairs of the nation which is declared to be normal. The term gained currency near the end of President Wilson's term of office. He had sponsored many domestic reforms during his first term and the United States had entered World War I during his second term. Therefore in the 1920 campaign the Republicans called for a "return to normalcy," which by their definition meant the conditions which existed before the Wilson Administration.

North Atlantic Treaty Organization (NATO) The alliance of North Atlantic nations to preserve their freedom and common heritage and to provide for their collective defense. It was established by the North Atlantic Treaty signed in 1949 by the Foreign Ministers of Belgium, Canada, Denmark, France, Iceland, Italy, Luxembourg, the Netherlands, Norway, Portugal, the United Kingdom, and the United States. Greece and Turkey joined the organization in 1952 and West Germany in 1955. Under terms of the Treaty "the parties agree that an armed attack against one or more of them in Europe or North America shall be considered an attack against all of them. . . ." NATO was the response of the allied nations to the aggressive Soviet imperialism following World War II, and it has been a major factor in the containment of the Soviet Union. No territory in Europe has come under Soviet domination since NATO was established. The extraordinary feature of NATO has been the development of a commond command of naval, air and land forces assigned to NATO by the **109**

member nations, and the creation of its own defense installations.

Carmack, The Christian Science Monitor, 1957.
"FINDING THEY'RE NOT FEET OF CLAY."

Notary Public A minor public official who performs many routine services such as administering oaths and certifying that a signature on a document was made in his presence and is therefore authentic.

NSC See **National Security Council.**

Nullification A doctrine which holds that a state has the right to "nullify," that is, to declare void and of no effect, an act of Congress or a decision of the Supreme Court. The doctrine

has never been widely accepted and, of course, is in clear contradiction of the Constitution. It continues to manifest itself in the rather extreme expression of "states' rights," and in recent years has gained some support under the name of "interposition," a basis upon which Supreme Court decisions affecting racial segregation supposedly can be opposed or ignored. See also **States' rights.**

Seibel, 1956. Wide World Photos.
THE CHALLENGE

Nuremberg Trials The name given the trials of the Nazi leaders who were captured in World War II. In the course of the trials, 12 top Nazi officials were condemned to death. The first trial was held before the International Military Tribunal established by the United States, Great Britain, France, and the Soviet Union. Later each of the four powers occupying Germany held additional trials in its own zone. From 1946 to 1949, the United States held 12 additional trials at Nuremberg. The most disputed question was not so much the guilt of many of the defendants as the absence of positive international law under which they could be prosecuted.

Fitzpatrick, St. Louis Post-Dispatch, 1945.

OAS See **Organization of American States.**

OASI See **Old Age and Survivors Insurance.**

Oath A solemn swearing before God that one's statement is true. Persons entering United States government service or the military are required to take an oath supporting the United States Constitution and promising to execute their office faithfully.

An oath that has been the cause of considerable controversy is the loyalty oath required of students who borrow money under the National Defense Education Act.

Oath of Office The solemn and formal declaration required of all holders of major public office. The oath taken in the name of God declares that the person taking it will uphold, support, protect, and defend the Constitution of the United States or of a state and that he will faithfully execute the office to which he has been elected or appointed. The oath of office of a newly elected President of the United States is administered by the Chief Justice of the United States Supreme Court. In taking the oath the President places his left hand on a Bible and raises his right hand. Governors usually take the oath of office from the Chief Justice of the State Supreme Court.

OCDM See **Office of Civil and Defense Mobilization.**

Office Column Ballot A ballot on which the names of the candidates are listed under the offices they seek either with or without party designation. This kind of ballot encourages **split ticket** voting. If a voter wishes to vote for all the candidates of one party, he must go through the entire ballot picking out his party's candidate for each office. Often the practice of rotating the names of the candidates is followed which makes the selection even more difficult. See also **Party column ballot.**

Office of Civil and Defense Mobilization (OCDM) The agency which has primary responsibility for civil defense and for maintaining the power to mobilize the nation's resources for defense purposes. OCDM is also responsible for administering federal disaster relief when floods, hurricanes, and other catastrophies strike a community or region. In 1961 the principal responsibility for civil defense was transferred to the Department of Defense, and the name of the organization, now with limited authority, was changed to the *Office of Emergency Planning.*

Office of Education See **Department of Health, Education, and Welfare.**

Office of Emergency Planning See **Office of Civil and Defense Mobilization.**

Old Age and Survivors Insurance (OASI) A compulsory nationwide contributory retirement system under which employers and employees pay a fixed sum to provide pensions for the employees when they reach retirement age. This plan was initiated in 1935 to meet the needs of the increasingly large number of older persons who had no means of livelihood or support. Money for this pension program is collected by the federal government through the social security tax which is imposed upon basic wages and salaries.

The coverage of social security has been gradually extended since it was initiated until now the only significant group excluded are the members of the medical profession. The wage base, too, has been increased to $4,800, and the rate of contribution by both employer and employee has also been increased until today it is 3 per cent; in the case of self-employed the rate is 4.5 per cent. If the wage earner dies before he reaches the retirement age, his widow and family receive pension benefits. Full retirement benefits may be drawn at age sixty-five; reduced benefits at age sixty-two.

Old Guard Any persons who represent the older and more traditional views in a political party. Specifically, the term is usually applied to very conservative Republicans.

Oligarchy A form of government wherein political power is exercised by only a few people. The term is also applied, more loosely, to any group of persons who control a party or government even if the method of their selection is democratic.

Open Door Policy An agreement among the Great Powers to allow all commercial-minded nations equal access to trade with China and to preserve the unity and independence of that nation. The motive was not primarily concern for China. Secretary of State John Hay stated the policy

Bartholomew. The Bettmann Archive.

in a note to the Great Powers in 1899, and it was generally accepted. The policy was restated in the Nine-Power Pact at the Washington Conference in 1922. The Japanese invasion of Manchuria in 1931 and of China in 1937 broke the agreement, and the United States did not choose to go to war to defend it.

Open Shop A business or industry

having no requirements for union membership of its employees. The employees may be union members, however, and a union may be the sole bargaining agent for the entire plant.

Ordinance The official enactment of a municipal body such as a city council or town board; in other words, a local law.

Organization for Economic Cooperation and Development (OECD) An organization created in 1960 to provide an institutional framework for economic cooperation between European countries and Canada and the United States. The OECD is the successor to the **Organization for European Economic Cooperation.** It includes the countries in the **European Free Trade Association,** the **European Economic Community,** and Greece, Iceland, Ireland, Turkey, Canada, and the United States. The United States Senate ratified the OECD treaty in 1961.

Organization for European Economic Cooperation (OEEC) An organization of 17 European states established in 1948 in order to bring about economic improvement through common efforts for modernization of industrial and agricultural equipment, reduction in trade barriers, and promotion of full employment and other devices. Representatives of each of the member nations met regularly in Paris to discuss their economic problems and to work out solutions. Spain became a member in 1959. In 1960 the OEEC members were joined by the United States and Canada in establishing the **Organization for Economic Cooperation and Development.**

Organization of American States (OAS) The organization of the 21 republics of the Western hemisphere established in 1948 to promote the solidarity of the American countries and to advance economic, social, and cultural relations among them. The Organization of American States is a regional agency within the **United Nations** and is the successor to the International Union of American States established in 1890 and later designated as the Pan American Union. The Council of the OAS is made up of one representative, with rank of ambassador, from each member state, and in its decisions each state has one vote. Among the duties of the Council is that of seeking peaceful solutions to controversies between member nations. The Pan American Union is the permanent secretariat of the OAS. It is located in Washington, D.C.

Oriental Exclusion See **Immigration laws.**

Original Jurisdiction See **Jurisdiction.**

Pacifism The philosophy of belief which holds that violence in the use of power is immoral and ineffective, and that neither persons nor nations should ever use force even in self-defense. However, most of those who are called "pacifists"—those who accept pacifism—agree on the necessity for such things as police forces and jails; therefore the term is usually used in connection with international affairs. Pacifists generally argue that war is inherently immoral, that it seldom or never produces anything of any lasting value, and that it is therefore better and wiser for a person or a nation to accept defeat rather than pursue the immoral course of war. Pacifism has received new impetus since the development of nuclear weapons.

Pact   An agreement, usually formal, between two or more nations or groups or individuals.

Pair   The arrangement between two members of a legislative body by which they agree to be recorded on opposite sides of an issue if one or both are absent when a vote is taken. In either case their declarations are not a part of the actual vote count. A pair does, however, make the legislator's position known, even though his vote is not counted.

There are many kinds of pair arrangements in American legislatures. A *general pair* usually refers to an agreement which is of indefinite duration and applies when both members are absent. A *live pair* refers to a situation in which one of the parties to the pair is actually on the floor at the time the vote is taken and announces the pair. A live pair may be on a single issue or may cover a number of votes. The usual form for announcing a live pair is as follows: "Mr. President, on this vote I have a live pair with the Senator from [X State]. If he were present, he would vote 'no'; if I were permitted to vote, I would vote 'aye.' I therefore refrain from voting." Some pairs are merely announced without designating how the members would have voted.

Palace Guard   The term applied in criticism, usually by those who feel left out, to those who are good friends and close advisers to the President or to a governor. Almost every executive in high office develops, in order to meet his own needs and to give him some protection, a kind of palace guard.

114   Palko *v*. Connecticut (1937)   A case in which the court laid down certain criteria which must be met in order that the protections of the Bill of Rights may apply against the state governments as well as the federal government. Those rights listed in the Bill of Rights are protections against the federal government, not the states. The Fourteenth Amendment, adopted shortly after the Civil War, required among other things that no person or state shall "deprive any person of life, liberty or property, without due process of law." Many questions were raised by this amendment. What, for example, does "due process of law" mean? Was the Bill of Rights now a protection against the states, as well as federal encroachments on individual rights? The Court has consistently held that the Fourteenth Amendment does not give the individual all of the protections of the Bill of Rights against the state, but it has selected certain ones which do apply.

In determining which rights are protected by the Fourteenth Amendment "due process" clause, the Court has generally used a standard like the one laid down by Justice Cardozo in *Palko v. Connecticut.* According to this ruling, rights in question must be "of the very essence of a scheme of ordered liberty." They must be so crucial that neither "liberty nor justice would exist if they were sacrificed"; and violation of them would have to be "shocking to the sense of justice of the civilized world." If all these standards are met, then the right is protected against state encroachment by the "due process" clause of the Fourteenth Amendment. All of the First Amendment is now so regarded, as are certain other portions of the Bill of Rights.

Pallbearer   A name given to a type

of political hanger-on who generally sees the worst in every situation and seems happier in defeat than in victory.

Pan American Union See **Organization of American States.**

Pardon An official act of the President or governor of a state remitting the punishment for a crime and obliterating all legal disabilities arising from the conviction. A pardon restores the person to all legal rights he had prior to conviction. Legally, after a pardon he has the same status as if he had never been convicted.

A general pardon given to a group is called an *amnesty*.

Parish A geographical and political subdivision in the State of Louisiana; the equivalent to a county in other states of the union. The word *parish* also has reference to units of church organization on a geographical basis.

Parity Price The price which a farmer should receive for a specific product to assure him of purchasing power equal to that which an equal production would have assured him during some period which is accepted as a fair standard, usually 1910–14. Federal farm programs usually assure farmers a certain percentage of the parity price if they adhere to requirements such as acreage limitations.

Parliament Commonly used to refer to the legislature of Great Britain. It is composed of two bodies: the House of Lords and the House of Commons. The House of Lords for the most part has been stripped of its legislative power and the major responsibility for government rests in the House of Commons from which the cabinet is drawn. Other countries also have legislatures called "parliament."

Parliamentarian A person who is an expert in the accepted rules and procedures in a legislature as well as in the special rules adopted by a particular legislative body. He advises the presiding officer when technical questions come up and also advises members who may make inquiries about procedures. A parliamentarian is necessary in order to maintain orderly procedures and often becomes an extremely important person when controversy develops over rules.

Parliamentary Procedure The body of rules generally accepted as appropriate for the conduct of legislative affairs. These rules grew out of the practices of the British Parliament which developed them over centuries of experience. All legislatures have their own set of rules and procedures in addition to these more general prescriptions.

Parliamentary System A system of government wherein a cabinet, selected from among the members of the legislature (parliament), administers the government as long as it retains the support of the legislature. This system, especially associated with Great Britain, differs markedly from the American system in which the administration is under a President who is elected by the people, not by the legislature (Congress).

Parole The conditional release from prison prior to the expiration of the sentence in the case of those persons who are serving indeterminate sentences or who demonstrate good behavior in carrying out their sentences. The parolee must report regularly to his assigned parole officer who prescribes and supervises his activities during the period of parole.

Party See **Political party.**

Party Column Ballot A ballot on which the names of the candidates of each party are listed in separate columns. This kind of ballot makes it easy for a voter to vote a **straight ticket.** He can, if provision is made, make a mark at the top of the column which has the effect of casting his vote for everyone in that column, or he may go down the column marking the ballot for each of the candidates for that party. See also **Office column ballot.**

Party Designation The practice of designating party affiliation or identity on the ballot. Practice with regard to party designation varies from state to state. In some states only candidates for national office and for the highest offices in the state are identified as belonging to a particular political party. In such a state, candidates for the state legislature must run without any official party designation. A rather widespread practice is to have candidates for the judiciary and candidates for county and municipal offices run without any party identification.

Party Line A set of policies accepted and advanced by a political party. The term is frequently used in an exclusive sense with reference to the Communist party which has a very clearly defined, well-published party position. A party liner is a person who supports the party program even when that program contradicts earlier positions or changes very radically. A party line is not as permanent or as fundamental as a party's **ideology.**

Passport An official document identifying a citizen, permitting him to leave and reenter his country, and requesting other governments to grant him protection while he is in their territory. The compulsory passport system arose in the sixteenth and seventeenth centuries and was extended at the time of the French Revolution. Then under the liberal doctrine of freedom of movement in the nineteenth century, it was generally abandoned. With World War I there was a strong revival of the compulsory passport, and it has been retained since that time. In the United States passports are issued by the Department of State, are valid for two years, and after that time may be renewed for another two years. See **Visa.**

Patent The grant by the United States government to an individual of the rights to an invention or idea. A patent in this country is good for 17 years.

The Patent Office was established in 1790 to administer the patent laws enacted in accord with the Constitution (Article I, Section 8). Since 1925 the Patent Office has been a part of the Department of Commerce.

Paternalism Practices and policies which place the government and its citizens or business management and employees in a relationship like that of a father to son. A paternalistic government is generally viewed as one which provides necessary and desirable services for its citizens without calling upon them to accept full responsibility. In labor-management relationships paternalism is usually applied to the policy on the part of management which seeks to prevent or discourage union organization or activity by making concessions or by granting them essentially the same things that unions are demanding for other employees.

Patriotism An attitude expressed in

a strong sense of loyalty and devotion to one's own country and to its causes.

Patronage Jobs, contracts and other economic and honorary rewards which are available for distribution by political leaders and organizations. Although patronage has always been one of the major incentives for participation in politics and remains so today, many jobs, especially in the federal government and in some states, have been taken out of the patronage category and made into permanent positions to be held by trained civil servants.

Morris, 1961. Wide World Photos.

IT TAKES PATIENCE, WAITING FOR THE PLUMS

Pauper's Oath A solemn declaration made by an individual that he owns no earthly possessions of any real value. This oath is required by some government boards and bureaus before they will give relief to the needy.

Peace Corps A United States government program for training and sending a limited number of United States citizens overseas to assist the people of underdeveloped nations in educational and technical projects. The program was established by President Kennedy in 1961 and later approved by the Congress. Members of the Peace Corps are carefully selected. They live and work with the people of the countries to which they are sent and receive only maintenance and a small termination payment for their service.

Carmack, The Christian Science Monitor, 1960.

Peanut Politics A disparaging expression used to describe political action inspired by petty or mean motives. Politicians are accused of peanut politics when in order to win popularity they exploit trivial matters while refusing to deal with the important issues.

Peer An equal, or one of equal rank or station in life. The term is frequently used in the declaration that a person coming into court is entitled to be tried by a jury of his peers. Historically, a peer is a member of the **117**

British nobility. The Peers of the Realm constitute the House of Lords in parliament. A peer can be tried for treason or a felony only by his peers, thus the modern usage to designate one's equals.

Pension A payment made to a person on a regular basis in recognition of previous services or previous financial contributions. In the United States the most expensive pension systems are the veterans' pension program and the **Old Age and Survivors' Insurance,** commonly known as the social security system. Veterans' pensions are paid out of the general revenue of the federal government for recognition of military service. The OASI pensions are paid out of contributions which are made under the **Social Security Act.**

Pentagon See **Department of Defense.**

Per Capita A term usually used in describing an individual citizen's share of a tax or a share in the distribution of money or property. A per capita tax is one applied equally to each person who must pay the tax.

Permanent Court of International Justice An international court established by the **League of Nations** at the Hague in 1920. It is often referred to as the World Court. During its history this Court has rendered many decisions regarding disputes between member nations. Its effectiveness was limited since the Court generally had no jurisdiction over any state unless that state consented to submit to its jurisdiction. The Court also gave advisory opinions on disputes referred to it by the Council or the Assembly of the League of Nations. Under the United Nations the World Court was replaced by the

International Court of Justice. The United States never became a member of the World Court.

Perquisites Payments or benefits accruing to an officeholder or public official over and above his salary. They may include such things as a chauffeur-driven limousine, personal flag, free transportation on government aircraft, use of special dining rooms, elevators, extra office space, additional personnel, parking privileges, and other similar benefits.

Persona non Grata A person who is not welcome in a given country. If, for example, country A believes that a diplomatic representative of country B is a spy or for some other reason finds his presence undesirable, country A will declare the representative *persona non grata*. This automatically results in his removal.

Petit Jury A group of twelve persons charged with the responsibility of rendering a judgment as to the facts in a case. Their conclusion must be unanimous. The right to trial by jury is regarded as one of the foundations of our judicial system. It is based upon the assumption that a cross-section of one's fellow citizens is more likely to reach a fair judgment about guilt or innocence than a single judge who might be arbitrary and unfair.

Petty Offense See **Criminal case.**

PHA See **Housing and Home Finance Agency.**

Picketing The action by the membership of a labor union or its representatives in patrolling or standing before a plant entrance or a place of business in order to demonstrate disapproval of the labor policies of the respective plant or business. Picketing workmen usually carry placards calling attention to the union's demands in the strike or describing the practices against which the protest is being registered. The purpose of picketing usually is to deter striking workers, prospective employees, or customers from entering the struck plant or store. Picketing is usually nonviolent.

Pigeonhole To put off action indefinitely; hence, to defeat. The expression developed out of the practice of putting papers or legislation in a small compartment or hole in a desk, which was sometimes called a "pigeonhole," and then ignoring it.

Pink A person or policy which tends to follow the communist **party line** or which is said to follow that line. The word implies that the person or policy is dangerously communistic or close to communist **ideology** or program. The term is used very loosely in American politics, frequently in an attempt to smear a political opponent.

Plaintiff See **Suit.**

Plank See **Platform.**

Planning Any systematic effort to provide adequately for the future. If a city hires a specialist to study its problems and make formal suggestions about what steps it should take to improve the city now and in the future, this specialist is defined as a planner.

Platform The set of principles, policies, and promises adopted by a convention or by a candidate. The *plank* is one provision of a platform. Platforms are generally rather comprehensive and somewhat lacking in clarity and should be accepted as a general indicator of what the party or the candidate hopes to accomplish. Failure to accomplish provisions of a campaign platform is usually made an issue by the opposition party.

Pledge of Allegiance Declaration of loyalty made by United States citizens. It is used on patriotic occasions such as national holidays and at events where the United States flag plays a central role. The words of the Pledge of Allegiance are these: "I pledge allegiance to the flag of the United States of America and to the republic for which it stands; one nation under God, indivisible, with liberty and justice for all."

Plenary Session The term used to describe a meeting of a deliberative body when all members are present.

Plenipotentiary See **Ambassador.**

Plessy v. Ferguson (1896) A case involving public transportation facilities in which the Supreme Court held that states could require segregation of the races but that the facilities must be equal. This was the origin of the famous "separate but equal" doctrine which prevailed for over a half a century, despite many efforts to have it overturned and despite the fact that facilities generally were "separate but not equal." This rule was finally struck down in 1954. See **Brown v. Board of Education.**

Plumping Campaigning for or urging the election of a candidate. Another application describes the practice of casting a single vote for one's own candidate in an election in which the voters are called upon to pick two or three or even more for certain offices. An example would be that of the election of a city councilman in which the voter is called upon to choose six out of twelve candidates. By casting one vote for one candidate and voting for none of the other candidates, the voter gives protection to the one person for whom he has voted. This is a common practice among minorities

Pluralistic Society

who have only one of their own members on the ticket. The same meaning is expressed by the terms *bull's eye, single shot,* and *bullet ballot.*

Pluralistic Society A society composed of persons and groups with many different racial, ethnic, religious, social, and cultural characteristics. In the United States we tend to take this for granted since we are so obviously a pluralistic society. However, many nations are composed of persons who have many of these charactertistics in common, and therefore do not face the same problems, tensions, and opportunities as exist in a pluralistic society.

Plurality The difference between the highest number of votes and the second highest in a race between more than two candidates. If candidate A polled 50,000 votes and candidate B 40,000 votes, and candidate C 20,000 votes, then candidate A's plurality over candidate B was 10,000, and his plurality over candidate C was 30,000. Candidate A in this election would not have received a majority of the votes cast. See also **Majority. Runoff primary.**

Pocket Veto See **Veto.**

Point Four Program The technical assistance and economic aid provided to underdeveloped nations, particularly in Asia and in Africa, by the United States government. The program received its name as it was submitted as the fourth point in the inaugural address of President Truman in 1949 when he called upon the nation to "embark on a bold new program for making the benefits of scientific advances and industrial progress available for the improvement and growth of underdeveloped areas. . . ." The Point Four program

was not submitted as a separate plan, but was incorporated in the general **Mutual Security Program** and other forms of foreign aid.

Point of Order An objection raised in a legislative body or in a committee in which it is charged that the rules of procedure are being violated. When a point of order is raised, the presiding officer, in consultation ordinarily with the parliamentarian, determines whether the point of order is valid. If a member of the legislative body disagrees with the ruling of the chair, he may appeal that ruling; that is, he may call upon the body itself to sustain or reject the ruling of the presiding officer.

Police That branch of state or local government charged with preserving law and order, preventing crime, and safeguarding the health, welfare, and safety of the citizens. The state police are concerned primarily with preserving the safety of the highways, but they often have additional functions. Sheriffs are the county police officers. They are usually elected. In cities the police chief is oftentimes appointed, subject to an elected commissioner of public safety. There is no federal police force, but the FBI and the Treasury agents perform some police functions.

Police Courts Courts in municipalities having jurisdiction over minor crimes and misdemeanors. Their jurisdiction in the city usually corresponds to that which is exercised by the Justice of the Peace courts in rural areas.

Police Power The general power of the state to regulate the actions of persons and groups and the use of property for the protection of the public health, safety, and morals. In

120

the United States this power resides primarily with the states, but the federal government exercises a similar power through the authority of the Congress over the mails, taxation, and interstate commerce. The power of the state to license, inspect, zone, quarantine, establish safety regulations, and to impose a variety of restraints comes from its police power. States also have the authority to set wages and hours and establish minimum working conditions by virtue of their police power. The police power is limited by the rights guaranteed citizens in the federal and state constitutions, particularly by the *due process of law* provisions. See also **Bunting *v*. Oregon 1917.**

Policy Committee A committee composed of leaders of the same party in a legislative body. The policy or steering committee coordinates the party legislative program and attempts to secure its adoption. In the case of the majority party the policy committee may determine the order and time for bills to be taken up on the **floor.** In Congress the Senate Democratic Policy Committee and the Senate Republican Policy Committee are more formally organized and more important than those in the House of Representatives, but none of the committees actually create an over-all legislative program or policy for the party.

Political Party A group of persons organized to develop a party position, to choose candidates, to have those candidates put into office, and to make the party position effective. Party activities include the nomination of candidates for public office and the support of those candidates, the solicitation of funds, to support campaigns, the organization and conduct of campaigns, determination of party policy and program, and in some cases the handling and distribution of **patronage.** Political parties in this country are rather loose coalitions of persons representing many interests and points of view. For the most part political activity in the United States is concentrated in the two major parties—the Democratic party and the Republican party—although in some states third parties or splinter groups within major parties are politically significant.

The national parties are nominally controlled by their respective **national committees.** Actually a national committee may be quite unimportant, especially when the President of the United States is of the same party, since he then almost always becomes the undisputed leader of his own party.

Political Science A branch of the social sciences which studies political and government affairs. It has become a regular academic subject in universities only within this century.

Politician A person actively engaged in politics either as a candidate for public office or as one actively involved in political affairs such as party organization activities, campaign management and direction, and the like. The term is sometimes applied in a derogatory sense with the implication that anyone engaged in politics is either corrupt or verges on the corrupt.

Politics A term which has been variously defined. Taken in its most comprehensive meaning, it is the art and the science of government. It is applied also, of course, to those activities and organizations through which individuals or political parties seek to be established in positions of power and authority. Politics is essential to de- **121**

mocracy since it provides the way through which people can be informed on political problems and also provides the methods, procedures, and institutions through which the judgment of the people can be translated into policy and action.

Morris, 1959. Wide World Photos.
SPEAKING OF TIDAL WAVES

Poll (a) to take a vote, as in a delegation or a legislature, or the results of such a vote.

(b) to ask a number of persons how they intend to vote in a given election or what their opinion about certain matters is, or the results of such a procedure.

(c) Polls: the collective word used to designate the voting places.

Poll Tax A tax levied in some of the Southern states, or a charge imposed upon everyone who votes in an election. The unofficial purpose of the tax is to discourage poorer citizens, especially Negroes, from voting. Five states still have poll taxes: Alabama, Arkansas, Mississippi, Texas, and Virginia. In Alabama, Mississippi, and Virginia, the tax is cumulative; that is, it is necessary to pay the taxes

one failed to pay in earlier years of residence if one wishes to vote in any given election. Despite the fact that poll taxes are usually small in amount, running about one or two dollars a year, they have been an effective barrier to voting for persons in the lower income groups in those states which do have poll taxes.

Pierotti, New York Star, 1948.

Pollsters Those persons who conduct public opinion polls or make special inquiries with regard to the position of the general public or selected groups in society on particular questions or issues. The most famous pollsters are George Gallup and Elmo Roper.

Populist Party A party organized in the late nineteenth century to give expression to the economic discontent of the farmers in the South and the West, and to other dissatisfied elements who found little to choose from between the Democratic party and the Republican party. The Populist demands included a greatly expanded

122

supply of printed money, a **graduated income tax,** and government ownership of the railroads. After making a strong showing in the election of 1892—in which it polled over one million popular votes and captured 22 votes in the electoral college—it was virtually absorbed by the Democrats in 1896 when William Jennings Bryan and his followers gained control of the Democratic convention and endorsed most of the Populist program. The Populists then endorsed the Democratic Bryan for the presidency, but with his defeat, virtually vanished.

Pork Barrel The popular term applied to the money spent by the federal government for local projects such as the deepening of rivers, the improvement of harbors, and the construction of post offices, and other public buildings or projects. The term is intended to imply that this money is spent for the political benefit of congressmen and senators or other officeholders rather than for any pressing need or economically justified purpose. See also **Log rolling.**

Pork Chopper Name applied to leaders in some state legislatures (Florida, for example), who direct and largely control the legislative program of the state.

Postmaster General See **Post Office Department.**

Post Office Department A cabinet-level department of the federal government established in 1872. It was called a department long before 1872, however, and the Postmaster General has been a member of the cabinet since 1829. The Post Office Department is responsible for familiar services such as mail delivery, the issue and sale of postage stamps, and the sale of postal money orders. It has been called the "largest business in the world." In 1960 it employed over 550,000 persons.

Carrying the mail has been an accepted government responsibility since the founding of the nation. There have been no serious demands that the Post Office Department be turned over to private enterprise. Traditionally the Postmaster General has been a close political friend and adviser to the President on political matters. The appointment of postmasters and the assignment of rural mail carriers make up quantitively the major area in which political patronage, subject to some degree of civil service regulation, is still operative.

PR See **Proportional representation.**

Precinct The smallest voting unit. Each precinct usually has one polling place on election days and voting statistics are usually compiled and reported on a precinct by precinct basis. The precinct also is used as a unit for political organization and activity.

Precinct Captain A local party official charged with insuring that as many members of his party as possible are politically alert, registered, and vote on election day. The precinct captain in a large city with an effective political **machine** or organization is an important link between the voter and the party. In return for carrying out these party duties, the precinct captain is frequently given the right to make appointments—the right of **patronage**—or is given a job himself. Depending upon the nature of the city and the political machine, these favors may cover a wide range from the very corrupt practice of insuring a "not guilty" verdict by a judge to the humane one of providing food for unemployed families.

123

Premier   See **Prime Minister.**

Preparedness   The condition of being militarily and economically ready, or prepared, for war. The term frequently enters partisan debate in this country as the party out of power charges that the party in power is neglecting the nation's defenses and that the country therefore lacks preparedness.

Presidency   The general term applied to the executive branch of the United States government. The Constitution decrees that "the executive power shall be vested in a President of the United States." This provision in the Constitution was a most significant one as it established clearly that the presidency would be an office of great power as well as of symbolic importance. Among the duties and powers of the presidency are these listed by the Constitution: The President shall be Commander-in-Chief of the armed forces. He shall make treaties and appoint ambassadors and other officers of the United States. He is charged with the responsibility for taking care that the laws be faithfully executed. These three phrases from the Constitution give the President control of the military establishment, impose upon him a great share of responsibility for foreign policy, and assign to him the obligation to administer the federal laws and the programs of the federal government. As the country has grown and its government services have been extended and its foreign policy has become more important, the presidency has become increasingly important and powerful.

President of the Senate   The Vice President of the United States, or if there is no Vice President, a senator elected by the Senate. Actually the Vice President presides infrequently, and his duties as presiding officer are often fulfilled by a member of the Senate. The current practice in the Senate is to elect a *president pro tempore*—that is, a temporary president —who is responsible either for presiding himself or for assigning the job to someone else each day.

During the routine conduct of affairs, a senator with very little seniority is usually called upon to preside. When the subject matter under consideration is of great importance or when special rulings of importance may be called for from the presiding officer, the Vice President himself is likely to occupy the chair. This is especially true if he is at the same time a declared or potential candidate for the presidency. For routine rulings the presiding officer depends very much upon the parliamentarian of the Senate.

President *pro Tempore*   See **President of the Senate.**

President's Oath of Office   See **Inauguration.**

Presidential Press Conference   A meeting between representatives of newspapers, magazines, radio, and television, and the President wherein the press is free to ask the President questions on matters of public concern. The press conference has become an important custom, providing the nation with an insight into the President's thinking and vice versa. Conferences are held as frequently or infrequently as the President desires. Originally they were rather confidential, "off the record" meetings, and reporters were not allowed to quote the President directly. Now they are "on the record," and everything the President says is immediately reported to the nation and the world.

Presidential Succession The order in which officials would succeed to the presidency in case of the death or removal of the incumbent President. The Constitution names the Vice President as next in line and leaves it to Congress to determine succession in the event something happens to the Vice President.

Before 1947 a law in effect since 1886 listed the heads of seven cabinet departments in line to succeed the Vice President in case something happened to him. In 1947 Congress rewrote the law and established the following order of succession after the Vice President: the Speaker of the House of Representatives, the President pro tempore of the Senate, the Secretary of State, the Secretary of the Treasury, the Secretary of Defense, the Attorney General, the Postmaster General, the Secretary of Interior, the Secretary of Agriculture, the Secretary of Commerce, and the Secretary of Labor. With the establishment of the new Department of Health, Education, and Welfare, that secretary is in line to succeed after the Secretary of Labor. It is hard to imagine a case in which he might become eligible other than some kind of massive destruction of the seat of government of the United States. The action in 1947 followed a decision by President Truman and Congress that it would be more appropriate for an elective official of the Congress to follow the Vice President in the line of succession.

Presidential Timber A person who is regarded as qualified to be a party's nominee for the presidency. One who is said to be "presidential timber" should have the following attributes to a greater or lesser degree: wide public following, good reputation, political experience, attractive personality, the ability to win elections, acceptability to party regulars, political strength or leadership in a large or pivotal state, campaign financing, and a record of achievement in public service. The entrance of Madison Avenue, and such things as "people predictors," may bring about some changes in what has been traditionally defined as "presidential timber."

Darling, Des Moines Register, 1932.

HEAVENS! MAYBE WE'VE BEEN DOING IT WRONG

President's Press Secretary See **White House office.**

Press Newspapers and magazines; more broadly, the entire **mass media.**

Press Gallery The portion of a gallery above a legislative chamber reserved for representatives of news- **125**

papers, magazines, television, and radio. Behind the actual gallery, there is frequently a large area given over to the special needs of the press, providing telephone booths, teletype machines, ticker tapes, and the like.

Morris, Wide World Photos.

POLITICAL TORTURE CHAMBER

Pressure Group An organization or a group of organizations which endeavor in a variety of ways to influence government policies. They may print pamphlets, advertise in newspapers or on radio and television, hire lobbyists, and otherwise attempt to create a favorable climate of opinion. The word *pressure* is frequently used in an unfavorable sense, sometimes improperly so. However, in a democratic society, all persons and groups do have the right to attempt to influence public policy, and such efforts should not be generally denounced, but should be examined according to their specific objectives and specific methods. Some pressures are good and some are bad.

Pretrial Conference A meeting in the judge's chambers between lawyers representing opposing parties to a lawsuit to attempt to settle the suit out of court, or at least to eliminate from the trial those issues upon which the lawyers can agree beforehand. The pretrial conference is designed to speed the trial of a case and to eliminate unnecessary issues from a trial. It often results in settlement of the case without a trial.

Previous Question A motion "to move the previous question." When adopted it ends debate on an issue and brings it to a vote. The rules of the United States Senate make no provision for such a motion.

Price Support A payment or purchase program carried out by the federal government in an effort to raise prices received by farmers for their produce. Price support programs are generally carried out through the **Commodity Credit Corporation,** which buys or makes loans on farm commodities which are held off the market until market prices rise above a set level.

Primary Election An election held to determine who will be the candidates of the various parties in the general election. Primaries became popular in many states in the early part of the century as a means of having the public decide who the candidates should be rather than having party leaders or conventions make that choice. It has been only moderately successful in that respect since the party leaders' choices are frequently able to win the primary elections.

Prime Minister The first, or leading, official of government. This usually means that he is the actual leader of government, but sometimes the Prime Minister is subordinate to a president—as in the French Fifth Republic, or a king—as in Saudi Arabia.

Prison A place of confinement for persons convicted by a court of major crimes. Each state has its own state prison for those who violate state laws. The federal government operates a number of prisons for persons convicted of federal crimes. The largest and best known of the federal prisons or penitentiaries are Alcatraz, Atlanta, Joliet, and Leavenworth. State prisons are usually operated by a state bureau of corrections and are under the direct supervision of a warden. See also **Jail.**

Private Bill A bill providing for special treatment, monetary or otherwise, for an individual or a corporation. In the Congress there are two major types of private bills: those involving claims against the government which grow out of property damage or personal injury; and second, those involving special handling of immigration and citizenship cases. Congress has passed a law prohibiting certain kinds of private bills, such as those correcting a military record. All private bills are subject to presidential veto. In 1960, Congress passed 256 private bills; the President vetoed 11 of them.

Private Enterprise The term applied to any business operated by and for its owners. It is also used to describe the United States economy as a private enterprise economy˙ in which most decisions are made by individuals or nongovernmental institutions as distinguished from decisions in economies controlled by the government. The expression usually has reference to business and economic activities largely free from government interference and regulation.

Privileged Question A motion in a legislative body which must be considered ahead of other motions. In general, the most privileged motion is the motion to adjourn.

Probate (a) A procedure of proving before a court that a will is authentic.
(b) The name of the court which takes testimoney bearing on the validity of a dead person's will and declares the will to be valid or invalid. It then orders the distribution of property in accordance with the terms of the will. If there is no will, the probate court orders distribution of property according to the laws of the state. Some probate courts also hold sanity hearings.

Probation A procedure whereby juvenile offenders and persons convicted of less serious crimes are not sent to prison, but given a suspended sentence and the opportunity to prove they can be law abiding. Most courts have probation officers who establish conditions for probationers' behavior and who supervise their conduct during the probation period.

Probe An investigation—usually by a committee of the Congress.

Proclamation A formal executive declaration. It can range from the insignificant to historic; an example of the latter kind was Lincoln's Emancipation Proclamation.

Progressive In American politics, one who advocates change. The word is sometimes used as being synonymous with the word **liberalism,** although in a somewhat stricter sense the word *progressive* applies primarily to a program of action, and the word *liberalism,* in modern usage, applies to an attitude and general approach to political problems.
See also **Progressive party.**

THE EMANCIPATION PROCLAMATION. THIS DOCUMENT WAS ISSUED BY PRESIDENT LINCOLN IN 1862.

Progressive Moderation A term developed about the middle of the Eisenhower Administration to describe the policies of that Administration. It is suggested by critics of that Administration that moderate progress or moderate progressivism would have served the country better.

Progressive Party The name taken by several third parties in the course of American history. Usually Progressive parties have been organized by dissatisfied members of a major party and have gained prominence through following the leadership of an established political figure. The Progressive party of 1912, popularly called the Bull Moose party, was formed by liberal Republicans and others who rallied around former President Theodore Roosevelt when he lost his bid for the Republican party nomination. Roosevelt received more than four million votes and 88 electoral votes, running ahead of the Republican candidate, President Taft. The Progressive party of 1924 was also formed primarily by dissatisfied Republicans led by Senator Robert LaFollette of Wisconsin. The party had great strength among Midwest farmers. LaFollette received nearly five million votes and 13 electoral votes in that election. In 1948 a new Progressive party was organized with former Vice President Henry Wallace as its leader. It was made up of those who thought both parties were far too conservative. Wallace polled more than one million votes but won no electoral votes in the 1948 election.

Progressive Tax A tax which is greater for high incomes than for lower. An income tax, for example, which increases in percentage as the income rises is a progressive tax. See **Regressive tax.**

Prohibition In American politics, the movement to outlaw or prohibit the sale of intoxicating liquor. The Eighteenth Amendment, adopted in 1919, prohibited "the manufacture, sale, or transportation of intoxicating liquors" in the United States. This amendment was repealed by the Twenty-first Amendment in 1933.

Proletariat The working class as distinguished from the propertied class, the bourgeois, and the nobility. In Marxist ideology, the proletariat plays a decisive role, and the term has come to be rather closely identified with Marxian usage.

Propaganda Any kind of information or news—either true or false—used by a government to influence other governments and persons. Propaganda has been used by governments for centuries, but it has achieved a special importance in recent years because of the development of radio and television. Such United States programs as the Voice of America make every effort to present straight factual information. Generally the word is used as indicating immoral or undignified methods, although within recent years it has become somewhat more respectable.

Proportional Representation A system of allocating seats in a legislature in such a way that each political party or faction is given a percentage of seats roughly equivalent to their percentage of the popular vote. Proportional representation is not used in the United States, but it is used in some foreign countries. This is an example of how proportional representation, or "PR" as it is called, might work. Assume that a nation were divided into large legislative districts, each sending five representa-   **129**

tives to the legislature and with the voters voting for parties and not for individual candidates. If party A received 40 per cent of the votes, party B 36 per cent of the vote, party C 20 per cent of the vote, and party D 4 per cent of the vote, under proportional representation A and B would each win two seats in the legislature, C would win one, and D would have no representation. PR tends to promote many parties, because minor parties can hope to get some representation. Under the American system of single-member districts, the competition tends to center around the two major parties.

Prosecution In criminal law, the procedure whereby the district attorney institutes and tries on behalf of the government a lawsuit against a person accused of a crime. The purpose of the prosecution is to determine guilt or innocence.

Prosecutor See **Suit.**

Protocol Traditional ceremonies, procedures, and etiquette observed on occasions of state. Protocol also is used with reference to a diplomatic document which shows the area of agreement between representatives of different states on matters under discussion; when ratified, a protocol has the force of a treaty.

Proxy (a) A person who is delegated to act for another, as in casting the vote of an absent member at a meeting.

(b) The document authorizing one person to act for another. Stockholders sign proxy statements authorizing other stockholders to vote for them at meetings of boards of directors. Political groups often allow votes to be cast by proxy.

Public Assistance Help given by government agencies to specifically defined categories of persons. Public assistance programs include such things as the Old Age and Assistance program, aid to the blind, aid to dependent children, and aid to the permanently and totally disabled. The federal government and the state governments share the cost of administering these programs and also make contributions to the payment of benefits. Extensive federal participation in public assistance programs began with the **Social Security Act** of 1935. See also **General Assistance.**

Public Bill A bill dealing with matters of general public policy. Public bills constitute almost all legislation which receive publicity or create noticeable controversy. An example of a public bill would be a bill to change the Social Security Act.

Public Debt The amount of money which is owed by government at all levels—local, state, and federal. In 1960 the total state and local indebtedness had risen to something over $60 billion. This amount added to the total federal debt gives a grand total of public debt in the United States of approximately $350 billion.

Public Defender The attorney designated by the court to defend those persons accused of crimes and brought to trial who do not have an attorney and cannot afford one. The public defender is generally paid a small salary from public funds. It is a burden usually imposed upon young lawyers.

Public Domain The term usually applies to an area of land in which ownership rights are vested in the general public. It is also applied to such things as patents and copyrights when they pass from private ownership and become available to the general public.

Public Health All health services which are supplied by a local, state, or federal government. Public health frequently refers only to those services which are provided at public expense to needy persons, but can also mean any kind of health service generally available to the public and paid for out of taxes. An example of the latter is the mobile x-ray units provided by many city or county departments of health.

Public Health, Safety, and Morals A phrase used to describe the **police power** of the government. This is a kind of catch-all authority under which legislatures can justify the enactment of any law which even remotely relates to any one of these terms.

Public Health Service See **Department of Health, Education, and Welfare.**

Public Housing Housing projects financed by government funds and operated by a governmental agency. In the United States public housing has been used chiefly in connection with slum clearance and in providing housing for low-income families. See **Housing and Home Finance Agency.**

Public Housing Administration See **Housing and Home Finance Agency.**

Public Law 480 See **Agricultural Trade Development and Assistance Act.**

Public Roads, Bureau of See **Department of Commerce.**

Public Utilities Those enterprises having a public character which are usually subject to government regulation. The major public utilities in the

United States are telephone, telegraph, and power transmission industries; all forms of transportation: airline, railroad, bus, streetcar, and taxicab companies; gas and oil pipelines, wharves, and docks. These businesses, though privately owned, are generally regulated by local or state public utilities commissions, and nationally by such bureaus and agencies as the **Civil Aeronautics Board,** the **Interstate Commerce Commission,** and the **Federal Power Commission.** These governmental agencies usually have power to set rates, distribute routes, and compel a firm to provide adequate services to the public. In some cities the public utilities are actually owned by the municipalities or the government. The only public utility owned by the federal government of the United States is the postal service.

Public Utilities Commission See **Railroad and Warehouse Commission.**

Public Works Those services provided by a government, usually a city, to improve the physical environment and protect the health and safety of its citizens. They include public buildings, transportation, street construction and maintenance, lighting, bridges, sewers, and water supply. Often these services and activities are grouped under a department of public works, although the jurisdiction may be divided among several departments at the city or state level.

Pump Priming The name applied to an economic technique of increasing the supply of money in the hands of consumers to increase their purchasing power and in turn increase demand, thereby stimulating the whole economy. The term was often applied   **131**

to government spending programs designed to revive or stimulate economic activity. John Maynard Keynes, a British economist, is credited with first advancing this theory.

Purge Removal from office or party or position of influence. Purges in the United States are usually conducted in a peaceful manner through elections, and the purged individual survives. Many purges abroad, however, become violent and the deposed persons lose their lives. Stalin and Hitler have been notorious in modern times for purges conducted within their own parties.

Quisling The proper name of a Norwegian who became an agent of the Nazis. It is applied more broadly in politics to anyone who abandons his own party and goes over to the other side.

Quorum The number of members of a legislative body who must be present before that body or committee can conduct official business. Ordinarily a quorum is a majority of the members.

Quota A proportionate share which is assigned to various groups or countries. Quotas are used by government to control many types of transactions. In international trade, quotas are frequently used to limit the amount of goods which can be imported or exported, and they serve to supplement tariffs as a device for protecting a share of the domestic market. The quota system has also been used in the United States in immigration legislation since 1921 in order to give a preferential ratio to emigrants from countries in northwestern Europe.

Radical A person who favors a fundamental change in government or society. There are radicals of the **right wing** and radicals of the **left wing,** but the term is usually applied to the latter. A radical of the right, for example, might propose the abolition of the income tax or the restriction of voting rights to persons owning property. A radical of the left might propose government ownership of the major means of production or the elimination of inherited wealth by means of taxation. In the United States, radicals have rarely exerted great immediate influence, although their ideas have had some bearing upon the course of government policy and action. See also **Conservative, Liberal, Reactionary.**

Railroad and Warehouse Commission A state commission established generally to fix rates and routes of railroads, trucking companies, bus lines and to set rates for public utilities and telephone companies operating within the state. The commission is generally composed of three or more members elected at large or appointed by the governor or by the legislature. It is sometimes called the "Public Utilities Commission."

Ranking Member The member of a legislative committee who **(a)** is a member of the same party as the committee chairman and who ranks next in line in seniority, or **(b)** the senior member of the minority party. The former is called "the ranking majority member"; the latter is called "the ranking minority member."

Reactionary A person who strongly disapproves of current policies and practices and who generally favors a return to those of an earlier and of a simpler time. In America today a reactionary is likely to favor such things as the abolition of the social security system or a withdrawal from defense alliances with foreign nations or from the United Nations. The term is rather loosely used in American political debate. Since it has a rather unfavorable meaning, it is sometimes unfairly applied to persons who are genuinely **conservative** but not reactionary.

Readings of a Bill Formal steps in the passage of legislation. Older parliamentary practice required that there be three full readings of a bill at various stages in its passage through a legislative body. This was in a time when printing was not as easy or as fast as it is today. Now the three readings are largely formality. In Congress the *first reading* consists of a bill being introduced and being presented by title only in the **Congressional Record.** When a bill is brought up on the **floor** for consideration, it has its *second reading.* Sometimes the bill is actually read at this time; more often it is simply reported by title and the full reading is passed over. When all amendments have been acted upon, the bill has its *third reading,* usually consisting again of the reading by title only. The purpose of the readings originally was to insure, or at least to make it quite sure, that the legislators understood what was in the bill before them. Now that the bills and amendments are printed rapidly and in great quantity, this time-consuming practice is generally not followed.

Reapportion To make a new allocation of congressional seats among the states or within the state. Since 1911 the size of the House of Representatives has been fixed at 435 members. This number rose to 437 when Hawaii and Alaska became states, since each is entitled to one member in the House of Representatives, but it is scheduled to go back to 435 in 1963 unless the Congress acts to change the existing law.

As the population grows and shifts, it is necessary to redistribute congressional seats among the states. The Constitution requires that a national census be taken every ten years, and Congress has the responsibility to reapportion seats after each census. See also **Redistrict** and **At large.**

Rebellion Organized armed action by a group of citizens against their own government. Historically, a rebellion is a revolt that fails while a successful assault in which the old government is overthrown is called a revolution. The Declaration of Independence states the right and even the duty of a people to rebel against a long-established tyranny, but obviously no government looks with favor on this principle in specific cases, and the line between treason and justified revolt is hard to draw. In the United States, Shays' Rebellion in 1786 against the government of Massachusetts failed, but it pointed up the need for a stronger central government than that provided under the Articles of Confederation. The Whiskey Rebellion of western Pennsylvania farmers against federal tax collectors in 1794 was quickly put down. The Civil War is given various classifications. Officially the federal government considered the Civil War the war of rebellion; others refer to it as the War Between the States. In fact, seven Southern states undertook to secede and formed the Confederacy before hostilities began. Virginia, North Carolina, Tennessee, and Arkansas joined the Confederacy after the attack on Fort Sumter.

Recall The procedure whereby a **133**

public official can be removed from office. Fourteen states provide for recall procedures. Under them, a specified percentage of the voters, usually about 25 per cent, can petition that a public official be removed from office and a new election held. Eight states permit recall of judges as well as legislators. See also **Initiative, Referendum.**

Recess   See **Adjournment.**

Recession   Place of the business cycle during which signs of economic distress such as rising unemployment, falling production, declining retail sales, and the like begin to show, but which have not reached the serious proportions which characterize a **depression.** An administration in power is likely to describe unfavorable economic conditions as a recession rather than as a depression.

Reciprocal Trade   See **Tariff.**

Recognition   Formal acknowledgment by one government of the existence of another government. Recognition can be extended in a variety of ways, including the sending or receiving of a diplomatic representative or the issuance of a proclamation.

Recommittal   The act by a legislative body of sending a bill or resolution back to the committee which reported it out. Recommittal usually means the death of the proposal but occasionally a recommittal resolution will require that the bill be reported back out to the floor.

Record Vote   See **Roll call vote.**

Red   A popular synonym for **communist** or, more loosely, any revolutionary person or policy. The use of the term arose from the fact that the communist flag is red, a color long associated with revolution.

Redistrict   The action of establishing new legislative districts for either the state legislature or the House of Representatives of the United States Congress. Some state constitutions require that the state legislature be redistricted every ten years to make allowance for shifts and changes in the population. Other constitutions make no such provision and redistricting often is put off for many years.

Congressional districts are usually redrawn when a state's representation in Congress is either increased or decreased. The drawing of new district boundaries usually hurts some persons or parties and helps others. It is a highly controversial political task. See also **At large, Reapportion, Gerrymander.**

Red Tape   Unnecessary delays in administrative action resulting from rigid adherence to forms and routine regulations. The expression arose from dissatisfaction with the time taken to tie and untie the red tape used to bind official documents.

Referendum   The submission to the public for approval or disapproval of drafts for state constitutions, constitutional amendments, or acts passed by the legislature. Twenty-two states now make it possible for a specified percentage, usually about 5 per cent, of the voters to petition within a stated period of time to have an act of the legislature submitted to the voters in a referendum. All of the states require that constitutional amendments be submitted in a referendum for ratification. See also **Initiative, Recall.**

Refugees   Those people who flee from their own nation in order to escape persecution or death, or who are forcibly moved out by a hostile government. Refugees, even in a friendly nation, are dispossessed of legal status and of the protections ordinarily given to citizens. In the course of World War II and the period following it, approximately 40 million people were classified as displaced persons or as refugees. The United Nations Relief and Rehabilitation Administration was established to provide aid and operated from 1943 to 1947, when its functions were taken over by other international organizations, particularly the International Refugee Organization. Many religious groups and voluntary agencies have done important service in meeting the problems of refugees. See also **Displaced persons.**

Register of Deeds A county official, usually elected, who records all real estate transactions in his county. The record of every deed and mortgage on county property is filed in his office. His records also show property ownership from the time of the original government grant of land in the county up to the present.

Registration A procedure whereby the voter establishes his qualifications for voting by appearing before election officials at some set time before an election. Periodic registration systems require voters to register before each election. A system of permanent registration used in most states requires voters to register only once. The name then remains on the voting register unless some cause, such as change in residence or failure to vote in two or more succeeding elections, results in removal of the name from the register.

Regressive Tax A tax which falls more heavily on low-income persons than on high-income groups. It is the opposite of a **progressive tax** which is applied according to the taxpayer's ability to pay.

Most sales taxes are regarded as regressive because persons with small incomes must pay the same amount of tax on purchases as do the people with high incomes. This means that a greater percent of the income of the low-income group goes for taxes unless necessities such as foods, medicines, and rents are exempted from the sales tax, or unless other taxes are used to equalize the burden.

Relief See **General Assistance, Public Assistance.**

Representative A member of the House of Representatives in the federal government or of the House legislative body in the various states. In the United States House of Representatives the number of representatives in each state is determined by population, but not all the states provide for state representative districts of equal size.

Representative Government Often equated with democracy. A form of government wherein the actual business of making laws is delegated by the citizens to duly elected public officials, or representatives. As a democratic form of government, "representative" democracy is technically distinguished from "pure" democracy in which the people themselves, not their representatives, make their laws.

Republic A state in which political power is broadly based and which elects its leaders. It is to be distinguished from an absolute **monarchy** or a dictatorship wherein political a few persons, not elected. A republic power is exercised by one person or   **135**

lic may or may not be a democracy, depending upon whether the right to vote and hold public office is enjoyed by selected groups of persons—such as landowners or persons paying a certain rate of tax—or whether that right is broadly diffused throughout the entire population. Efforts to make a clear distinction between a republic and a democracy are often made, but without much success. The United States is both a republic and a **democracy.**

Republican Party One of the two major political parties in the United States. It began as a party opposed to the extension of slavery in the territories and soon adopted other policies such as high tariffs and free land for homesteaders. The Republican party today is generally regarded as the more conservative of the two parties. It is generally opposed to government programs, especially in the welfare field, and tends to emphasize private enterprise and individual initiative. Among its adherents are most businessmen, the majority of the middle class and the professions, and many farmers. Compare with **Democratic party.**

Reserved Powers Those powers neither given to the federal government by the Constitution nor denied to the states by the Constitution. They include the right of the state to provide for the health, safety, welfare, education, morals, and convenience of its citizens. Since they are not clearly defined or described, reserved powers are generally subject to controversy, both in the legislatures and in the courts.

Resolution A measure proposed or passed by a legislature or by one house of a bicameral legislature. In the United States Congress a *simple resolution* is used by either the House or the Senate for such things as establishing a committee or expressing its sorrow over the death of one of its members.

A *concurrent resolution* requires approval by both the House and the Senate and is used to fix the time of final adjournment or to express the sense of Congress on some matter not directly within the jurisdiction of Congress. A recent example of the latter kind of concurrent resolution was one approved which declared congressional opposition to the recognition of Communist China. Concurrent resolutions are not sent to the President for approval or disapproval, and they do not have the force of law.

A *joint resolution* also requires approval of both houses of Congress and is used for such purposes as correcting errors in bills sent to the President or proposing amendments to the Constitution. Joint resolutions must be sent to the President for his signature, except proposed constitutional amendments, and they do have the force of law if signed by the President. They are virtually indistinguishable from ordinary bills, but usually deal with less important matters.

Revenue The money, or source of money, used to finance the activities of any unit of government. The principal source of funds for the financing of governments is taxation, although the sale of property, operation of services, and similar activities also supply some revenue.

When expenditures exceed revenues, governments generally obtain the necessary additional funds by issuing bonds or by borrowing money.

Revise and Extend A practice common particularly in the House of Representatives permitting members to revise their remarks and also to extend them. Under this practice, the words actually spoken may be modified greatly before they appear in the **Congressional Record** and what was originally a very short speech may appear as one which took a long time. There are no clear rules with regard to revising and extending. It is general practice, however, that when the original statement was issued in controversy with other members of Congress, it will not be corrected in such a way as to change the meaning or sense of the argument or of the controversy. A member may protect himself in bitter controversy, of course, by demanding that his opponent's words be taken down.

Revolution A fundamental change in the political order of a nation or society. There have been many different kinds of revolution. The American Revolution resulted in the end of British rule in the Colonies and the establishment of 13 free and independent states. The French Revolution abolished the **monarchy** and established a **republic.** The Russian Revolution ended the reign of the czars and resulted in the creation of the first communist government. Since the end of World War II there have been many revolutions in colonial areas of Asia and Africa resulting in the formation of new nations.

Revolving Fund A fund established for the purpose of carrying out a continuing function which will return money to the fund, theoretically enough to maintain the fund at its initial level. An example of such a fund would be one established by a municipality to operate a municipally owned transportation system.

Rider An amendment to a bill which deals with a subject different from the bill itself. Most riders are attached to

Berryman. Library of Congress.

appropriations bills. In Congress, they usually contain provisions which the President disapproves of but which he will accept rather than veto the entire bill.

Right-To-Work Laws   The declared purpose of such laws, which have been accepted in a few states, is to guarantee everyone the right to work. In effect they permit employers to hire nonunion workers in those plants that have closed or union shops. From the point of view of organized labor, therefore, right-to-work laws have the effect of undermining unions and in many cases of making unions ineffective.

Rights   Privileges and prerogatives which are due a person; that is, those things to which a person is entitled. In the United States, rights include such things as the right to a fair trial, the right to vote, and the right to speak freely.   See also **Civil rights** and **Natural Law.**

Right Wing   Persons or ideas which favor the maintenance of the *status quo* or a return to that which existed in the past. The term is lacking precision, but it is generally associated with **conservatism** and a strong emphasis on property rights in the United States.   See also **Left wing.**

Roll Call Vote   A vote taken in a legislative body by which the names of all the members are called and each one responds individually to that call. This procedure is known as recording the **"yeas and nays."** It is the voting method which makes it possible for the public to learn of the action of their representatives. It is also known as a "record" vote. Under the Constitution a roll call vote is mandatory in the House or in the Senate if one-fifth of the members request it.   See also **Voice vote, Division vote, Teller vote.**

Rubber Stamp   A person or organization that is controlled by an outside force. A legislature which invariably approves of the proposals made by the executive branch is called a "rubber stamp legislature."

Rugged Individualism   See **Individualism.**

Rules Committee   See **Committee on Rules.**

Runoff Primary   A primary election between or among persons who received the largest number of votes in the original primary without having received a majority or whatever percentage of votes may be necessary for nomination. Runoff primaries are common in the South where the Democratic nominee almost always wins in the general election. Three or more persons frequently enter a given Democratic primary and when none of them gets 50 per cent or more of the vote, the top two face each other in a runoff.

Rural Electrification Administration (REA)   An important agency, commonly called REA, within the Department of Agriculture. The REA provides low interest loans to local public bodies, to cooperatives, and to other private organizations for the construction of electrical and telephone service facilities in rural areas. Created in the days of the Great Depression in 1935, the REA has made available electricity and telephone to millions of farm houses which otherwise would be deprived of these necessary services.   See also **Department of Agriculture.**

Saint Lawrence Seaway Development Corporation A government corporation established in 1954 when Congress, after decades of controversy involving powerful economic interests on both sides, agreed to cooperate with Canada in the development of the Saint Lawrence River to permit ocean-going vessels to reach Great Lakes ports, and also to produce hydroelectric power. The corporation was made responsible for negotiating with Canada on such matters as construction of locks and dams and also on tolls, for supervising the American share of construction work, and for administering the American share of the actual maintenance and operation of the project. By 1959, the Seaway had a 27-foot channel, thus making such Great Lakes ports as Cleveland, Detroit, Chicago, and Duluth in effect ocean ports.

Sales Tax A percentage assessment levied upon the receipts from the sale of merchandise or services. More and more states are resorting to this tax as a revenue-providing device, supplementing other types of taxes.

Sandbag A term applied in politics drawn, of course, from the practice of trying to control floods by using sandbags to build up dikes and levees or to strengthen weak points in dikes and levees. In politics it refers to action whereby the political ambitions or desires of an individual or of a group are frustrated by counteraction which controls or regulates the desires or efforts of the opposition. It is sometimes also used to indicate blunt or crude political action.

Satellite Nation A nation or state that is economically and politically dependent upon some other power and which is either directly or indirectly controlled by the other nation. The term has special reference to nations whose governments are controlled through the local communist party under the domination of the Soviet Union.

Schecter Poultry Corporation v. United States (1935) A case in which the Supreme Court held that the wages and hours of employees at a slaughterhouse which purchased live poultry in New York and Philadelphia and slaughtered it in Brooklyn could not be regulated by the federal government because the slaughterhouse was not engaged in "transactions in interstate commerce."

WE DO OUR PART
The National Archives.

During the depression of the thirties, Congress passed many laws designed to help the economy. One such law provided for the National Recovery Administration (NRA) which established codes for wages and hours of industry and labor. It was such a code that the Court held could not apply to the Schecter Corporation. **139**

The Court's decision in this case sounded the death knell of NRA. This was a rather narrow interpretation of the **commerce clause** of the Constitution and was altered shortly thereafter by such decisions as **National Labor Relations Board v. Jones and Laughlin.** See also **Gibbons v. Ogden and United States v. Darby.**

Schenck v. United States (1919) A case in which the Supreme Court laid down its most famous rule for limiting free speech. Although the First Amendment protects freedom of speech, certain kinds of statements are, nonetheless, punishable by law. These include libel, obscenity, and contempt of court. The difficult distinctions are in the areas of politics and religion. The Court has been very careful to protect freedom of speech in these areas, but it has not taken the position that *all* speech is permissible. At issue in the Schenck case was the Espionage Act, passed during World War I, which prohibited false statement designed to impede the prosecution of the war. In upholding the conviction of some individuals who had mailed out circulars urging men to resist the draft, Justice Holmes declared: "The question in every case is whether the words used are used in such circumstances and are of such a nature as to create a clear and present danger that they will bring about the substantive evils that Congress has a right to prevent." This "clear and present danger" standard has not been universally accepted nor is its application easy or obvious in actual cases. There is always a tension between the claims of organized society or government and the freedoms of individuals. When the two conflict, the Court must decide in the light of the constitutional safeguards which shall prevail.

School District A quasi-municipal corporation of indeterminate area and population created for the purpose of providing land, buildings, and teachers for elementary, intermediate, and high-school education. The school district has the authority to levy taxes and to issue bonds to finance its activities.

SEATO See **Southeast Asia Treaty Organization.**

SEC See **Securities and Exchange Commission.**

Second Reading See **Readings of bills.**

Secondary Boycott Union pressure brought to bear on an employer because of his relationship with a second employer who is the real object of the union's interest. It may take the form of a strike or of a refusal to handle goods supplied by the second employer unless all relationships are broken off between the two employers or until the second employer agrees to the union's conditions. See **Taft-Hartley Act.**

Secretariat The working staff of the **United Nations** which services its agencies and carries out directives of the **General Assembly** and the **Security Council.** The Secretary General is the chief administrative officer. He is nominated by the Security Council and elected by the General Assembly. With the development of the United Nations, the position of the Secretary General has become one of considerable influence and power.

Secret Service See **Department of the Treasury.**

Secretary of Agriculture See **Department of Agriculture.**

Secretary of Commerce See **Department of Commerce.**

Secretary of Defense See **Department of Defense.**

Secretary of Health, Education and Welfare See **Department of Health, Education, and Welfare.**

Secretary of the Interior See **Department of the Interior.**

Secretary of State At the state level he is the elected or appointed official who publishes and distributes the statutes adopted by the legislature, countersigns proclamations and commissions, issues certificates of incorporation and automobile licenses, supervises elections and accepts filings for office, and keeps the Great Seal of the state and the archives. For functions at the federal level, see **Department of State.**

Secretary of Treasury See **Department of the Treasury.**

Sectionalism The pursuit of interests which are of special concern to a region or section of the country. Sectionalism has traditionally played an important part in American political life. In the early days of the republic, the commercial North had interests which conflicted with the agricultural South, and the growing West had concerns which were special to that area. There are still sectional concerns which leave a great imprint on American politics—the most notable of these, of course, is the South's abiding problem of race. Fortunately, sectionalism is no longer the great force it used to be.

Securities and Exchange Commission (SEC) An independent regulatory commission of the federal government established in 1934. It is made up of five members appointed by the President with the consent of the Senate. They serve for five-year, staggered terms. The general purpose of the SEC is the protection of the public against malpractices and deception in securities and financial markets. The Commission is empowered to exercise broad authority over the buying, selling and advisory practices involving stocks, bonds and other securities sold in interstate commerce. It requires detailed registration of all such securities for the purpose of making such information public. The Commission also has special regulatory powers with respect to public utility holding companies.

Security Council The organ of the **United Nations** which has primary responsibility for preventing war and maintaining peace. It has the authority to investigate any dispute that threatens international security and to recommend action. The five powers—United Kingdom, France, China, the United States, and the Soviet Union—are the permanent members of the Council along with six others elected by the **General Assembly** for a two-year term. On procedural questions a vote of seven members carries, but on substantive matters the seven votes must include all five permanent members. The effectiveness of the Security Council has been limited by the frequent use of its veto power by the Soviet Union.

Sedition Activity in the form of meetings, speeches, and conversation which tend to incite people to overthrow the government by force. Sedition is not **treason** and does not involve an overt act.

Segregation The practice of keeping races separate from each other by the provisions of separate facilities or separate organizations. The areas or institutions in which segregation has been most discussed include schools, churches, clubs, unions, housing, public transportation, restaurants, hotels, and the employment practices of business. Segregation has been applied with special forces in Negro-white relationships in the South, but it is also widely practiced in a variety of forms in other areas of the country. See **Brown** *v.* **Board of Education, Jim Crow laws.**

Morris, 1961. Wide World Photos.

HOW CAN PEOPLE BE LIKE THAT!

Select Committee See **Standing committee.**

Selective Service System The name given an organization of the federal government which has been set up to administer the federal laws regarding induction of men into the armed forces. It is responsible for what is popularly or unpopularly called "the draft." Within statutory limits set by Congress, the director, who is appointed by the President with the consent of Congress, is responsible for establishing registration and classification systems and determining the monthly quotas of inductees. State directors, appointed by the President upon the recommendation of the governors, are responsible for selective service matters within their states. Local boards—the famous "draft boards"—consist of three or more civilian residents and have the authority to determine who shall be drafted and who shall be temporarily or permanently exempted in accordance with the law. Their decisions are appealable to an appeal board established in each federal judicial district.

Self-Determination A principle that people with common language, culture, and traditions should have their own government and independence as a national state. This principle was particularly popular in Europe at the turn of the nineteenth century and was used as a justification for breaking up the old empires. It has been looked upon with less favor when advanced by Asiatic and African peoples against the colonial powers in Europe. The granting of self-determination was one of the major pledges made by the Allies in World War I. Its application led to the creation of several small states in what had formerly been part of the German, Russian, Austrian, and Turkish empires. Political and economic realities in Europe following World War I prevented recognition of every nationality group that sought to be recognized. Somewhat similar problems are manifest today, especially in Africa.

Senate The second body of the legislative branch of the United States government. The term is also used for the similiar branch in state legislatures. The United States Senate is made up of two senators elected from each state in the union and when all states are fully represented has 100 members. According to the Constitution, the Senate has special responsibility in the field of foreign affairs and also in the confirmation of appointees by the executive branch of the government.

Senator A member of the United States Senate or of the Senate in the various states. In the United States Senate each state is entitled to two senators, regardless of population, and in the states the senatorial districts generally are larger and different from the House districts.

Senatorial Courtesy A tradition and practice in the United States Senate of not approving any presidential appointment which directly affects a state when the senator or senators of that state who belong to the majority party object to the appointment. This applies most frequently to appointments such as local postmasters and district attorneys, and also to the appointment of federal judges in the respective states.

Senior Senator In the United States Senate the term used to distinguish the senator from each state who has the longer continuous service in the United States Senate. The other senator from the state is referred to as the "junior senator." Neither term has any legal or institutional significance.

The term is also used more broadly to refer to any member of the United States Senate who has been there for a long time and is therefore high on the seniority scale.

Seniority The tradition widely observed in the United States Congress as well as in state legislatures of assigning committee positions, office space, as well as symbols of authority on the basis of length of service in the legislative chamber. In Congress the rule is applied quite strictly in naming the majority party member who has served for the longest time on the committee as chairman of the committee. The seniority system gives power to those who are able to maintain themselves in office for long periods of time. It is frequently criticized as undemocratic and unfair, especially by those from areas of a state or nation where close competition between the parties results in frequent turnover among representatives. It is a somewhat unreasonable basis for assigning chairman and committee members. However, there is that measure of good in it which was attributed by Chesterton to the practice of having the eldest son of the king succeed his father. This practice, Chesterton osberved, was without any basis in reason, but it saved a lot of trouble.

Separation of Church and State See **Church and State.**

Separation of Powers A theory and also a practice of government whereby power is separated or divided, some resting in the executive branch, some in the legislative branch of the government, and some in the judiciary. The Constitution of the United States established a government of separated powers. Perhaps a better description would be "shared powers," since these powers are not absolutely and clearly separated in our government. Foreign policy, for example, is largely an executive responsibility, but Congress also plays an important role in appropriating funds and conducting investigations. The primary legislative responsibility rests with the Congress, but through the exercise of the veto **143**

the President can also indirectly influence legislation.

Sergeant at Arms An officer of a legislative body who is responsible for keeping order in and around the chamber, insuring that only authorized persons gain access to the floor, and generally performing such duties as the presiding officer may require.

Session (a) A formal meeting of a legislative body or a legislative committee.

(b) A particular series of meetings of a legislative body. For example, each new Congress, elected every two years, has at least a first session and a second session. It may also have more sessions, called "special sessions," if called by the President. A bill passed in 1959 was passed by the Eighty-sixth Congress, First Session. A bill passed in 1960 was passed by the Eighty-sixth Congress, Second Session. In the United States Congress, work begun in the first session may be continued in the second session.

Shadow Cabinet See **Cabinet.**

Sheriff Elected county official in every state excepting Rhode Island. The sheriff directs law enforcement activities within the county and outside the municipalities in which city police have jurisdiction. Sheriffs usually have a number of assistants or deputies. The duties of the sheriff include maintenance of the county jail and care of prisoners, enforcement of traffic, liquor and gambling laws, making arrests, and generally preserving the peace in the county.

Sherman Act See **Antitrust.**

Short Ballot See **Ballot, short.**

Simple Majority See **Majority.**

144 **Simple Resolution** See **Resolution.**

Sit-Down Strike A strike wherein the workers refuse either to work or to leave the premises until an agreement is reached. Sit-down strikes were rather prominent in the thirties but are a rarity today.

Sit-In A term used since 1960 in connection with a series of efforts by Negroes and whites to obtain service at lunchcounters in the South which were segregated, that is, reserved for Negroes or whites. It is a variation on the technique of the **sit-down strike.**

Slate A list of candidates for public office. Usually the slate contains the names of the candidates of one party; or in the case of primaries, conventions, or nonpartisan elections, it presents a list of candidates approved by one group or **faction.**

Slush Fund A slang term used in politics to refer to money kept for various purposes such as influencing elections or influencing public officials.

Small Business Administration (SBA) An independent agency of the federal government established in 1953. It is headed by an administrator appointed by the President with the consent of the Senate. The purpose of this agency is to protect and advance the interests of small business. It has a broad range of powers for this purpose including the following: to advise small business concerns on such matters as financial practices and government contracts; to make loans to small businesses for specified purposes; to insure that a fair proportion of government purchases and contracts are placed with small businesses by certifying such firms for certain projects and by trying to influence agencies of the government to make purchases from small businesses; and to enter into government contracts and assign work to small businesses and industries.

Smithsonian Institution Usually is applied to a single building in Washington sometimes called the "Nation's Attic." It is in fact an establishment of the federal government, created in 1846 in accordance with the will of James Smithson of England, who left his fortune to the United States to be used for "the increase and diffusion of knowledge among men." It administers many subordinate institutions, including the following: the United States National Museum, the Museum of Natural History, the Museum of History and Technology, the National Air Museum, the National Zoological Park, the National Collection of Fine Arts, the National Gallery of Art, and the Astrophysical Observatory of Cambridge, Massachusetts.

Smoke-Filled Room The room in which political leaders supposedly meet to hold private and confidential sessions in order to reach agreement on such things as nominations and political policy. Perhaps the most famous smoke-filled room was the one at the Republican National Convention in 1920 at which time the leaders gathered to select a compromise candidate, Warren G. Harding. The term is usually applied in a critical way, implying unsavory **deals** between dishonest politicians or decisions which do not reflect the popular will and are made in secret, away from the press and the public.

Soapbox Any improvised speaking platform from which informal speeches are made in public. Presumably, the term grew out of the practice of some orators of using a soapbox from which to speak. Soapbox speeches are usually associated with somewhat unusual persons talking in a somewhat irrational manner about political or religious subjects, or under unusual or unplanned circumstances.

Social Security See **Social Security Act.**

Social Security Act (1935) One of the major social welfare programs adopted during the Roosevelt New Deal administration. The original act, approved in 1935, had three principal sections. It provided for a public assistance program wherein the federal government makes grants to the states to help pay for welfare aid to the needy, the aged, the blind, and dependent children. Second, it established a federally administered program of old-age insurance whereby workers and employers contribute a percentage of wages over the years into a retirement fund which then makes monthly payments to the employees upon retirement. This aspect of the Act—the **Old Age and Survivors Insurance**—is what is popularly known as "social security." Third, the Act established a federal-state employment insurance program whereby employers pay an amount equal to a percentage of their employees' wages to an unemployment fund established in each state. Benefits are then paid to eligible unemployed workers; the amounts paid and the duration of the benefits vary widely from state to state.

Social Security Administration See **Department of Health, Education, and Welfare.**

Socialism The set of beliefs or doctrines—the ideology—which favors public government ownership of all of the major means of production, transportation, and communication. There are many different kinds of socialism. **145**

Marxist socialism is derived from but not completely dependent upon the writings of Karl Marx; it tends to be doctrinaire and inflexible. The socialism of the British Labour party, on the other hand, is sometimes called "soft socialism": it favors public ownership of many industries, but not all, and bases its policies on the needs of a nation as they develop rather than relying on the rigid doctrines of any person or group.

The term *socialism* is used by communists to describe their own beliefs and system. We, however, call it "communism." This leads to a great deal of confusion, but the distinction between the noncommunist and communist use of the word is obviously of very great importance.

Soil Conservation Service (SCS) A federal agency to provide the information and technical assistance necessary to carry out good soil conservation practices in all the agricultural districts of the country. The agency operates under the Department of Agriculture in providing service to the soil conservation districts, of which there were 2,868 in 1960.

Solicitor General See **Department of Justice.**

Solid South The descriptive term applied to those southern states which in the past have almost always voted Democratic. The term has never had any precise geographical meaning, but ordinarily has referred to the eleven former Confederate states with the possible addition of Oklahoma and Kentucky. The Solid South traditionally elected Democrats to Congress and voted Democratic in presidential campaigns. There were very few exceptions from the end of **carpetbagger** rule in the South until 1928 when

seven of the thirteen states voted for the Republican candidate for president. In 1952, 1956, and 1960, a total of seven of the so-called Solid Southern states voted at least once for the Republican presidential candidate. In the 1960 election there were ten Republicans elected to Congress from these states. Obviously the Solid South is not a sure thing for Democratic congressional candidates, and more and more Republicans are challenging in the congressional elections.

Southeast Asia Treaty Organization (SEATO) The alliance designed to prevent communist aggression in Southeastern Asia. It is also one of the three major collective defense organizations, **NATO, CENTO,** and **SEATO,** whose purpose is to contain the imperialism of communist nations. SEATO was established in 1954 by a treaty signed in Manila by Australia, Great Britain, France, New Zealand, Pakistan, the Philippines, Thailand, and the United States. Its headquarters are in Bangkok, Thailand.

Southern Democrat A member of the **Democratic party** from one of the Southern states. Southern Democrats have traditionally voted differently from northern and western Democrats on some issues, most notably on questions of race. There have been other sources of division, largely economic, which have resulted in splits between Southern Democrats and other members of the Democratic party. In general Southern Democrats tend to be more **conservative.**

Sovereignty Final authority in a given area. A nation has sovereignty if it controls its own affairs without dictation from another country. The term is often used rather loosely in the United States, as when someone refers to one of the fifty states as being "the sovereign state of. . . ." Although it is true that many powers are reserved to the states under the Constitution, none of the fifty states is sovereign in the basic sense of having supreme authority in all those fields which are properly subject to government action.

Soviet Union (the Union of Socialist Soviet Republics) The first and the leading communist state. Until the Russian Revolution of 1917, the nation was known as Russia and was ruled by czars.

Speaker of the House of Representatives The presiding officer of the House in the national and state legislatures. He is elected by the House from among its members. The Speaker of the United States House of Representatives, usually a person of great importance, is the leader of the majority party in the House. He has a powerful voice in making committee assignments. He has wide discretionary authority in recognizing or failing to recognize members who wish to speak or to offer motions. Under the Presidential Succession Act of 1948, he does in case of death or disability of both the President and the Vice President succeed to the office of President.

Special Committee See **Standing committee.**

Special Districts Governmental corporations created from one or more cities, towns, or villages in order to provide for a specific governmental function or service such as water, gas, electricity, transportation, schools, sewage, and the like. In rural areas the special districts may take the form of irrigation, drainage, or reclamation districts.

Special Session A meeting of a legislature which is not ordinarily required by constitution or law. In the case of the federal government the Constitution provides that the President "may, on extraordinary occasions, convene both Houses, or either of them. . . ." Regular sessions of Congress are convened on January 3 of each year, unless Congress fixes another date. State legislatures are sometimes convened by the governor of the state for sessions over and above those required under the state constitution.

More loosely, it is any session of a legislature which takes place under unusual conditions. If Congress should recess for a month in the summer and return for a brief period to complete its work, the short meeting is often popularly called a special session.

Spellbinder A colorful and persuasive speaker who is able to hold the attention of his audience and whip up great enthusiasm; a speaker who has the audience under his spell. The term is used to designate the manner of a speaker rather than the quality of what he says.

Split Ticket Balloting whereby one casts votes for candidates of more than one party. More and more Americans seem to be voting split tickets. In 1956, for example, the voters overwhelmingly reelected President Eisenhower, a Republican, but at the same time elected a Congress with a Democratic majority. See also **Straight ticket.**

Spoils System The distribution of government jobs exclusively or almost exclusively to the victorious party-faithful, without regard to the desirability of establishing a career service and sometimes without regard to the abilities of the persons being employed.

Stalking Horse   A candidate who is not a real contender, but is put forward to divide the opposition or to conceal the real candidacy of someone else. The term comes from the practice of a hunter using a horse, or imitation of one, as a cover in order to get within range of game.

Standards, National Bureau of   See **Department of Commerce.**

Standing Committee   A permanent and officially established committee of a legislative body which is given authority over certain kinds of legislation. There are currently (1961) 20 standing committees in the House of Representatives and 16 in the Senate. A standing committee should be distinguished from *select* or *special committees* which are appointed for a limited period of time to investigate and report on special problems. An example of this kind of committee was the Select Committee to Investigate Improper Activities in Labor-Management Relations which was popularly called the "Rackets Committee."

Star Spangled Banner   See **National anthem.**

Stare Decisis   The practice of basing judicial decisions on precedents. As a general rule, *stare decisis* provides continuity and uniformity in decision-making. It is not binding on the courts and in recent years the Supreme Court has shown a considerable willingness to depart from earlier findings. As a matter of fact, the use of precedents is a somewhat artificial basis upon which to form immediate judgment. Its use, however, often can save a great deal of trouble.

148

State, Department of   See **Department of State.**

State Militia   The military establishment of the individual states organized for the protection of the states and the preservation of law and order. Members of the militia are civilians who assume military status periodically and who undergo special training. They are called into active duty only in cases of emergency. Two classes of state militia are the reserves and the organized. The last group is known as the **National Guard.**

State of the Union Message   An annual message from the President to Congress. The Constitution requires that the President "shall from time to time give to the Congress information on the state of the nation, and recommend to their consideration such measures as he shall judge necessary and expedient." The President always submits such a message, usually in person, near the opening of each session of Congress and can also send special messages, as he often does, on particular matters of concern to him. The President is now required by law to submit two other annual messages to the Congress, the **Economic Report** and the **Budget Message.**

States' Rights   Strictly speaking, states' rights are those rights which under the Constitution are reserved to the states. Just what these rights are has been subject to continuous dispute. The advocates of states' rights rest their case primarily upon the Tenth Amendment to the Constitution, which declares that "the powers not delegated to the United States by the Constitution, nor prohibited by it to the States, are reserved to the States respectively, or to the people." The term *states' rights* is frequently applied to the view of those advocating extreme positions like **nullification,** secession, and interposition. It is often applied also to those who recognize the need for a strong central government, but who are genuinely concerned that the states remain active and distinct political entities, and that certain decisions, particularly those in the cultural field, be reserved to the states or to other smaller units of government.

State, Secretary of See **Department of State**

Statesman A person in public office who is judged to exhibit strength of character and concern for the general welfare of the nation.

Statute A written law. The act of a legislature authorizing, declaring, or prohibiting something.

Statute of Limitations A law establishing a time limitation within which certain types of legal actions may be started. These statutes usually state that no legal action may be taken after a certain number of years have passed since the alleged action occurred.

Steering Committee See **Policy committee.**

Straight Ticket Voting for the candidates of one party only. Many printed ballots and voting machines make provision for a voter to select one box or one lever by which he can vote for the entire slate of candidates of one party. This saves the voter the trouble of checking all of the boxes or pulling all the levers. See also **Split ticket.**

Straw Vote A sample or preliminary vote taken unofficially and usually prior to an official vote. Straw votes may be samplings taken by newspapers or by political organizations for the purpose of determining ahead of time the sentiment of the voters. Political parties resort to this device to test public response to campaign techniques, candidates, and issues and as a basis for planning future strategy and policy. A straw vote is usually considered to be less scientific than a public opinion poll.

Strict Construction See **Elastic clause.**

Strike A work stoppage organized by employees for the purpose of forcing employers to accede to their demands for higher wages, shorter hours, or some other change in working conditions or compensation.

A sympathy strike is one organized to support the efforts of employees in some other firm or business. See **Taft-Hartley Act, National Labor Relations Act, Secondary Boycott.**

Stump (a) to make campaign speeches.

(b) the location of a political campaign, usually implying a rural setting.

(c) relating to a political campaign in style and content, as "stump oratory," which is highly partisan and colorful.

Subpoena An official order by a legislature or one of its committees or by a court requiring the attendance of a person at a hearing or requiring the presentation of certain evidence such as documents or checks. Failure to answer a subpoena may result in fine or imprisonment or both.

Subsidy A gift or financial grant by one unit of government to another or to individuals or groups performing some service deemed necessary or   **149**

Opper, 1880. Culver Pictures.

GREAT POLITICAL EXCITEMENT IN INDIANA

beneficial to the public. The subsidy best known in the United States today is the subsidy of farmers under the agricultural program of the federal government. The federal government, however, grants subsidies to many other business activities including shipowners, airlines, and the like. The term is also applied to **grants-in-aid** given by one branch of the government to another as in the case of federal subsidies to the states or sub-

sidies of state governments to county and municipal units.

Subversive A person who attempts to weaken or destroy—to subvert—an organization or a government. It is sometimes difficult to distinguish between a subversive and a harsh critic. The difference is primarily one of means or methods, the harsh critic using legal means and open methods, the subversive generally using any method, legal or illegal, moral or immoral, open or secret. The term today is applied particularly to the communists' methods of influencing governments outside Russia.

Subversive Activities Control Board An independent agency established in 1950, consisting of five members appointed by the President with the consent of the Senate for five-year, staggered terms. When asked by the Attorney General, the Board determines whether an organization is a "Communist-action organization," a "Communist-front organization," a "Communist-infiltrated organization," or none of these, within the meaning of the Subversive Activities Control Act of 1950. It also makes determinations about the relationship of individuals with such organizations.

Suffrage Simply the right to vote. This right has been gradually extended in the United States beginning with universal manhood suffrage, extending the right to vote to Negro men, followed by the granting of women suffrage in the Nineteenth Amendment. At the present time there is agitation for the general lowering of the voting age to include those between eighteen and twenty-one. Georgia and Kentucky are the only states in the Union which do permit voting at the age of eighteen. Alaska permits it at nineteen and Hawaii at twenty.

Suffragette A woman who works to secure **suffrage** and other political rights for women.

Suit Action taken in court by one party against another. In a civil suit, the person bringing the suit is called the *plaintiff,* and the person sued is called the *defendant.* In a criminal case, the one who brings the action is the *prosecutor,* or the state, and the

one called upon to defend himself is the defendant.

Summons A notice served on a defendant named in a lawsuit, notifying him that a lawsuit has been started against him and requiring him to answer the complaint within so many days, or to appear in court on a particular day.

Kirby. Museum of the City of New York.
THE END OF THE CLIMB

Superintendent of Education The executive manager of a local educational system. He is usually hired by the school board and in turn he hires, promotes, and transfers teachers, generally subject to approval of the board of education. A superintendent is expected to combine the qualities of an educator and an administrator together with some political sense.

Superintendent of Public Instruction 151

A state officer who directs educational activities within the state. Sometimes he is named in the constitution of the state. His duties are generally supervisory and advisory. He may also administer the laws dealing with education and the apportionment of funds for education. In about half the states the superintendent of public instruction is elected; in the others he is appointed by a state board of education or by the governor.

Supreme Court (United States) See **Judiciary.**

Supreme Court (State) In most states the highest court of the state. In New York and a few other states the highest state court is known as the Court of Appeals. The Supreme Court of the state is the final court of appeals for most cases originating in lower state courts. Its decisions are final, except for those cases that can be appealed to the United States Supreme Court. The state Supreme Courts usually have five or seven justices, including the chief justice.

Surtax A tax which is imposed in addition to the normal tax. It may be applied to income or to goods.

Tabling A parliamentary maneuver which results in the defeat of a measure. The effect of a motion to table if it passes is to lay a bill aside and to remove it from consideration. Usually a two-thirds vote is required to bring up a measure which has been tabled by a majority vote.

Taft-Hartley Act Popular name of the Labor-Management Relations Act of 1947, derived from the names of its two authors. The Act imposed the following restrictions, many of which were opposed by unions:

1. Recognized the right of workers not to join a union.

2. Required that each union which desires to use NLRB procedures file with that body complete lists of members, officers, rules, and finances.

3. Outlawed the **closed shop.**

4. Permitted a **union shop** only if a majority of workers desired it.

5. Outlawed **featherbedding, secondary boycotts,** and jurisdictional strikes.

6. Forbade expenditures from union funds in any national election campaign.

Tammany Hall The popular name for the Democratic organization of New York County, comprising the borough of Manhattan. It is also the name of the building in which this organization meets. Tammany Hall has a long history as a large and effective city **machine.** It has lost much power within recent years. The symbol or totem animal of Tammany is the tiger.

Tariff The rate of duty imposed by a government on goods imported from other nations; also used to describe the whole system of import tax rates. Tariffs are a source of national revenue, but they have been of greater importance as a device to protect domestic producers from foreign competition. The United States has had a tariff since 1789, and from the Civil War to recent times the "high tariff *vs.* free trade" issue was a constant controversy. Industrial interests and the Republican party generally favored higher tariffs, while agriculturists and the Democratic party advocated low tariffs.

The Trade Agreements Act of 1934 introduced the policy of reciprocal tariffs. It authorized the President to enter into agreements with other nations to stimulate mutual trade concessions and gave him the authority to raise or lower tariff rates by as much as 50 per cent. Under the "most favored nation" provision, a tariff concession to one nation was extended to all other nations with which the United States had such agreements. The reciprocal tariff policy has been effective in promoting international trade. It has also reduced the pressure on Congress for protecting specific items. As a result, the tariff issue has become less important and less partisan in politics. See **United States Tariff Commission.**

Tariff Commission See **United States Tariff Commission.**

Tax Financial obligation imposed upon citizens by the government in order to pay costs of government. The principal types of taxes are the income tax, the sales tax, and the real estate and personal property taxes.

Tax, Withholding A method of collecting taxes by which the employer withholds a portion of each employee's salary and turns it over to the government as a partial tax payment. This method is used principally in the collection of federal income tax, unemployment compensation, and social security taxes.

Tax Court of the United States This court reviews disputed tax decisions made by the Bureau of Internal Revenue. It is technically not a court but is rather a tribunal within the executive branch. It is composed of 16 members, appointed for 12-year terms.

Teamsters Union (International Brotherhood of Teamsters, Chauffeurs. Warehousemen and Helpers) The largest major labor union not affiliated with the AFL-CIO. The Teamsters, with approximately 1.5 million members, represent most of the truck drivers and many of the other occupations connected with the transportation of goods. Because of this great power and because of recent scandals involving the highest officers of the union—which led to expulsion of the union from the AFL-CIO—the Teamsters are one of the most controversial organizations in America.

Technical Assistance Program One of the important programs carried out by the **United Nations** and its specialized agencies. It is designed to provide advice and aid to governments of developing nations. Groups of experts are sent to those underdeveloped nations which request assistance, and fellowships are granted to enable their technicians to study in other nations. The major areas in which technical assistance has been provided are these: agricultural production, surveys of resources and economic planning, health services, industrial research and research related to improvement of public utilities, power, communications, transportation, community development, and public administration. The term is also applied to similar programs developed by the United States under the **Point Four** and the **Mutual Security** programs.

Teller Vote A vote taken in a legislative body by having members walk past designated "tellers" who count first those who are in favor of the action and then those who are opposed. Under this procedure an actual count of the vote is taken, but there is no official record of how individual legislators have voted. A member's vote may, of course, be reported by observers in the gallery or by other **153**

members of the legislature. See also **Roll call vote, Voice, vote, Division vote.**

Tennessee Valley Authority (TVA) A government corporation created in 1933 and headed by a board of three men appointed by the President with the consent of the Senate for nine-year, staggered terms. Its purpose has been the general development of the Tennessee River basin, which covers 40,000 square miles and serves a population of about 3.5 million people. About three-fourths of the area is rural. The TVA has produced and sold hydroelectric power, provided a navigable channel in the Tennessee River, and improved flood control facilities by the construction of dams on the Tennessee River and its tributaries. It also manufactures and sells fertilizer and has fostered soil conservation in the area.

Through these and other activities, TVA has been a boon to both agriculture and industry in the area. Since it was created by the government and still is financed in part through congressional appropriations, it has been the cause of a great deal of controversy, some persons charging that it constitutes socialism. Others claim, however, that it has been a noble and successful experiment in the development of a region handicapped by floods, poor soil conditions, and a lack of utilities.

Tenth Amendment Provides that powers not delegated to the United States by the Constitution, nor prohibited by it to the states, are reserved to the states respectively or to the people. This amendment has been subject to continuous controversy, debate, and varied interpretations. It is considered by some to have been a kind of "catch-all" amendment to take care of what was not specifically covered in the Constitution. Its placement as the last of the ten amendments in the Bill of Rights gives support to this view. It is considered by others, however, as a vital amendment and the basis for the **states' rights** cause.

Territorial Courts Special courts established by Congress to hear cases in territories of the United States. Their number, if not their importance, has declined as more and more territories became states. Territorial courts hear cases under both federal and territorial law. The judges are appointed for specific periods of time, rather than for life as is in the case with federal judges generally.

Third Degree Extremely harsh treatment of a prisoner by the police in an effort to obtain information from him or a confession. In the popular mind it consists of beatings, long hours of questions under bright lights, and deprivation of food or similar treatment, although in fact it may consist simply of harsh questioning in uncomfortable surroundings.

Third Party A party other than the two major parties. The only third party in the United States which has significant effect today—and that is limited to one state—is the Liberal party in the State of New York. The Nonpartisan League in North Dakota, which does not call itself a political party, does exert an influence similar to that of a third party, and the Farmer-Labor party, which until 1944 was a significant third political party in the State of Minnesota, is now fused with the Democratic party so that candidates in the State of Minnesota officially run as Democratic-Farmer-Labor candidates. See also **Two-party system, Populist party, Progressive party.**

Third Reading See **Readings of bills.**

Thirteenth Amendment See **Civil War amendments.**

Tort A wrong done by one person to another for which the law establishes a remedy. Tort cases involve property damage, personal injury, and other wrongful acts (not involving a **breach of contract)** caused by the negligence or malicious acts of another for which a civil suit can be brought for damages.

Total War A modern concept of warfare in which it is accepted that the total population and all of the resources of each belligerent are directly involved in the contest. The theory of total war assumes that a mass attack with modern weapons on cities and the civilian population, as well as upon military targets and military personnel, will destroy a people's will to resist as well as destroy the nation's capacity to supply and maintain its armed forces and military organization. See **War, Limited war.**

Totalitarian State A state in which almost every aspect of life is controlled by the government. The word *totalitarian* is drawn from the word total, meaning that the whole of one's life is subject to government determination. The economy, educational system, religious institutions, family life—all may be in greater or lesser degree regulated and controlled.

Town A New England unit of government having many of the powers of a municipal corporation such as the right to sue, to levy taxes, to borrow money, and to enact ordinances.

Towns are governed through a town meeting made up of qualified voters. A board of from three to nine selectmen is usually chosen to act as an executive committee of the town meeting, and they actually conduct the government of the town.

In some areas a town is a unit of rural administration similar to the New England town, but with less authority. The term is used in popular speech in reference to any municipality.

Town Board A board of three to nine elected officials (selectmen) who serve as an executive committee of a town meeting and govern a town between town meetings. Powers are limited, and the board merely executes actions taken at the town meeting. Functions usually include granting licenses, caring for town property, supervising elections, and the care of the poor.

Town Meeting An old-fashioned assembly of an entire town's population which acts as a legislature. Town meetings are still the governing bodies in many parts of New England. This is *direct democracy,* that is, the people themselves make governmental decisions instead of having representatives who do it on their behalf.

Township A political geographic division of a county provided in several states. It is a basic unit of rural government within the county. The size and character vary greatly from one area to another. See also **Town.**

Trade Association An organization made up of businesses and persons engaged in the same kind of commercial activity. There are trade associations for almost every conceivable kind of product and business in the United States, including, for example, sugar **155**

processors, steel producers, insurance companies, realtors, and beauticians.

Trademark A unique mark placed by the manufacturer on his product to identify it as his own, and to distinguish it from the products of others. Trademarks are registered with a register of trademarks in the United States Patent Office in order to guarantee their exclusive use by their owners.

Treason An act of disloyalty to one's nation. Such things as joining the armed forces of an enemy nation or giving government secrets to a foreign power are clearly acts of treason. The Constitution defines it as follows: "Treason against the United States, shall consist only in levying War against them, or, in adhering to their Enemies, giving them Aid and Comfort." See **Sedition.**

Treasurer The official charged with collecting the revenue and paying the obligations upon direction of the auditor or comptroller. Generally he is an elected official in a state or municipality. For Treasurer of the United States, see **Department of the Treasury.**

Treasurer of the United States See **Department of the Treasury.**

Treasury, Department of See **Department of the Treasury.**

Treasury, Secretary of See **Department of the Treasury.**

Treaty A contract between two or more nations, formally signed and ratified by the appropriate authorities of each nation. Treaties are usually about important matters and provide a means for long-range cooperation between nations or for eliminating areas of conflict. Enforcement of a treaty rests largely on the good faith of each nation, although unilateral breaking of a treaty may lead to various kinds of sanctions on the part of the offended nation. Treaties may be permanent or they may carry a termination date.

In the United States the making of treaties is reserved to the federal government (Article I, Section 10), and the authority to negotiate treaties is vested in the President. However, a treaty is not binding unless ratified by two-thirds of the voting members of the Senate. The President is not required to consult the Senate in advance of his negotiations. The Senate has approved the great majority of treaties submitted, but in 1919 it rejected the Treaty of Versailles with its provision for the League of Nations, demonstrating the power of the Senate to change the direction of foreign policy on a major matter. Under the Constitution, all treaties have the full force of federal law (Article VI). In recent times the President has frequently used the **executive agreement** in international relations rather than the more difficult treaty process.

Trial Balloon See **Leak.**

Tribunal The place where justice is dispensed, for example, a courtroom. The term is also applied to include all of the judges of a particular court. The Supreme Court is sometimes referred to as the "supreme tribunal." The term is derived from the tribunes of ancient Rome. The tribunes were magistrates elected to protect the rights of citizens. They could initiate laws, veto measures of the Senate, and defend a citizen against the unjust or arbitrary act of a judge.

Truce An agreement for a temporary ending of hostilities, either on the

156

battlefield or in a political struggle of some kind.

True Bill An **indictment** signed by a grand jury charging a person or persons with violation of a criminal law.

Truman Doctrine A departure in American foreign policy by which the United States pledged support to "free peoples" to resist subjugation by communist forces. It grew out of an address to the Congress in 1947 by President Truman, calling for economic and military aid for Greece and Turkey to resist communist aggression. His position was that totalitarian regimes threaten international peace "and hence the security of the United States." In practice it has not meant automatic intervention or indiscriminate aid to any nation asking for it, but a policy of containment of Soviet

influence and expansion by long-term economic, military, and informational programs to noncommunist nations. See **Marshall Plan.**

Trust **(a)** An association of a number of firms for the purposes of controlling the price and market of a product. In this sense, it is sometimes used as a synonym for monopoly.

(b) A property right where one person—the trustee—holds property for the benefit and use of another. It is common for high government officials to place their investments in trust for the duration of their service.

Trust Busting The name given to legal action taken by the Antitrust Division of the United States Department of Justice to break up monopolies or trusts which, under the law, are determined to be illegally restraining competition.

Rogers. 1904. Culver Pictures.

THE LION TAMER

Trusteeship Council The department of the **United Nations** responsible for the welfare of territories held in trust and of certain non-self-governing territories. It supervises the policies of member nations which administer territories, such as those formerly held by Japan and Italy or which were mandated areas under the **League of Nations.** The members of the Trusteeship Council include the permanent members of the **Security Council,** countries which administer trust territories, and as many other countries as are required to keep an equal representation on the Council of administering and nonadministering nations. A number of trust territories have become independent nations in recent years.

TVA See **Tennessee Valley Authority.**

Two-Party System A political system wherein there are only two important or major political parties. This has long been the case in the United States and on the record of history seems to be important for effective working of democratic government. Many factors discourage the formation and development of nationally strong third parties in the United States, including the two-party tradition and the method of electing a president which requires that one candidate receive a majority of the electoral college vote. Third party or splinter groups in the United States are generally short-lived and eventually have their ideas adopted by one of the major parties or are themselves absorbed by one of the two major parties.

Tyranny A regime which rules with great harshness, uses coercive methods freely, permits no opposition, and has little or no regard for the wishes or rights of the people.

Unconstitutional Action in violation of a constitution and therefore illegal. Parts of the United States Constitution are subject to various interpretations, and it is traditional for Americans to argue over whether a proposal or action is constitutional. One of the Supreme Court's gravest responsibilities is to pass judgment on the constitutionality of measures or actions which come before it. It is common in political debate to declare that one's own position is constitutional. The Supreme Court is the only body, however, that can determine constitutionality in federal matters.

Unemployment Insurance The federal-state system to provide a limited number of weekly benefits to the unemployed. It was created as one of the basic divisions of the **Social Security Act,** and it is designed both to alleviate the hardships of the unemployed and to maintain purchasing power in the economy. The program is operated by the federal government in cooperation with the individual state systems. The federal government imposes a 3.1 per cent unemployment tax on employers for wages paid, but the employer receives a tax credit of approximately 90 per cent of his contribution if he participates in his state system of unemployment compensation. In general the eligibility requirements and the amount and duration of benefits are determined by the individual state. The state may also vary the percentage of the tax it imposes on each employer in terms of the experience rating with unemployment in his business, and many employers pay much less than the maximum. It was anticipated that the unemployed would receive about 50 per cent of their average weekly wage in benefits but in many instances the benefits are less. The maximum duration of benefits also varies widely from state to state, with 26 weeks being the most common figure.

Unicameral Legislature A legislature which has only one legislative body. A **bicameral** legislature has two. Nebraska is the only state which has a unicameral legislature.

Union An association of the employees in a particular industry or craft for the purposes of bargaining collectively with their employer or employers on questions involving wages, hours, working conditions, pensions, and other matters. Prior to the merger of the CIO (Congress of Industrial Organizations) and the AFL (American Federation of Labor), the CIO was an industrial union and the AFL was made up of worker groups organized on the basis of special crafts or skills. See **Taft-Hartley Act, National Labor Relations Act.**

Union of Soviet Socialist Republics See **Soviet Union.**

Union Shop A business or industry which hires nonunion employees on the condition that they join the union within a given number of days. The Labor-Management Act of 1947 permits union shop agreements only if adopted in an election in which a majority of the eligible employees support it.

Unitary State A government wherein all authority resides in a central government. The central government

delegates as much or as little responsibility to local units of governments as it sees fit. A unitary state may be a democracy, as in Great Britain, or it may be a dictatorship, as in Hitler's Germany. See also **Confederation** and **Federation.**

United Nations (UN) An international organization designed to prevent war and foster international cooperation. The Charter was signed by representatives of 50 nations on June 26, 1945 following a conference at San Francisco. The permanent head-

Crawford, The Newark News, 1949.
"THERE'S STILL A BRIDGE"

quarters of the United Nations is in New York City. The UN has 104 members (1961), and it includes all the major powers except Red China. The United Nations has no power to tax, and it has no permanent armed forces. But it has called upon member nations with success to back its decisions, as in the case of the Korean conflict in 1950 and in the Congo crisis in 1960. The principal organs of the UN are the **General Assembly,** the **Security Council,** the **Secretariat,** the **Trusteeship Council,** the **Economic and Social Council,** and the **International Court of Justice.** Other

159

United Nations activities include the United Nations Children's Fund (UNICEF), the **Technical Assistance** program, and assistance to refugees. In addition there are a number of **United Nations Specialized Agencies** associated with the central organization. The permanent representative of the United States to the UN and our representative on the Security Council has the rank of ambassador. This position has developed into an important instrument of United States foreign policy.

United Nations Educational, Scientific and Cultural Organization (UNESCO) Created as a special agency of the **United Nations** in 1946 to promote cooperation among the nations through educational, scientific, and cultural efforts to "further universal respect for justice, for the rule of law and for the human rights and fundamental freedoms which are affirmed for the peoples of the world, without distinction of race, sex, language, or religion, by the Charter of the United Nations." UNESCO holds a biennial General Conference to determine the policy and major activities of the group. It has an Executive Board of 24 members and a secretariat headed by the Director General. It conducts research and publishes reports in the fields of education, science and culture. There are 82 member nations (1960). UNESCO headquarters are in Paris, France.

United Nations Specialized Agencies The thirteen agencies related to the **United Nations** by special agreements and working in partnership with it to achieve specific objectives. Membership in the specialized agencies is by application of the individual nations which subscribe to the objectives of the agency. Each has its own budget, personnel, and headquarters. The agencies are: the International Atomic Energy Agency (IAEA) concerned with peaceful uses of atomic energy; the **International Labor Organization** (ILO); the **Food and Agricultural Organization** (FAO); the **United Nations Educational, Scientific and Cultural Organization** (UNESCO); the **World Health Organization** (WHO); the **International Bank for Reconstruction and Development** (World Bank); the **International Finance Corporation** (IFC); the **International Monetary Fund;** the International Civil Aviation Organization (ICAO) created to establish international standards for civil aviation; the Universal Postal Union (UPU) which facilitates the reciprocal exchange of mail; the International Telecommunication Union (ITU) for the regulation of various communication services; the World Meteorological Organization (WMO) for improvement of meteorological efforts; the Inter-Governmental Maritime Consultative Organization (IMCO) for the promotion of international shipping. In addition a Charter was drawn up at Havana in 1948 to establish an International Trade Organization, but it has never been implemented. Its proposed functions are achieved to some extent by the **General Agreement on Tariffs and Trade** (GATT).

United States Attorney The attorney appointed in each judicial district of the United States to represent the United States in all lawsuits in his district in which the government is a party. The United States Attorneys are appointed by the President.

United States Civil Service Commission (CSC) An independent agency of the federal government established in 1883. It is made up of three commissioners appointed by the President with the consent of the Senate. They serve six-year, staggered terms. One member is designated chairman, and he becomes the chief executive officer of the organization. The Commission was established by the law which created the first merit system for many federal positions under which appointment, promotion, and retention on the job through changing administrations are determined on the basis of merit and service rather than party allegiance. The Commission has many responsibilities, including the establishment of standards for employees of the federal government, giving examinations for those seeking employment with the federal government, providing lists of available persons to the various agencies seeking employees, administering and enforcing certain preferences granted veterans by law, classifying positions according to duties and responsibilities, and recommending improvement in personnel practices.

United States Commissioner An administrative officer attached to United States Courts for the purpose of holding preliminary hearings on criminal cases and issuing search and arrest warrants.

United States Courts of Appeals A system of federal courts between the District Courts and the United States Supreme Court. Cases are appealed to these courts from the District and legislative courts and certain major federal boards and commissions. Their decisions may be appealed to the Supreme Court but generally are not. A Court of Appeals is located in each of ten regions or circuits across the nation and another is established in the District of Columbia. At least three judges are appointed to each

court and additional ones for heavily populated circuits. See **Judiciary.**

United States Information Service (USIA) An independent agency of the federal government established in 1953. It is administered by a director appointed by the President with the consent of the Senate. USIA was established to centralize, expand, and make more effective the overseas information programs which were previously conducted by a number of agencies. Its purpose is to inform the rest of the world about Americans, American life, and American government and policies. It is therefore sometimes referred to as the propaganda agency of the government. One of the important functions of the USIA is the *Voice of America,* its international broadcasting service. It broadcasts programs in the local language to communist nations—both behind and outside the Iron Curtain—and to other areas of the free world. It operates information centers and libraries in many cities throughout the world. It distributes and shows motion pictures and television films produced either privately or under its own direction, and it distributes pamphlets, magazines, and other printed material.

United States Marshal A federal official attached to a United States District Court who serves arrest warrants, arrests federal offenders, and takes prisoners from jail to court and back again. His duties for the federal government are comparable to those of a sheriff for a county. Marshals are appointed by the President with the consent of the Senate for four-year terms. They are one of the chief sources of patronage still available to the party which controls the presidency.

United States Tariff Commission
An independent agency of the federal
government established in 1916. It
is made up of six members appointed
by the President with the consent of
the Senate for six-year, staggered
terms. This commission is not a regulatory commission. Its primary responsibility is to investigate certain
tariff and foreign trade questions and
report its findings. It conducts investigations and makes reports on its own
initiative or upon the request of the
President or the Ways and Means
Committee of the House of Representatives or the Finance Committee
of the Senate—these are the tax committees of Congress. It can also make
investigations upon request of either
branch of Congress. These investigations generally deal with such matters
as the general effect of the tariff laws,
the impact of specific imports on domestic producers, the tariff relations
between the United States and foreign
countries, and comparative production costs in the United States and in
foreign countries. The Commission
has special responsibilities with respect to the negotiations of trade
agreements between the United States
and foreign nations.

**United States v. Curtiss-Wright Cor-
poration (1936)** A case in which the
Court determined that the authority
of the federal government in the conduct of foreign affairs is virtually absolute. The Constitution itself lists
some specific functions and responsibilities in this area, but the Supreme
Court has accepted that federal
authority is inherent in any sovereign
entity. The language of the Court in
this case included the following:
". . . the investment of the federal government with the powers of
external sovereignty did not depend
upon the affirmative grants of the
Constitution. The powers to declare
and wage war, to conclude peace, to
make treaties, to maintain diplomatic
relations with other sovereignties, if
they had never been mentioned in the
Constitution, would have vested in the
federal government as necessary con-
comitants of nationality."

United States v. Darby (1941) A
case in which the Supreme Court upheld a federal law prohibiting the
transportation in interstate commerce
of goods produced by child labor. The
court held this to be a proper exercise
of Congress' power to regulate commerce, thereby overturning its decision in **Hammer v. Dagenhart.** See
also **Gibbon v. Ogden**

United States Secret Service See
Department of the Treasury.

Unit Rule An arrangement under
which a **delegation** to a convention
casts all of its votes as the majority of
that delegation decides. For example,
if a state delegation to a national convention is operating under the unit
rule and is split 12 to 11 over a resolution before the convention or on two
candidates for nomination, the position advocated by the 12 would receive all 23 votes. The unit rule is
designated to give a delegation more
influence at a convention. It is widely
used.

Universal Postal Union See **United
Nations Specialized Agencies.**

Upper House The name usually
given to that branch of a bicameral
legislature which by prior association
is identified with the aristocracy or a
special class in society, or which does
not directly or immediately represent or reflect popular opinion. The
Senate of the United States is our

"upper" house. The term *upper* is derived from European systems in which one chamber of a parliament represented the aristocracy and the other (*lower* house) represented the population at large. The terms *upper* and *lower* no longer have the historical meaning in the United States Congress or in the legislatures of the states, nor do the terms signify any level of political or legislative power.

Urban Renewal Administration See **Housing and Home Finance Agency.**

Use Tax A tax imposed only on the users of a particular service. For example, the tolls paid by motorists on turnpikes and toll bridges.

USIA See **United States Information Agency.**

USSR The abbreviation for the Union of Soviet Socialist Republics. See **Soviet Union.**

Utopia An imaginary place where mankind lives in peace and harmony. As an adjective—"utopian"—the word is applied to proposals which are regarded as unrealistic, or even dangerous. The term comes from a Greek word meaning "no place." It is the title of a book by Thomas More, Prime Minister of England under Henry VIII, which describes life in an ideal republic.

VA See **Veterans Administration.**

Veterans Administration (VA) An independent agency of the federal government created in 1930 by consolidating a number of agencies which had been dealing with veterans' affairs. The VA is headed by an administrator who is appointed by the President with the consent of the Senate. The Veterans Administration has more employees than any of the cabinet-level departments except the Department of Defense and the Post Office. It administers the great number of laws which provide benefits to veterans of the armed forces and to their dependents. Included among these benefits are pensions, disability compensation, vocational rehabilitation assistance, education allowance— as under the "G.I. Bill," insurance of various kinds, and hospitalization.

Veterans of Foreign Wars of the United States (VFW) A national organization of military veterans who have served overseas in a war, campaign or an expedition for which Congress has authorized a campaign medal. Its purposes are fraternal, patriotic, educational and historical. It was founded in 1899 and has its headquarters in Kansas City, Missouri. With a membership of about 1,700,-000, it is the second largest veterans' organization in the nation. Compare with **American Legion.**

Veto The act of an executive returning to a legislature unsigned and with stated objections a bill which has passed the legislature and which requires the executive's approval before it can become law. Under the federal Constitution, it takes a vote of two-thirds of those present and voting in the House and also in the Senate to override the veto and make the bill a law despite the President's objection. While Congress is in session, a bill becomes law if the President does not sign or return the bill to Congress within ten days—Sundays excepted. If, however, Congress adjourns after sending a bill to the President and he fails to sign it, it does not become law. The latter instance is what is defined **163**

as a *pocket veto:* the President simply puts the bill in his pocket, supposedly, without signature and it dies when the session of Congress expires.

In 1960, 49 state governors were empowered to veto bills—North Carolina being the only exception. The number of legislators required to override a governor's veto varies from merely a majority of those present to three-fourths of those elected. Forty-two state governors also have the right to exercise the *item veto* on appropriations bills. This enables governors to veto specific parts of an appropriations bill without nullifying the rest. The President does not have the power of item veto despite repeated requests by many presidents, and Congress is not likely to grant it. The President can, of course, veto the whole bill and ask Congress to delete the items of which he disapproves. This is risky since Congress may retaliate by deleting some of the President's own favorites. It is generally held that by granting the President item veto, over-all appropriations would be cut down. This is not necessarily true. Recent history shows that Congress for the most part has appropriated less money than was asked for by administrations, both Democratic and Republican.

The veto has received a great deal of attention in relation to the activities of the United Nations, since the veto power is held in that body by each of the five permanent members of the Security Council. Any one of them can prevent a decision by refusing to concur in it. These nations are China, France, United Kingdom, USSR, and the United States.

Vice President   The elected federal officer who succeeds to the presidency in the case of the latter's death or removal from office. The Vice President is the only national official besides the President who is elected by a national constituency. His only important constitutional duty is to preside over the Senate and to vote in case of a tie. Whatever else he may be officially assigned to do is at the discretion of the President.

Village   (a) (Incorporated)   A small community or cluster of houses in a rural area organized for the purpose of providing the inhabitants with necessary services such as fire and police protection, schools, roads, and other facilities not generally provided by the township or county government. Incorporation gives the village legal status, permitting it to levy taxes, to borrow money, to sue and be sued, and to perform other activities requiring the fixing of legal responsibility. Villages are generally governed by from three to nine trustees or burgesses elected by the voters.

(b) (Unincorporated)   Similar to an incorporated village, but lacking legal status and the accompanying powers. An unincorporated village need not meet standards of area and population required of incorporated villages.

Virginia Plan   A set of fifteen resolutions presented to the Constitutional Convention by the Virginia delegation. These fifteen resolutions became the rallying center for the large states represented at the Constitutional Convention. Generally these resolutions favored a strong central government and a bicameral legislature. Representation in both houses was to be based on either wealth or numbers, thereby favoring the large and wealthy states.   See also **Connecticut Compromise, Constitutional Convention,** and the **New Jersey Plan.**

Visa Official document of a foreign country that permits a visitor to enter that country. The visa is attached to the visitor's passport and is ordinarily obtained without difficulty unless there is tension between the nations involved, or unless the individual is held to be politically undesirable for some reason. The visa system does not operate universally. See **passport.**

Voice of America See **United States Information Agency**

Voice Vote A vote in a legislative body by which the presiding officer asks all those in favor of a proposal to say "aye" and then asks all those opposed to say "no." He then determines which side has the largest support and declares that side to be the winner. Obviously this is not an exact gauge of the position of the members; it is ordinarily used on non-controversial matters. Occasionally it is used rather arbitrarily on a matter which the presiding officers and other leaders wish to pass or to defeat very quickly without recording the position of the members. See also **Roll call vote, Division vote, Teller vote.**

Voting Machine A mechanical device through which persons can record their vote. Voting machines are becoming increasingly popular in the United States. They are rather easy to operate. It is much more difficult to tamper with them than with paper ballots, and they provide a fast and accurate count of the total vote.

Voting Qualifications Those conditions required for eligibility to vote. Most states require that the voter be a citizen of the United States, twenty-one years of age, a resident of the state for at least one year, and a resi-dent for at least three months in the county or township in which he seeks to vote. Some states require the payment of a poll tax, and some few states undertake to impose a literacy test.

Wagner Act See **National Labor Relations Act, New Deal.**

Wall Street The most important financial area in the country, located in New York City. The New York Stock Exchange and many important banking establishments are on or near Wall Street. The term has become the symbol in American political life for financial interests. Wall Street has long been the **whipping boy** or target of agrarian reformers and Western interests, but this usage of the term is becoming less popular.

War Armed conflict between nations or between powerful factions in the same nation, in which case it is called civil war. In the classical sense, war involves military action and acknowledgment by authorities on both sides of the existence of a state of war and a declared intention to bring about a settlement. Modern nations have entered into various international agreements in an effort to regulate the conduct of war and to give some protection to the rights of neutrals, civilians, prisoners of war, and medical personnel who are not directly involved in conflict, and also to some extent to regulate the types of weapons and the manner in which weapons may be used. Unfortunately, many guarantees are not respected when the difficult test arises and the threat of retaliation remains one of the principal restraints in time of war.

Under the Constitution of the United States the right to declare war is reserved to the Congress, but the President in his executive capacity and as Commander-in-Chief has great responsibility for actions which may lead to the declaration of war. In World War I and World War II, the United States formally declared war. In the Korean conflict there was no formal declaration of war, but President Truman committed American forces under his authority to respond to the call of the United Nations. See **Limited war, Total war, ABC warfare, Cold war.**

War, Department of See **Department of Defense.**

War Powers Special and temporary authority given the President during wartime. Because the President is Commander-in-Chief of the armed services, and in order that the war effort can be carried out effectively, Congress has always granted the President war powers beyond those which he normally possesses. The courts, moreover, have consistently upheld these congressional grants as constitutional and have also been very tolerant of executive action during war, even when that action was not specifically authorized by Congress. War and the preparation for war requires a speed-up of the normal processes of democracy: military forces must be created and maintained; the economy must be converted from peacetime production to the production of war materiels; military strategy in the modern age must be worked out with military leaders of other nations and with allies. To accomplish all these things, a wartime President does within certain limits become a kind of "constitutional dictator."

Ward A legal subdivision of a city which frequently serves as a legislative district for the city council. It is often chosen by a party as a unit for a political organization and political activity. Wards are usually further subdivided into **precincts.**

Ward Heeler A person who works for a political party in a **ward** or **precinct.** The term is usually applied to those who perform routine but important tasks like passing out literature and urging citizens to register. Sometimes the term is used in a derogatory manner, implying that the person is insignificant in party affairs, that he is a "hanger-on," or perhaps even corrupt.

Warrant **(a)** A written order from a judge or other competent authority directing a marshal or sheriff or other officer to arrest the named person, or to search a stated premise, or seize a particular thing.

(b) It may be an order issued by one person, such as a comptroller, authorizing another to pay money. Warrants are issued to draw money to meet a city payroll or to obtain funds for running a department of government.

(c) It is the name given to an official certificate which appoints a person to an office or a position.

Ways and Means Committee A **standing committee** of the House of Representatives which has charge of legislation dealing with taxes, the national debt, tariffs, trade agreements, unemployment compensation, and social security. It is one of the most important committees of the Congress. Since under the Constitution revenue matters must originate in the House of Representatives, this committee is the revenue committee of the House—the body which originates and gives substantial form to tax legislation in the United States government. The Democratic members of this committee also serve as the **Committee on Committees** for House Democrats. They are elected to this committee by the Democratic **caucus.**

Welfare Programs The term generally applied to the many different types of assistance given to the poor and those unable to care for themselves. In the United States it includes an extensive system of private welfare programs conducted by voluntary and religious groups as well as public programs operated by the local, state, and federal governments. There is a growing tendency to include such things as the **social security** program in the term.

Welfare State The name popularly applied to a government which has extensive programs for the welfare needs of citizens. Such programs include hospitals, medical aid programs, unemployment insurance, old-age assistance or pensions, and special programs for those who have some unusual handicap. The term is often applied critically by those people who are opposed to having government intervention or government programs in these areas. On the other hand, it is accepted by many people as descriptive of a necessary government role.

Whig Party A major party in the United States for about twenty years beginning in 1834. Its great distinction was its opposition to President Andrew Jackson and the strong presidency which he represented. The name *Whig* was taken from the party in England which supported the growing power of Parliament as opposed to

the king. The Whig party was the more conservative party and elected presidents in 1840 and 1848. It disintegrated after a smashing defeat in 1852 and many of its members joined the newly developing Republican party. One of these was Abraham Lincoln who had served a single term in Congress, 1847–49, as a Whig.

Whip A member of a legislative body who is chosen to serve as the assistant to the leader. Both the majority party and the minority party in the United States Congress have whips. The whip is usually responsible for seeing that members of his party are present when critical votes are taken and is charged with responsibility for keeping members of his party informed as to the legislative program and floor action. He or his staff generally arrange **pairs** and explain or authorize absences to the legislature. Holding the office of whip is often preliminary to selection as majority or minority leader.

Whipping Boy A person or institution blamed for the troubles and difficulties of someone else.

Whispering Campaign The communication by word of mouth rather than by publication or through public discussion of false and malicious rumors about a candidate for public office.

White House The residence of the President of the United States located at 1600 Pennsylvania Avenue in Washington, D.C. In the popular use and in the press, it has come to apply not only to the residence of the President, but to the office of the presidency itself. The press, for example, frequently refers to the White House in terms such as this: "White House reaction was. . . ."

Kirby, 1932. Library of Congress.

SHE TURNS UP EVERY FOUR YEARS

White House Office The name given to the President's immediate aides. Their roles depend in large measure on what the President expects of them, rather than on their titles. The White House Office includes the following: the *Assistant to the President,* who can assist a great deal or very little depending upon the demands of the President; the President's *Press Secretary,* who may be simply a person who transmits information to the press. He may also be called upon to explain what the President meant to say. He may be called upon to say what the President intends to say, or in some cases what the President intended to say. Frequently the Press Secretary is a close personal friend

and adviser to the President. An important position in the White House Office is that of *Special Counsel,* who is expected to advise the President on legal questions primarily. The *Deputy Assistant for Congressional Affairs* endeavors to establish and maintain a close working relationship between the executive branch of the government and the legislative branch. In addition to these more or less regular officers, the White House Office is likely to contain several special assistants who undertake whatever task the President assigns to them, a *Staff Secretary,* who supervises staff procedures, and several military aides who may perform both in ceremonial and advisory roles. In 1960 the White House Office consisted of approximately 50 staff personnel plus the necessary complement of clerical assistants.

White Primary A primary election in which Negroes and other nonwhites are systematically excluded from voting. The white primary in its various guises has been repeatedly declared unconstitutional by the Supreme Court in recent years but there are still many areas in the South where voting is restricted almost exclusively to whites. The means of barring Negroes have ranged all the way from state laws prohibiting Negro voting to subtle economic and psychological pressures or threats of violence.

Whitewash To gloss over or cover up corruption or mistakes in office. Charges of whitewash are sometimes unfairly raised by spokesmen for an opposition party when the majority party exonerates a person from charges of corruption or malpractice.

Witch Hunt Any investigation or prosecution conducted in an unfair manner which deals with imagined dangers, or is conducted without any very clear purpose other than to gain some partisan advantage or to discredit some person or officer. The term has been transferred to politics from the early practice in certain communities in the United States and other parts of the world of solving all of their problems by eliminating some person from the community, either by exile or death, who was believed to be possessed by a devil.

Withholding Tax See **Tax, withholding.**

Women's Bureau See **Department of Labor.**

Workmen's Compensation A program established by law under which workers can collect from employers for sickness or injuries arising out of and in the course of their employment. Most states require the employer to carry insurance which pays the workers benefits decreed by the state industrial commission or some similiar agency which examines the claim and makes an award based upon duration and nature of the disability.

World Bank See **International Bank for Reconstruction and Development.**

World Court See **Permanent Court of International Justice, International Court of Justice.**

World Health Organization (WHO) Created in 1948 as a specialized agency of the **United Nations** to promote the health of the people of the world and to prevent disease by attacking it at its source. The structure of WHO provides for an annual World Health Assembly of representatives of all member states which sets policy and determines programs,

an Executive Board, and the Secretariat, headed by the Director General, which carries out the programs. WHO projects include technical assistance to countries to strengthen public health services, to improve environmental sanitation, maternal and child health, mental health and other health programs, and to control communicable diseases. WHO also is active in medical research, in establishing uniform standards, and in publishing reports to assist in improvement of international health. There are 87 member nations (1960), and the principal office is located at Geneva, Switzerland.

World Meteorological Organization See **United Nations Specialized Agencies.**

Writ A court order requiring certain kinds of action. There are many kinds of writs, for example, **habeas corpus** and writ of certiorari.

Writ of Certiorari See **Judiciary.**

Xenophobia Hatred, distrust or fear of foreigners derived from the Greek *xenos,* a stranger. In politics, extremely restrictive immigration policies and strong opposition to efforts at international cooperation are often cited as examples of xenophobia.

Yalta Conference The meeting of Franklin D. Roosevelt, Churchill, and Stalin at a conference held at Yalta (on the Black Sea in Soviet Russia), February, 1945, shortly before the end of the war in Europe. Decisions

Marcus, 1955. Culver Pictures.

ONCE BITTEN, TWICE SHY

were reached regarding the occupation of Germany, reparations, establishing governments in liberated areas with a guarantee of free elections, creation of the United Nations, and Soviet participation in the war against Japan in return for concessions. The failure of the Soviet Union to honor many of its pledges and the belief by some that President Roosevelt had conceded too much to Stalin made the Yalta agreements the source of bitter controversy between Democratic and Republican leaders for nearly a decade.

Yeas and Nays See **Roll call vote.**

Z

Zoning The division of a city into districts or zones for the purpose of restricting the use to which property within that zone can be put. The purpose of municipal zoning ordinance is usually to protect purely residential areas. The basic zones are the following: heavy industry, light industry, multiple-family dwellings, two-family dwellings, single family dwellings, and general commercial.

Zorach v. Clauson (1952) A case in which the Supreme Court held, by a six to three vote, that a New York "released time" program which provided for religious instruction outside the schools was constitutional. This is considered by some as a modification of the **Illinois ex rel McCollum v. Board of Education** case.

SUPPLEMENTS

States, Territories, and Possessions

Alabama Admitted as a state in 1819. Capital, Montgomery. Pop. 3,266,740. Electoral votes, 11 (10 in 1964). Presidential vote: States Rights (1948), Democratic (1952, 1956, 1960, except 6 unpledged electors in 1960). Governor: 4-year term, cannot succeed himself; Democrat (1961). State legislature: Senate, 35 Democrats (1961); House, 106 Democrats (1961). U.S. Senators, 2 Democrats (1961); Representatives, 9 Democrats (1961). Voting requirements: 21 years of age, 2 years in state, 1 year in county, 3 months in precinct, $1.50 annual poll tax for those 21–45 except members of the Armed Services.

Alaska Admitted as a state in 1959. Capital, Juneau. Pop. 226,167. Electoral votes, 3. Presidential vote, Republican (1960). Governor: 4-year term, 2 term limitation; Democrat (1961). State legislature: Senate, 13 Democrats, 7 Republicans (1961); House, 20 Democrats, 18 Republicans, 2 Independents (1961). U.S. Senators, 2 Democrats (1961); Representatives, 1 Democrat (1961). Voting requirements: 19 years of age, 1 year in state, 30 days in precinct, must read and speak English.

Arizona Admitted as a state in 1912. Capital, Phoenix. Pop. 1,302,161. Electoral votes, 4 (5 in 1964). Presidential vote, Democratic (1948); Republican (1952, 1956, 1960). Governor: 2-year term; Republican (1961). State legislature: Senate, 30 Democrats, 10 Republicans (1961); House, 47 Democrats, 33 Republicans (1961). U.S. Senators, 1 Democrat, 1 Republican (1961); Repre-

sentatives, 1 Democrat, 1 Republican (1961). Voting requirements: 21 years of age, 1 year in state, 30 days in county, 30 days in precinct, literacy test.

Arkansas Admitted as a state in 1836. Capital, Little Rock. Pop. 1,786,272. Electoral votes, 8 (6 in 1964). Presidential vote, Democratic (1948, 1952, 1956, 1960). Governor: 2-year term; Democrat (1961). State legislature: Senate, 35 Democrats (1961); House, 99 Democrats, 1 Republican (1961). U.S. Senators, 2 Democrats (1961); Representatives, 6 Democrats (1961). Voting requirements: 21 years of age, 1 year in state, 6 months in county, 1 month in precinct, $1.00 annual poll tax for all voters except members of the Armed Services.

California Admitted as a state in 1850. Capital, Sacramento. Pop. 15,-717,204. Electoral votes, 32 (40 in 1964). Presidential vote: Democratic (1948), Republican (1952, 1956, 1960). Governor: 4-year term; Democrat (1961). State legislature: Senate, 30 Democrats, 10 Republicans (1961); House, 47 Democrats, 33 Republicans (1961). U.S. Senators, 1 Democrat, 1 Republican (1961); Representatives, 16 Democrats, 14 Republicans (1961). Voting requirements: 21 years of age, 1 year in state, 90 days in county, 54 days in precinct. New residents of 54 days or more may vote for presidential electors but no other officers. Literacy test.

Colorado Admitted as a state in 1876. Capital, Denver. Pop. 1,753,-947. Electoral votes, 6. Presidential vote: Democratic (1948), Republican (1952, 1956, 1960). Governor: 4-year term; Democrat (1961). State legislature: Senate, 19 Democrats, 16 Republicans (1961); House, 33 Democrats, 32 Republicans (1961). U.S. Senators, 1 Democrat, 1 Republican; Representatives, 2 Democrats, 2 Republicans (1961). Voting requirements: 21 years of age, 1 year in state, 90 days in county, 30 days in town, 15 days in precinct.

Connecticut Admitted as one of the thirteen original states in 1788. Capital, Hartford. Pop. 2,535,234. Electoral votes, 8. Presidential vote: Republican (1948, 1952, 1956), Democratic (1960). Governor: 4-year term; Democrat (1961). State legislature: Senate, 24 Democrats, 12 Republicans (1961); House, 176 Republicans, 118 Democrats (1961). U.S. Senators, 1 Democrat, 1 Republican (1961); Representatives, 4 Democrats, 2 Republicans (1961). Voting requirements: 21 years of age, 1 year in state, 6 months in town, literacy test.

Delaware Admitted as one of the thirteen original states in 1787. Capital, Dover. Pop. 446,292. Electoral votes, 3. Presidential vote: Republican (1948, 1952, 1956), Democratic (1960). Governor: 4-year term, limited to 2 consecutive terms; Democrat (1961). State legislature: Senate, 11 Democrats, 6 Republicans (1961); House, 20 Democrats, 15 Republicans (1961). U.S. Senators, 2 Republicans (1961); Representative, 1 Democrat (1961). Voting requirements: 21 years of age, 1 year in state, 3 months in county, 30 days in district, literacy test.

District of Columbia Pop. 763,956. Congress is the legislature for the District of Columbia. Each House has a committee for the District. A commission of three members actually directs District affairs. Two members are appointed by the President and confirmed by the Senate, and one is detailed from the Corps of Engineers of the Army. Residents of the District of Columbia have no elected representatives in the Congress nor do they elect municipal officials. The ratification of the Twenty-third Amendment in 1961 extended to District residents the right to vote for the President. The number of presidential electors for the District will be equal to that of the least populous state, which is three. District residents may also vote in a presidential primary.

Florida Admitted as a state in 1845. Capital, Tallahassee. Pop. 4,951,560. Electoral votes, 10 (14 in 1964). Presidential vote: Democratic (1948), Republican (1952, 1956, 1960). Governor: 4-year term, cannot succeed himself; Democrat (1961). State legislature: Senate, 37 Democrats, 1 Republican (1961); House, 88 Democrats, 7 Republicans (1961). U.S. Senators, 2 Democrats (1961); Representatives, 7 Democrats, 1 Republican (1961). Voting requirements: 21 years of age, 1 year in state, 6 months in county.

Georgia Admitted as one of the thirteen original states in 1788. Capital, Atlanta. Pop. 3,943,116. Electoral votes, 12. Presidential vote: Democratic (1948, 1952, 1956, 1960). Governor: 4-year term, cannot succeed himself; Democrat (1961). State legislature: Senate, 53 Democrats, 1 Republican (1961); House, 203 Democrats, 1 Republican, 1 vacancy (1961). U.S. Senators, 2 Democrats; Representatives, 10 Democrats (1961). Voting requirements: 18

years of age, 1 year in state, 6 months in county. Under 1949 law, all voters had to reregister and pass literacy test. Those failing had to answer 10 of 30 questions prescribed by law.

Guam   Created a territory in 1950. Capital, Agena. Pop. 59,498. Governor: 4-year term. Unicameral legislature. Voting requirements: 18 years of age, 2 years in territory, 90 days in precinct.

Hawaii   Admitted as a state in 1959. Capital, Honolulu. Pop. 632,772. Electoral votes, 3 (4 in 1964). Presidential vote: Democratic (1960). Governor: 4-year term; Republican (1961). State legislature: Senate, 14 Republicans, 11 Democrats (1961); House, 33 Democrats, 18 Republicans (1961). U.S. Senators, 1 Republican, 1 Democrat (1961); Representatives, 1 Democrat (1961). Voting requirements: 20 years of age, 1 year in state, 3 months in district, literacy test in English or Hawaiian.

Idaho   Admitted as a state in 1890. Capital, Boise. Pop. 667,191. Electoral votes, 4. Presidential vote: Democratic (1948), Republican (1952, 1956, 1960). Governor: 4-year term; Republican (1961). State legislature: Senate, 23 Republicans, 21 Democrats (1961); House, 30 Republicans, 29 Democrats (1961). U.S. Senators, 1 Democrat, 1 Republican (1961); Representatives, 2 Democrats (1961). Voting requirements: 21 years of age, 6 months in state, 30 days in county (county elections, 6 months in county), 90 days in precinct.

Illinois   Admitted as a state in 1818. Capital, Springfield. Pop. 10,081,158. Electoral votes, 27 (26 in 1964). Presidential vote: Democratic (1948, 1960), Republican (1952, 1956).

Governor: 4-year term; Democrat (1961). State legislature: Senate, 31 Republicans, 27 Democrats (1961); House, 89 Republicans, 88 Democrats (1961). U.S. Senators, 1 Democrat, 1 Republican (1961); Representatives, 14 Democrats, 11 Republicans (1961). Voting requirements: 21 years of age, 1 year in state, 90 days in county, 30 days in precinct.

Indiana   Admitted as a state in 1816. Capital, Indianapolis. Pop. 4,662,498. Electoral votes, 13. Presidential vote: Republican (1948, 1952, 1956, 1960). Governor: 4-year term, cannot succeed himself; Democrat (1961). State legislature: Senate, 26 Democrats, 24 Republicans (1961); House, 66 Democrats, 34 Republicans (1961). U.S. Senators, 1 Democrat, 1 Republican (1961); Representatives, 7 Republicans, 4 Democrats (1961). Voting requirements: 21 years of age, 6 months in state, 60 days in township, 30 days in ward or precinct.

Iowa   Admitted as a state in 1846. Capital, Des Moines. Pop. 2,757,537. Electoral votes, 10 (9 in 1964). Presidential vote: Democratic (1948), Republican (1952, 1956, 1960). Governor: 2-year term; Republican (1961). State legislature: Senate, 35 Republicans, 15 Democrats (1961); House, 78 Republicans, 30 Democrats (1961). U.S. Senators, 2 Republicans (1961); Representatives, 6 Republicans, 2 Democrats (1961). Voting requirements: 21 years of age, 6 months in state, 60 days in county.

Kansas   Admitted as a state in 1861. Capital, Topeka. Pop. 2,178,611. Electoral votes, 8 (7 in 1964). Presidential vote: Republican (1948, 1952, 1956, 1960). Governor: 2-year term; Republican (1961). State legislature: Senate, 32 Republicans, 8 Democrats

(1961); House, 82 Republicans, 43 Democrats (1961). U.S. Senators, 2 Republicans (1961); Representatives, 5 Republicans, 1 Democrat (1961). Voting requirements: 21 years of age, 6 months in state, 30 days in township and ward.

Kentucky Admitted as a state in 1792. Capital, Frankfort. Pop. 3,038,-156. Electoral votes, 10 (9 in 1964). Presidential vote: Democratic (1948, 1952), Republican (1956, 1960). Governor: 4-year term, cannot succeed himself; Democrat (1961). State legislature: Senate, 29 Democrats, 8 Republicans, 1 vacancy (1961); House, 79 Democrats, 20 Republicans, 1 vacancy (1961). U.S. Senators, 2 Republicans (1961); Representatives, 7 Democrats, 1 Republican (1961). Voting requirements: 18 years of age, 1 year in commonwealth, 6 months in county, 60 days in precinct.

Louisiana Admitted as a state in 1812. Capital, Baton Rouge. Pop. 3,257,022. Electoral votes, 10. Presidential vote: States Rights (1948), Democratic (1952, 1960), Republican (1956). Governor: 4-year term, cannot succeed himself; Democrat (1961). State legislature: Senate, 39 Democrats; House, 101 Democrats (1961). U.S. Senators, 2 Democrats (1961); Representatives, 8 Democrats (1961). Voting requirements: 21 years of age, 1 year in state, 3 months in parish.

Maine Admitted as a state in 1820. Capital, Augusta. Pop. 969,265. Electoral votes, 5 (4 in 1964). Presidential vote: Republican (1948, 1952, 1956, 1960). Governor: 4-year term; Republican (1961). State legislature: Senate, 30 Republicans, 3 Democrats (1961); House, 113 Re-

publicans, 38 Democrats (1961). U.S. Senators, 1 Republican, 1 Democrat (1961); Representatives, 3 Republicans. Voting requirements: 21 years of age, 6 months in state, 3 months in town or plantation, literacy test.

Maryland Admitted as one of the thirteen original states in 1788. Capital, Annapolis. Pop. 3,100,689. Electoral votes, 9 (10 in 1964). Presidential vote: Republican (1948, 1952, 1956), Democratic (1960). Governor: 4-year term, limited to 2 consecutive terms; Democrat (1961). State legislature: Senate, 26 Democrats, 3 Republicans (1961); House, 116 Democrats, 6 Republicans, 1 vacancy (1961). U.S. Senators, 2 Republicans (1961); Representatives, 6 Democrats, 1 Republican (1961). Voting requirements: 21 years of age, 1 year in state, 6 months in county or district.

Massachusetts Admitted as one of the thirteen original states in 1788. Capital, Boston. Pop. 5,148,578. Electoral votes, 16 (14 in 1964). Presidential vote: Democratic (1948, 1960), Republican (1952, 1956). Governor: 2-year term; Republican (1961). State legislature: Senate, 25 Democrats, 14 Republicans, 1 vacancy (1961); House, 156 Democrats, 83 Republicans, 1 vacancy (1961). U.S. Senators, 1 Republican, 1 Democrat (1961); Representatives, 8 Democrats, 6 Republicans (1961). Voting requirements: 21 years of age, 1 year in commonwealth, 6 months in city or town, literacy test.

Michigan Admitted as a state in 1837. Capital, Lansing. Pop. 7,823,-194. Electoral votes, 20 (21 in 1964). Presidential vote: Republican (1948, 1952, 1956), Democratic (1960).

Governor: 2-year term; Democrat (1961). State legislature: Senate, 22 Republicans, 12 Democrats (1961); House, 56 Republicans, 54 Democrats (1961). U.S. Senators, 2 Democrats (1960); Representatives, 11 Republicans, 7 Democrats (1961). Voting requirements: 21 years of age, 6 months in state, 30 days in city or township.

Minnesota Admitted as a state in 1858. Capital, St. Paul. Pop. 3,413.-864. Electoral votes, 11 (10 in 1964). Presidential vote: Democratic (1948, 1960), Republican (1952, 1956). Governor: 2-year term (extended to 4 years in 1962); Republican (1961). State legislature: Senate, 45 Conservatives, 22 Liberals (1961); House, 72 Liberals, 59 Conservatives (1961). Candidates for the legislature run without party designation. Legislators caucus as liberals and conservatives. U.S. Senators, 2 Democrats (Democratic-Farmer-Labor Party) (1961); Representatives, 6 Republicans, 3 Democrats (1961). Voting requirements: 21 years of age, 6 months in state, 30 days in district.

Mississippi Admitted as a state in 1817. Capital, Jackson. Pop. 2,178,-141. Electoral votes, 8 (7 in 1964). Presidential vote: States Rights (1948), Democratic (1952, 1956), unpledged electors (1960). Governor: 4-year term, cannot succeed himself; Democrat (1961). State legislature: Senate, 49 Democrats (1961); House, 139 Democrats, 1 vacancy (1961). U.S. Senators, 2 Democrats (1961); Representatives, 6 Democrats (1961). Voting requirements: 21 years of age, 2 years in state, 1 year in election district, city, town or village; poll tax of $2.00 by all persons between ages of 21 and 60 except members of Armed Forces, the deaf, dumb, blind, or maimed; literacy test.

Missouri Admitted as a state in 1821. Capital, Jefferson City. Pop. 4,319,813. Electoral votes, 13 (12 in 1964). Presidential vote: Democratic (1948, 1956, 1960), Republican (1952). Governor: 4-year term, cannot succeed himself; Democrat (1961). State legislature: Senate, 29 Democrats, 5 Republicans; House, 100 Democrats, 57 Republicans (1961). U.S. Senators, 2 Democrats (1961); Representatives, 9 Democrats, 2 Republicans (1961). Voting requirements: 21 years of age, 1 year in state, 60 days in city or county. Some counties require 10 days' residence in precinct. New residents of 60 days or more may vote for President or Vice-President, but not for other offices.

Montana Admitted as a state in 1889. Capital, Helena. Pop. 674,767. Electoral votes, 4. Presidential vote: Democratic (1948), Republican (1952, 1956, 1960). Governor: 4-year term; Republican (1961). State legislature: Senate, 38 Democrats, 17 Republicans, 1 Independent (1961); House, 54 Republicans, 40 Democrats (1961). U.S. Senators, 2 Democrats (1961): Representatives, 1 Democrat, 1 Republican (1961). Voting requirements: 21 years of age, 1 year in state, 30 days in county.

Nebraska Admitted as a state in 1867. Capital, Lincoln. Pop. 1,411,-330. Electoral votes, 6 (5 in 1964). Presidential vote: Republican (1948, 1952, 1956, 1960). Governor: 2-year term; Democrat (1961). State legislature: Nonpartisan 43. Nebraska is the only state with a unicameral legislature; elected for a 2-year term. U.S. Senators, 2 Republicans (1961); Rep-

177

resentatives, 4 Republicans (1961). Voting requirements: 21 years of age, 6 months in state, 40 days in county, 3 months in city, 10 days in precinct, township, or ward.

Nevada. Admitted as a state in 1864. Capital, Carson City. Pop. 285,278. Electoral votes, 3 (1961). Presidential vote: Democratic (1948, 1960), Republican (1952, 1956). Governor: 4-year term; Democrat (1961). State legislature: Senate, 10 Republicans, 7 Democrats (1961); House, 32 Democrats, 15 Republicans (1961). U.S. Senators, 2 Democrats (1961); Representative, 1 Democrat (1961). Voting requirements: 21 years of age, 6 months in state, 30 days in county, 10 days in precinct.

New Hampshire Admitted as one of the thirteen original states in 1788. Capital, Concord. Pop. 606,921. Electoral votes, 4. Presidential vote: Republican (1948, 1952, 1956, 1960). Governor: 2-year term; Republican (1961). State legislature: Senate, 18 Republicans, 6 Democrats (1961); House, 259 Republicans, 138 Democrats, 1 Independent, 2 vacancies (1961). U.S. Senators, 2 Republicans (1961); Representatives, 2 Republicans (1961). Voting requirements: 21 years of age, 6 months in state and precinct, literacy test.

New Jersey Admitted as one of the thirteen original states in 1787. Capital, Trenton. Pop. 6,066,782. Electoral votes, 16 (17 in 1964). Presidential vote: Republican (1948, 1952, 1956), Democratic (1960). Governor: 4-year term, limited to 2 consecutive terms; Democrat (1961). State legislature: Senate, 11 Republicans, 10 Democrats (1961); House, 34 Democrats, 26 Republicans (1961). U.S. Senators, 1 Republican,

1 Democrat (1961); Representatives, 8 Republicans, 6 Democrats (1961). Voting requirements: 21 years of age, 6 months in state, 60 days in county.

New Mexico Admitted as a state in 1912. Capital, Santa Fe. Pop. 951,023. Electoral votes, 4. Presidential vote: Democratic (1948, 1960), Republican (1952, 1956). Governor: 2-year term, limited to 2 consecutive terms; Republican (1961). State legislature: Senate, 28 Democrats, 4 Republicans (1961); House, 58 Democrats, 7 Republicans, 1 vacancy (1961). U.S. Senators, 2 Democrats (1961); Representatives, 2 Democrats (1961). Voting requirements: 21 years of age, 1 year in state, 90 days in county, 30 days in precinct.

New York Admitted as one of the thirteen original states in 1788. Capital, Albany. Pop. 16,782,304. Electoral votes, 45 (43 in 1964). Presidential vote: Republican (1948, 1952, 1956), Democratic (1960). Governor: 4-year term; Republican (1961). State legislature: Senate, 33 Republicans, 25 Democrats (1961); House, 83 Republicans, 67 Democrats (1961). U.S. Senators, 2 Republicans (1961); Representatives, 22 Democrats, 21 Republicans (1961). Voting requirements: 21 years of age, 1 year in state, 4 months in county, city or village, 30 days in election district. Persons who became eligible to vote after January 1, 1922, must be able to read and write English.

North Carolina Admitted as one of the thirteen original states in 1787. Capital, Raleigh. Pop. 4,556,155. Electoral votes, 14 (13 in 1964). Presidential vote: Democratic (1948, 1952, 1956, 1960). Governor: 4-year term, cannot succeed himself; Democrat (1961). State legislature: Senate, 48 Democrats, 2 Republicans (1961); House, 105 Democrats, 15 Republicans (1961). U.S. Senators: 2 Democrats (1961); Representatives, 11 Democrats, 1 Republican (1961). Voting requirements: 21 years of age, 1 year in state, 30 days in precinct, ward or district.

North Dakota Admitted as a state in 1889. Capital, Bismarck. Pop. 632,446. Electoral votes, 4. Presidential vote: Republican (1948, 1952, 1956, 1960). Governor: 2-year term; Democrat (1961). State legislature: Senate, 28 Republicans, 21 Democrats (1961); House, 72 Republicans, 41 Democrats (1961). U.S. Senators, 1 Democrat, 1 Republican (1961); Representatives, 2 Republicans (1961). Voting requirements: 21 years of age, 1 year in state, 90 days in county, 30 days in precinct.

Ohio Admitted as a state in 1803. Capital, Columbus. Pop. 9,706,397. Electoral votes, 25 (26 in 1964). Presidential vote: Democratic (1948), Republican (1952, 1956, 1960). Governor: 4-year term; Democrat (1961). State legislature: Senate, 20 Republicans, 18 Democrats (1961); House, 84 Republicans, 55 Democrats (1961). U.S. Senators, 2 Democrats (1961); Representatives, 16 Republicans, 7 Democrats (1961). Voting requirements: 21 years of age, 1 year in state, 40 days in county, 40 days in precinct. New residents of less than 1 year may vote for President and Vice-President only.

Oklahoma Admitted as a state in 1907. Capital, Oklahoma City. Pop. 2,328,284. Electoral votes, 8. Presidential vote: Democratic (1948), Republican (1952, 1956, 1960). Governor: 4-year term, cannot succeed

himself; Democrat (1961). State legislature: Senate, 40 Democrats, 4 Republicans (1961); House, 107 Democrats, 14 Republicans (1961). U.S. Senators, 2 Democrats (1961); Representatives, 5 Democrats, 1 Republican (1961). Voting requirements: 21 years of age, 1 year in state, 6 months in county, 30 days in precinct.

Oregon Admitted as a state in 1859. Capital, Salem. Pop. 1,768,687. Electoral votes, 6. Presidential vote: Republican (1948, 1952, 1956, 1960). Governor: 4-year term, 2-term limitation; Republican (1961). State legislature: Senate, 20 Democrats, 10 Republicans (1961); House, 31 Democrats, 29 Republicans (1961). U.S. Senators, 2 Democrats (1961); Representatives, 2 Democrats, 2 Republicans (1961). Voting requirements: 21 years of age, 6 months in state, literacy test.

Pennsylvania Admitted as one of the thirteen original states in 1787. Capital, Harrisburg. Pop. 11,319,366. Electoral votes, 32 (29 in 1964). Presidential vote: Republican (1948, 1952, 1956), Democratic (1960). Governor: 4-year term, cannot succeed himself; Democrat (1961). State legislature: Senate, 25 Democrats, 25 Republicans (1961); House, 109 Democrats, 99 Republicans, 2 vacancies (1961). U.S. Senators, 1 Republican, 1 Democrat (1961); Representatives, 16 Republicans, 14 Democrats (1961). Voting requirements: 21 years of age, 1 year in commonwealth, 1 month as citizen of the United States, 2 months in district or precinct.

Puerto Rico Became a territory in 1898. Became a self-governing commonwealth in 1952. Capital, San **179**

Juan. Pop. 2,345,983. Governor: 4-year term; Popular Democrat. Legislative Assembly: Senate, 23 Popular Democrats, 8 Republicans, 1 vacancy (1961); House, 47 Popular Democrats, 16 Republicans, 1 vacancy (1961). Voting requirements: 21 years of age, 1 year in state, 1 year in district.

Rhode Island Admitted as one of the thirteen original states in 1790. Capital, Providence. Pop. 859,488. Electoral votes, 4. Presidential vote: Democratic (1948, 1960), Republican (1952, 1956). Governor: 2-year term; Democrat (1961). State legislature: Senate, 28 Democrats, 16 Republicans (1961); House, 79 Democrats, 20 Republicans, 1 vacancy (1961). U.S. Senators, 2 Democrats (1961); Representatives, 2 Democrats (1961). Voting requirements: 21 years of age, 1 year in state, 6 months in city.

South Carolina Admitted as one of the thirteen original states in 1788. Capital, Columbia. Pop. 2,382,594. Electoral votes, 6. Presidential vote: States Rights (1948), Democratic (1952, 1956, 1960). Governor: 4-year term, cannot succeed himself; Democrat (1961). State legislature: Senate, 46 Democrats; House, 124 Democrats (1961). U.S. Senators, 2 Democrats (1961); Representatives, 6 Democrats (1961). Voting requirements: 21 years of age, 2 years in state, 1 year in county, 4 months in precinct, literacy test (ownership of property is alternative to literacy test).

South Dakota Admitted as a state in 1889. Capital, Pierre. Pop. 680,514. Electoral votes, 4. Presidential vote: Republican (1948, 1952, 1956, 1960). Governor: 2-year term, 2-term limitation; Republican (1961). State

legislature: Senate, 22 Republicans, 13 Democrats (1961). House, 57 Republicans, 18 Democrats (1961). U.S. Senators, 2 Republicans (1961); Representatives, 2 Republicans (1961). Voting requirements: 21 years of age, 5 years in the United States, 1 year in state, 90 days in county, 30 days in district.

Tennessee Admitted as a state in 1796. Capital, Nashville. Pop. 3,567,-089. Electoral votes, 11. Presidential vote: Democratic (1948), Republican (1952, 1956, 1960). Governor: 4-year term, cannot succeed himself; Democrat (1961). State legislature: Senate, 27 Democrats, 6 Republicans (1961); House, 80 Democrats, 19 Republicans (1961). U.S. Senators, 2 Democrats (1961); Representatives, 7 Democrats, 2 Republicans (1961). Voting requirements: 21 years of age, 1 year in state, 3 months in county.

Texas Admitted as a state in 1845. Capital, Austin. Pop. 9,579,677. Electoral votes, 24 (25 in 1964). Presidential vote: Democratic (1948, 1960), Republican (1952, 1956). Governor: 2-year term; Democrat (1961). State legislature: Senate, 31 Democrats (1961); House, 150 Democrats (1961). U.S. Senators, 2 Democrats (1961); Representatives, 21 Democrats, 1 Republican (1961). Voting requirements: 21 years of age, 1 year in state, 6 months in county or district, poll tax of $1.75 annually which must be paid by all between ages of 21 and 60 prior to January 21 of the election year.

Utah Admitted as a state in 1896. Capital, Salt Lake City. Pop. 890,627. Electoral votes, 4. Governor: 4-year term; Republican (1961). State legislature: Senate, 14 Democrats, 11 Republicans (1961); House, 36 Democrats, 28 Republicans (1961). U.S. Senators, 1 Democrat, 1 Republican (1961); Representatives, 2 Democrats (1961). Voting requirements: 21 years of age, 90 days as United States citizen, 1 year in state, 4 months in county, 60 days in precinct.

Vermont Admitted as a state in 1791. Capital, Montpelier. Pop. 389,881. Electoral votes, 3. Presidential vote: Republican (1948, 1952, 1956, 1960). Governor: 2-year term; Republican (1961). State legislature: Senate, 23 Republicans, 7 Democrats (1961); House, 187 Republicans, 51 Democrats, 7 Independents, 1 contested (1961). U.S. Senators, 2 Republicans (1961); Representative, 1 Republican (1961). Voting requirements: 21 years of age, 1 year in state, 3 months in town for local offices. To register: take Freeman's Oath before the board of civil authority for each election.

Virginia Admitted as one of the thirteen original states in 1788. Capital, Richmond. Pop. 3,966,949. Electoral votes, 12. Presidential vote: Democratic (1948), Republican (1952, 1956, 1960). Governor: 4-year term, cannot succeed himself; Democrat (1961). State legislature: Senate, 38 Democrats, 2 Republicans (1961); House, 92 Democrats, 4 Republicans, 4 vacancies (1961). U.S. Senators, 2 Democrats (1961); Representatives, 8 Democrats, 2 Republicans (1961). Voting requirements: 21 years of age, 1 year in commonwealth, 6 months in county, city or town, 30 days in precinct, poll tax of $1.50 annually up to 3 years, literacy test.

Virgin Islands Purchased from Denmark in 1917. Formerly known as Danish West Indies. Capital, Charlotte Amalie, St. Thomas. Pop. St. Croix, 12,103, St. Thomas, 13,813, St. John, 749. Governor: appointed by the President and serves at his pleasure. Unicameral legislature: 4 Unity Party, 4 Democrats (1961). Voting requirements: 21 years of age, 1 year in Islands, 60 days in district, literacy test.

Washington Admitted as a state in 1889. Capital, Olympia. Pop. 2,853,-214. Electoral votes, 9. Presidential vote: Democratic (1948), Republican (1952, 1956, 1960). Governor: 4-year term; Democrat (1961). State legislature: Senate, 36 Democrats, 13 Republicans (1961); House, 59 Democrats, 40 Republicans (1961). U.S. Senators, 2 Democrats (1961); Representatives, 5 Republicans, 2 Democrats (1961). Voting requirements: 21 years of age, 1 year in state, 90 days in county, 30 days in city, town, ward or precinct, literacy test.

West Virginia Admitted as a state in 1863. Capital, Charleston. Pop. 1,860,421. Electoral votes, 8 (7 in 1964). Presidential vote: Democratic (1948, 1952, 1960), Republican (1956). Governor: 4-year term, cannot succeed himself; Democrat (1961). State legislature: Senate, 25 Democrats, 7 Republicans (1961); House, 82 Democrats, 18 Republicans (1961). U.S. Senators, 2 Democrats (1961); Representatives, 5 Democrats, 1 Republican (1961). Voting requirements: 21 years of age, 1 year in state, 60 days in county, 60 days in city to vote in municipal elections.

Wisconsin Admitted as a state in 1848. Capital, Madison. Pop. 3,951,777. Electoral votes, 12. Presidential vote: Democratic (1948), Republican (1952, 1956, 1960). Governor: 2-year term; Democrat (1961). State legislature: Senate, 20 Republicans, 13 Democrats (1961); House, 55 Republicans, 45 Democrats (1961). U.S. Senators, 1 Democrat, 1 Republican (1961); Representatives, 6 Republicans, 4 Democrats (1961). Voting requirements: 21 years of age, 1 year in state, 10 days in district or precinct. New residents may vote for President and Vice-President if eligible to vote in previous state.

Wyoming Admitted as a state in 1890. Capital, Cheyenne. Pop. 330,-066. Electoral votes, 3. Presidential vote: Democratic (1948), Republican (1952, 1956, 1960). Governor: 4-year term; Democrat (1961). State legislature: Senate, 17 Republicans, 10 Democrats (1961); House, 35 Republicans, 21 Democrats (1961). U.S. Senators, 2 Democrats (1961); Representative, 1 Republican (1961). Voting requirements: 21 years of age, 1 year in state, 60 days in county, 10 days in precinct, literacy test.

CAMPAIGN MEMORABILIA

1860 Lincoln and Hamlin campaign ribbon. Smithsonian Institution

McKinley and Hobart 1896 campaign parade umbrella. Smithsonian Institution.

1884 Cleveland and Hendricks wooden badge. Smithsonian Institution

1888 Harrison campaign pipe, Smithsonian Institution

1908 tin coaster. Smithsonian Institution

Franklin D. Roosevelt campaign sheet music. Library of Congress

1952 Eisenhower and Nixon "Clean-Up" bucket. Smithsonian Institution

Woodrow Wilson nut cracker. Smithsonian Institution

1960 Kennedy campaign hat. Smithsonian Institution

U.S. Army recruiting poster. Library of Congress

GOVERNMENT

The President's Seal
(National Archives)

Department of Labor

Department of State

The National Archives

Department of
Commerce

Department of the
Interior

Post Office Department

Department of the
Air Force
(Official U.S. Air
Force Photograph)

Department of the Army
(U.S. Army Photograph)

SEALS

Department of Justice

Department of Health,
Education, and Welfare

Department of the
Treasury

Department of
Agriculture
(USDA Photograph)

Smithsonian
Institution

The Great Seal
(Dept. of State)

Department of Defense
(U.S. Army Photograph)

Marine Corps Emblem
(Defense Dept.
Photograph)

Department of the Navy
(Official U.S. Navy
Photograph)

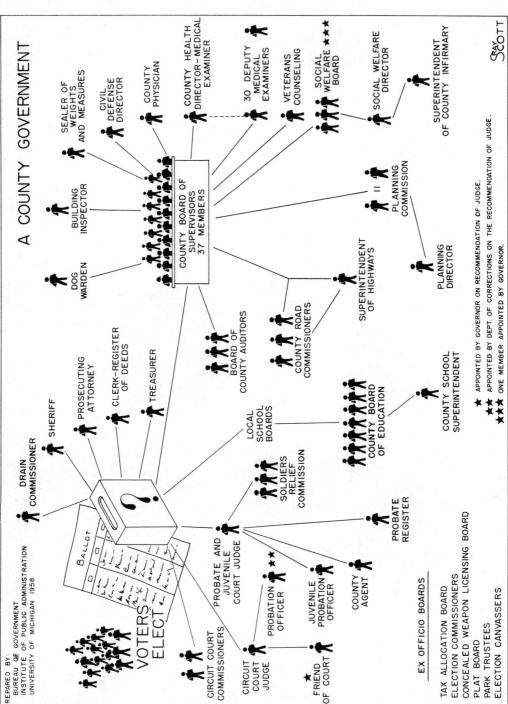

A COUNTY GOVERNMENT

PREPARED BY:
BUREAU OF GOVERNMENT
INSTITUTE OF PUBLIC ADMINISTRATION
UNIVERSITY OF MICHIGAN 1958

VOTERS ELECT

BALLOT

DRAIN COMMISSIONER
SHERIFF
PROSECUTING ATTORNEY
CLERK-REGISTER OF DEEDS
TREASURER
SEALER OF WEIGHTS AND MEASURES
CIVIL DEFENSE DIRECTOR
COUNTY PHYSICIAN
BUILDING INSPECTOR
DOG WARDEN

COUNTY BOARD OF SUPERVISORS 37 MEMBERS

COUNTY HEALTH DIRECTOR-MEDICAL EXAMINER
30 DEPUTY MEDICAL EXAMINERS
VETERANS COUNSELING
SOCIAL WELFARE BOARD ★★★
SOCIAL WELFARE DIRECTOR
SUPERINTENDENT OF COUNTY INFIRMARY

BOARD OF COUNTY AUDITORS
COUNTY ROAD COMMISSIONERS
SUPERINTENDENT OF HIGHWAYS
PLANNING COMMISSION
PLANNING DIRECTOR

CIRCUIT COURT COMMISSIONERS
CIRCUIT COURT JUDGE
FRIEND OF COURT ★
PROBATION OFFICER ★★
JUVENILE PROBATION OFFICER
COUNTY AGENT
PROBATE AND JUVENILE COURT JUDGE
PROBATE REGISTER

LOCAL SCHOOL BOARDS
SOLDIERS RELIEF COMMISSION
COUNTY BOARD OF EDUCATION
COUNTY SCHOOL SUPERINTENDENT

★   APPOINTED BY GOVERNOR ON RECOMMENDATION OF JUDGE.
★★ APPOINTED BY DEPT. OF CORRECTIONS ON THE RECOMMENDATION OF JUDGE.
★★★ ONE MEMBER APPOINTED BY GOVERNOR.

EX OFFICIO BOARDS

TAX ALLOCATION BOARD
ELECTION COMMISSIONERS
CONCEALED WEAPON LICENSING BOARD
PLAT BOARD
PARK TRUSTEES
ELECTION CANVASSERS

SCOTT

© by The University of Michigan

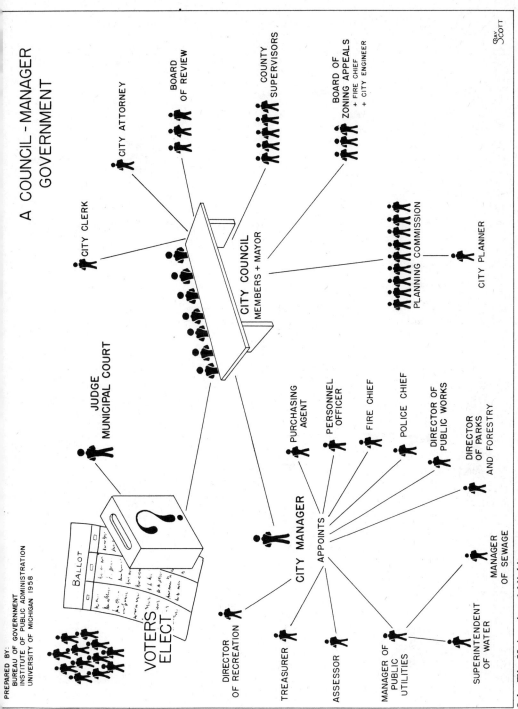

A COUNCIL - MANAGER GOVERNMENT

PREPARED BY:
BUREAU OF GOVERNMENT
INSTITUTE OF PUBLIC ADMINISTRATION
UNIVERSITY OF MICHIGAN 1958

VOTERS ELECT

BALLOT

JUDGE MUNICIPAL COURT

CITY CLERK

CITY ATTORNEY

BOARD OF REVIEW

COUNTY SUPERVISORS

BOARD OF ZONING APPEALS
+ FIRE CHIEF
+ CITY ENGINEER

CITY COUNCIL
MEMBERS + MAYOR

PLANNING COMMISSION

CITY PLANNER

CITY MANAGER
APPOINTS

PURCHASING AGENT

PERSONNEL OFFICER

FIRE CHIEF

POLICE CHIEF

DIRECTOR OF PUBLIC WORKS

DIRECTOR OF PARKS AND FORESTRY

MANAGER OF SEWAGE

SUPERINTENDENT OF WATER

MANAGER OF PUBLIC UTILITIES

ASSESSOR

TREASURER

DIRECTOR OF RECREATION

RAY SCOTT

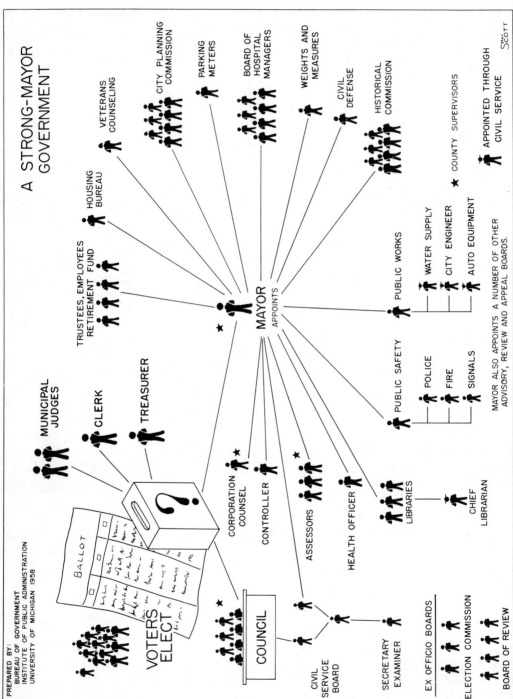

A STRONG-MAYOR GOVERNMENT

PREPARED BY:
BUREAU OF GOVERNMENT
INSTITUTE OF PUBLIC ADMINISTRATION
UNIVERSITY OF MICHIGAN 1958

VOTERS ELECT

BALLOT

MUNICIPAL JUDGES
CLERK
TREASURER

COUNCIL

CIVIL SERVICE BOARD

SECRETARY EXAMINER

EX OFFICIO BOARDS
ELECTION COMMISSION
BOARD OF REVIEW

CORPORATION COUNSEL
CONTROLLER
ASSESSORS
HEALTH OFFICER
LIBRARIES
CHIEF LIBRARIAN

MAYOR
APPOINTS

MAYOR ALSO APPOINTS A NUMBER OF OTHER ADVISORY, REVIEW AND APPEAL BOARDS.

PUBLIC SAFETY
POLICE
FIRE
SIGNALS

PUBLIC WORKS
WATER SUPPLY
CITY ENGINEER
AUTO EQUIPMENT

TRUSTEES, EMPLOYEES RETIREMENT FUND
HOUSING BUREAU
VETERANS COUNSELING
CITY PLANNING COMMISSION
PARKING METERS
BOARD OF HOSPITAL MANAGERS
WEIGHTS AND MEASURES
CIVIL DEFENSE
HISTORICAL COMMISSION

★ COUNTY SUPERVISORS
APPOINTED THROUGH CIVIL SERVICE

SCOTT

© by The University of Michigan

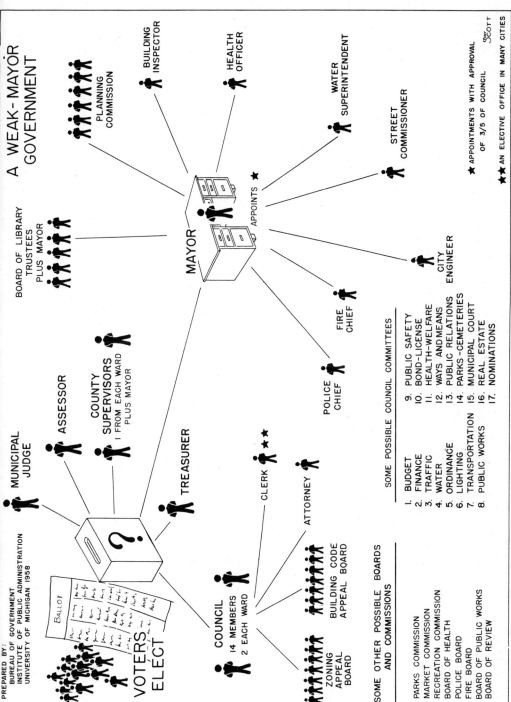

A WEAK-MAYOR GOVERNMENT

PREPARED BY:
BUREAU OF GOVERNMENT
INSTITUTE OF PUBLIC ADMINISTRATION
UNIVERSITY OF MICHIGAN 1958

BALLOT

VOTERS ELECT

MUNICIPAL JUDGE

ASSESSOR

COUNTY SUPERVISORS
1 FROM EACH WARD
PLUS MAYOR

BOARD OF LIBRARY TRUSTEES
PLUS MAYOR

PLANNING COMMISSION

BUILDING INSPECTOR

HEALTH OFFICER

WATER SUPERINTENDENT

STREET COMMISSIONER

MAYOR

APPOINTS ★

CITY ENGINEER

FIRE CHIEF

POLICE CHIEF

TREASURER

CLERK ★★

ATTORNEY

COUNCIL
14 MEMBERS
2 EACH WARD

ZONING APPEAL BOARD

BUILDING CODE APPEAL BOARD

SOME POSSIBLE COUNCIL COMMITTEES

1. BUDGET
2. FINANCE
3. TRAFFIC
4. WATER
5. ORDINANCE
6. LIGHTING
7. TRANSPORTATION
8. PUBLIC WORKS
9. PUBLIC SAFETY
10. BOND-LICENSE
11. HEALTH-WELFARE
12. WAYS AND MEANS
13. PUBLIC RELATIONS
14. PARKS-CEMETERIES
15. MUNICIPAL COURT
16. REAL ESTATE
17. NOMINATIONS

SOME OTHER POSSIBLE BOARDS AND COMMISSIONS

PARKS COMMISSION
MARKET COMMISSION
RECREATION COMMISSION
BOARD OF HEALTH
POLICE BOARD
FIRE BOARD
BOARD OF PUBLIC WORKS
BOARD OF REVIEW

★ APPOINTMENTS WITH APPROVAL OF 3/5 OF COUNCIL

★★ AN ELECTIVE OFFICE IN MANY CITIES

Scott

© by The University of Michigan

GOVERNMENT UNDER A STATE CONSTITUTION*

VOTERS ELECT

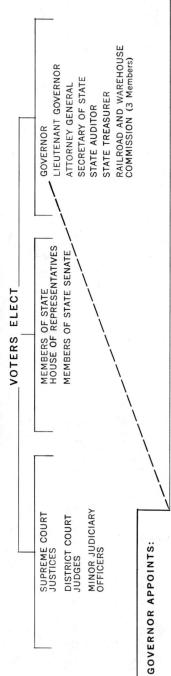

SUPREME COURT
JUSTICES

DISTRICT COURT
JUDGES

MINOR JUDICIARY
OFFICERS

MEMBERS OF STATE
HOUSE OF REPRESENTATIVES

MEMBERS OF STATE SENATE

GOVERNOR
LIEUTENANT GOVERNOR
ATTORNEY GENERAL
SECRETARY OF STATE
STATE AUDITOR
STATE TREASURER
RAILROAD AND WAREHOUSE
COMMISSION (3 Members)

GOVERNOR APPOINTS:

1. Heads of administrative departments and division, including Conservation, Taxation, Public Welfare, Highways, Banking, and Agriculture, Dairy and Food.

2. Members of administrative boards and commissions, including boards of Health, Education, Tax Appeals and the Industrial Commission, and the Fair Employment Practices Commission. These boards appoint the agency's chief executive officer.

3. Members of examining and licensing boards, including boards of Medical Examiners, Law Examiners, Electricity, and Barber Examiners.

4. Policy boards, commissions, and committees which have advisory functions or make quasi-legislative or quasi-judicial determinations which are then administered by other agencies.

*Minnesota, 1960

THE GOVERNMENT OF THE UNITED STATES

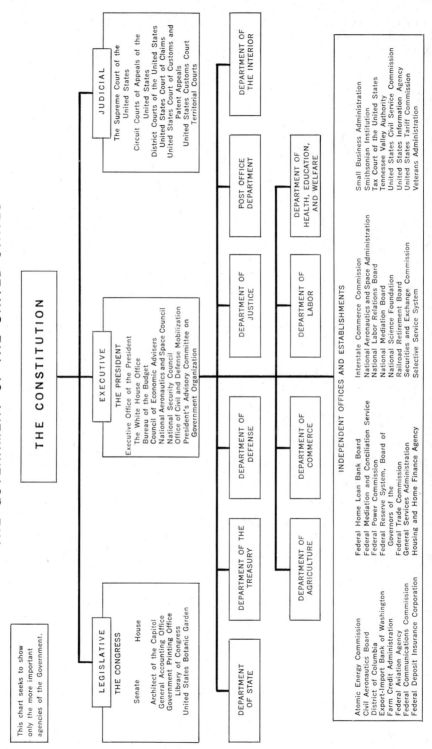

United States Government Organization Manual 1960-61

EXECUTIVE BRANCH OF THE GOVERNMENT

THE PRESIDENT OF THE UNITED STATES

EXECUTIVE OFFICE OF THE PRESIDENT

- BUREAU OF THE BUDGET — Director
- COUNCIL OF ECONOMIC ADVISERS — 3 Members
- WHITE HOUSE OFFICE
- NATIONAL SECURITY COUNCIL
- OFFICE OF CIVIL AND DEFENSE MOBILIZATION — Director

GENERAL SERVICES ADMINISTRATION — Administrator

NATIONAL CAPITAL TRANSPORTATION AGENCY — Administrator
FEDERAL AVIATION AGENCY — Administrator
NATIONAL AERONAUTICS AND SPACE ADMINISTRATION — Administrator
ST. LAWRENCE SEAWAY DEVELOPMENT CORPORATION — Administrator
UNITED STATES TARIFF AGENCY — Director

SELECTIVE SERVICE SYSTEM — Director

TEMPORARY AGENCIES

RENEGOTIATION BOARD — 5 Members
INDIAN CLAIMS COMMISSION — 3 Commissioners
TAX COURT OF THE UNITED STATES — 16 Judges
NATIONAL CAPITAL HOUSING AUTHORITY — 5 Members
NATIONAL CAPITAL PLANNING COMMISSION — 12 Members
AMERICAN BATTLE MONUMENTS COMMISSION — 11 Commissioners
COMMISSION OF FINE ARTS — 7 Commissioners
SMITHSONIAN INSTITUTION — 14 Regents
ADVISORY COMMISSION ON INTERGOVERNMENTAL RELATIONS — 26 Members
FEDERAL COAL MINE SAFETY BOARD OF REVIEW — 3 Members
SUBVERSIVE CONTROL BOARD — 5 Members
NATIONAL SCIENCE FOUNDATION — 25 Members
FOREIGN CLAIMS SETTLEMENT COMMISSION — 3 Members
ATOMIC ENERGY COMMISSION — 5 Commissioners
RAILROAD RETIREMENT BOARD — 3 Members
NATIONAL MEDIATION BOARD — 3 Members
FEDERAL HOME LOAN BANK BOARD — 3 Members
FARM CREDIT ADMINISTRATION — 13 Members
UNITED STATES TARIFF COMMISSION — 6 Commissioners
DEVELOPMENT LOAN FUND — 5 Directors
FEDERAL DEPOSIT INSURANCE CORPORATION — 3 Directors
TENNESSEE VALLEY AUTHORITY — 3 Directors
EXPORT-IMPORT BANK OF WASHINGTON — 5 Directors
CIVIL AERONAUTICS BOARD — 5 Members
NATIONAL LABOR RELATIONS BOARD — 5 Members
FEDERAL COMMUNICATIONS COMMISSION — 7 Commissioners
SECURITIES AND EXCHANGE COMMISSION — 5 Commissioners
FEDERAL POWER COMMISSION — 5 Commissioners
BOARD OF GOVERNORS OF THE FED. RESERVE SYSTEM — 7 Members
FEDERAL TRADE COMMISSION — 5 Commissioners
INTERSTATE COMMERCE COMMISSION — 11 Commissioners

AGENCIES

DEPARTMENTS

MULTI-HEADED AGENCIES

U.S. CIVIL SERVICE COMMISSION — 3 Commissioners

SMALL BUSINESS ADMINISTRATION — Administrator
FEDERAL MEDIATION AND CONCILIATION SERVICE — Director
HOUSING AND HOME FINANCE AGENCY — Administrator
VETERANS ADMINISTRATION — Administrator

DEPT. OF HEALTH, EDUCATION, AND WELFARE — Secretary
DEPT. OF LABOR — Secretary
DEPT. OF COMMERCE — Secretary
DEPT. OF AGRICULTURE — Secretary
DEPT. OF THE INTERIOR — Secretary
POST OFFICE DEPT. — Postmaster General
DEPT. OF JUSTICE — Attorney General
DEPT. OF DEFENSE — Secretary
DEPT. OF THE TREASURY — Secretary
DEPT. OF STATE — Secretary

EXECUTIVE OFFICE OF THE PRESIDENT BUREAU OF THE BUDGET

United States Government Bureau of the Budget

DEPARTMENT OF AGRICULTURE

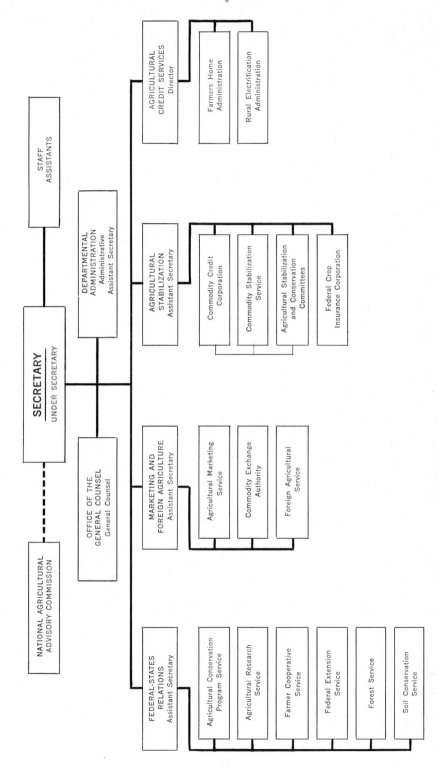

DEPARTMENT OF STATE

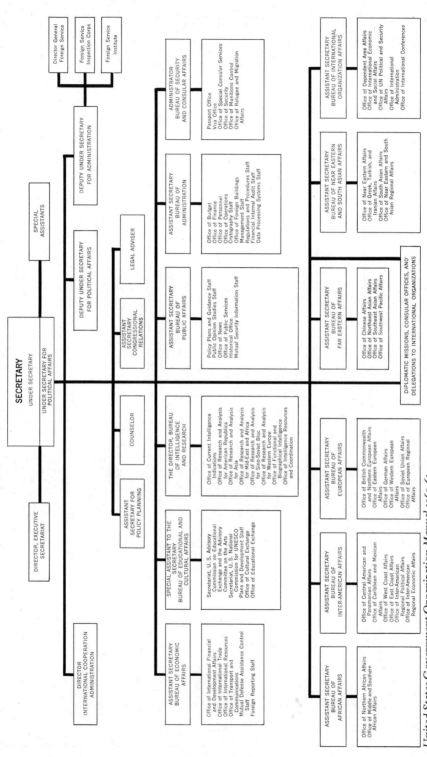

United States Government Organization Manual 1960-61

THE UNITED NATIONS AND RELATED AGENCIES

As of January 1959

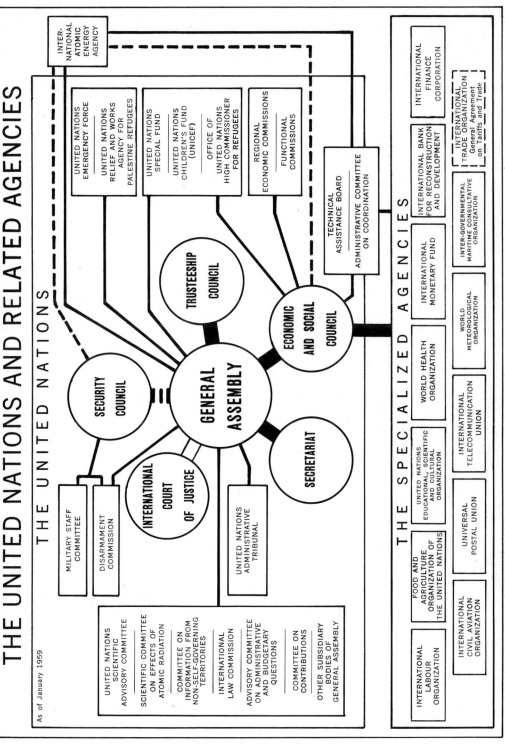

THE UNITED NATIONS

MILITARY STAFF COMMITTEE

DISARMAMENT COMMISSION

UNITED NATIONS SCIENTIFIC ADVISORY COMMITTEE

SCIENTIFIC COMMITTEE ON EFFECTS OF ATOMIC RADIATION

COMMITTEE ON INFORMATION FROM NON-SELF-GOVERNING TERRITORIES

INTERNATIONAL LAW COMMISSION

ADVISORY COMMITTEE ON ADMINISTRATIVE AND BUDGETARY QUESTIONS

COMMITTEE ON CONTRIBUTIONS

OTHER SUBSIDIARY BODIES OF GENERAL ASSEMBLY

INTER-NATIONAL ATOMIC ENERGY AGENCY

UNITED NATIONS EMERGENCY FORCE

UNITED NATIONS RELIEF AND WORKS AGENCY FOR PALESTINE REFUGEES

UNITED NATIONS SPECIAL FUND

UNITED NATIONS CHILDREN'S FUND (UNICEF)

OFFICE OF UNITED NATIONS HIGH COMMISSIONER FOR REFUGEES

REGIONAL ECONOMIC COMMISSIONS

FUNCTIONAL COMMISSIONS

TECHNICAL ASSISTANCE BOARD

ADMINISTRATIVE COMMITTEE ON COORDINATION

SECURITY COUNCIL

GENERAL ASSEMBLY

INTERNATIONAL COURT OF JUSTICE

TRUSTEESHIP COUNCIL

ECONOMIC AND SOCIAL COUNCIL

SECRETARIAT

UNITED NATIONS ADMINISTRATIVE TRIBUNAL

THE SPECIALIZED AGENCIES

INTERNATIONAL LABOUR ORGANIZATION

INTERNATIONAL CIVIL AVIATION ORGANIZATION

FOOD AND AGRICULTURE ORGANIZATION OF THE UNITED NATIONS

UNIVERSAL POSTAL UNION

UNITED NATIONS EDUCATIONAL, SCIENTIFIC AND CULTURAL ORGANIZATION

INTERNATIONAL TELECOMMUNICATION UNION

WORLD HEALTH ORGANIZATION

WORLD METEOROLOGICAL ORGANIZATION

INTERNATIONAL MONETARY FUND

INTER-GOVERNMENTAL MARITIME CONSULTATIVE ORGANIZATION

INTERNATIONAL BANK FOR RECONSTRUCTION AND DEVELOPMENT

INTERNATIONAL TRADE ORGANIZATION General Agreement on Tariffs and Trade

INTERNATIONAL FINANCE CORPORATION

United Nations Information Center, Washington